THE WORK OF RAPE

RANA M. JALEEL /

THE WORK OF RAPE

DUKE UNIVERSITY PRESS Durham and London 2021

Printed in the United States of America on acid-free paper ∞
Designed by Aimee C. Harrison
Typeset in Garamond Premier Pro
by Westchester Publishing Services

Library of Congress Cataloging-in-Publication Data
Names: Jaleel, Rana M., [date] author.
Title: The work of rape / Rana M. Jaleel.
Description: Durham : Duke University Press, 2021. | Includes
bibliographical references and index.
Identifiers: LCCN 2021005486 (print)
LCCN 2021005487 (ebook)
ISBN 9781478013570 (hardcover)
ISBN 9781478014508 (paperback)
ISBN 9781478021797 (ebook)
Subjects: LCSH: Rape as a weapon of war. | Sex crimes—
Rwanda. | Sex crimes—Yugoslavia. | Women and war. | Women
in war. | Women—Violence against—Rwanda. | Women—
Violence against—Yugoslavia. | Rape. | International criminal
law. | BISAC: SOCIAL SCIENCE / Gender Studies | SOCIAL
SCIENCE / Ethnic Studies / General
Classification: LCC KZ7162.J35 2021 (print) | LCC KZ7162
(ebook) | DDC 341.6/9—dc23
LC record available at https://lccn.loc.gov/2021005486
LC ebook record available at https://lccn.loc.gov/2021005487

Cover art: Walid Raad, *Appendix 137_100* (detail), 2018.
Archival inkjet print mounted on Sintra, 34 5/8 x 29 1/4 in.
Edition of 5, + 2 APs. © Walid Raad. Courtesy Paula Cooper
Gallery, New York.

Publication of this book is supported by Duke University Press's
Scholars of Color First Book Fund.

Contents

Acknowledgments

A short stint in Sweden helped kick-start this project and the dissertation from which it arose. I thank everyone involved in the GEXcel Centre of Gender Excellence at Linköping University for the opportunities and camaraderie of that fellowship.

A 2017 University of California Humanities Research Institute Research-In-Residence Fellowship in Transnational Feminisms was faith-restoring and came at just the right time. Thank you to Maylei Blackwell, Rachel Fabian, Monisha Das Gupta, Grace Hong, Zeynap Korkman, Karen Leong, Jessica Milward, and Judy Wu.

Thank you to my dissertation committee, whose members had the grace to let me be when I left graduate school for a crucial year to pursue union organizing full-time: Lisa Duggan, Katherine Franke, Ann Pellegrini, Crystal Parikh, and Andrew Ross. I truly loved thinking with you. What a gift.

To GSOC-UAW Local 2110 and generations of activists at NYU, union and beyond: I would not have been able to attend graduate school without the gains you earned.

To my dissertation writing group Mortal Kombat (Kari Hensley, Ariana Ochoa Camacho, Dacia Mitchell, Jan Padios, Dylan Yeats, and Zach Schwartz-Weinstein), thank you for your patience and kindness and your enormous brains. I forever draw little hearts next to your names.

Thank you to those I've known in various capacities, knocking around New York City, Ann Arbor, New Haven, and Atlanta, who sustained me or this work in various times and in various ways, especially Kate Bell, June Benjamin, Philip Carney, André Carrington, Maggie Clinton, Andrew Cornell, M. J. Durkee, Steve Fletcher, Patrick Gallagher, Manuel Gonzalez, Miles Grier, Michael Haskell, Madala Hilaire, Claudia Haupt, Caroline Henley, Joanna Holzman, Ronak K. Kapadia, Jonathan David Katz, Zenia Kish, Tamara Kneese, Johana Londoño, Elizabeth Loeb, Judy MC, Jack Minnear, Bich Beth Nguyen, Chairman Michael Palm, Lilian Radovac, Justin Rawlins, Adam Rodriguez, Maida Rosenstein, Incigul Sayman, Pavneet Singh, Christian Sweeney, Allison Tait, Emily Thuma, Susan Valentine, Erica Villanueva, Adam Waterman, Stefanie Wess, and Natan Zeichner.

Thanks to the Center for Reproductive Rights and Columbia Law School for an unparalleled postdoctoral experience, especially to Carol Sanger and Katherine Franke.

I do not understand California, much less the UCs, but what a formidable formation this university system is and can be. I appreciate my colleagues at UC Davis and across the UC campuses and those who emerged from them, including, but not limited to, Neel Ahuja, Javier Arbona, Neda Atanasoski, Toby Beauchamp, Alisa Bierria, Abigail Boggs, Caren Kaplan, Seeta Chaganti, Tim Choy, Ofelia Cuevas, Joe Dumit, Maryam Griffin, Angela Harris, Grace Hong, Lisa Ikemoto, Beenash Jafri, Mark Jerng, Tristan Josephson, Susan Kaiser, Susette Min, Nick Mitchell, Anjali Nath, Kimberly Nettles-Barcelón, Meaghan O'Keefe, Kathryn Olmsted, Sarah Perrault, Robyn Rodriguez, Eric Louis Russell, Leticia Saucedo, Eric Smoodin, Julie Sze, Kalindi Vora, and Claire Waters.

At UC Davis, I am especially pleased to work in Hart Hall alongside gender, ethnic, indigenous, and American studies faculty and staff who are dedicated to the well-being of our incredible students. Special thanks to Rodrigo Bonilla, Evelyn Farias, and Carlos Garcia for their efforts.

Queer fist bumps (from an appropriate physical distance, as needed) to Genevieve Clutario, Peter Coviello, Roberto C. Delgadillo, Wendy Ho,

Kathleen Frederickson, Elizabeth Freeman, Sara Giordano, Greta LaFleur, Sal Nicolazzo, Sara Mathiessen, Eli Meyerhoff, Jecca Namakkal, Lena Palacios, Cristina Jo Pérez, Evren Savci, Heather Steffen, Jeanne Vaccaro, and Jessica Kenyatta Walker.

More power to everyone involved in the abolitionist university formation and the American Association of University Professors, especially Tina Kelleher, Anita Levy, Risa Liebowitz, Joan Wallach Scott, and Donna Young, for our collective thinking about Title IX.

Thanks to my colleagues at the Vulnerability and the Human Condition Initiative at Emory Law School and those in its orbits, especially Martha Fineman and Stu Marvel.

Gratitude to the incomparable Jasmine Wade for calm and capable research assistance on portions of this project.

Thank you to the anonymous readers for their careful and sharp readings of the draft manuscript. You gave me more than you know.

Thank you to my long-admired editor, Courtney Berger. Thanks as well to Sandra Korn, Lisl Hampton, Aimee Harrison, and everyone at Duke University Press who saw this book to completion. Walid Raad's kind permission to use his stunning and provocative artwork for the cover was the icing on the cake.

Finally, thank you to my closest kith and kin: Hazel, Mohammed, Christy, Ryan, Ross, Robin, Lulu, Shahida, Avi, Coco, Randy, Marleah, Don, Ginny, Robin, Pete, Holly, my esteemed colleague Gertie, Mr. Doodles, Peanut (rest in chunky power), Dustin, Brandon, Brock, Bulbi, Imran, Irfan, Rafay and crew—far-flung across the world now.

To those I have omitted inadvertently, please excuse me. Acknowledgments assume that risk and are a vaguely awful genre of writing for exactly that reason.

This book is dedicated to the memory of Matt W. Robison. It is also dedicated to the memory of Cleo Hudson, who was the first person I understood to take my thinking seriously, and to the memory of my grandmother, who I think would be proud of me but who also knew very well that there is more to life than thought.

Introduction /
The Work of Rape

Although framing cannot always contain what it seeks to make visible or readable, it remains structured by the aim of instrumentalizing certain versions of reality. —JUDITH BUTLER, *Frames of War*

It has probably become more dangerous to be a woman than to be a soldier in armed conflict.—MAJOR GENERAL PATRICK CAMMAERT, in United Nations Human Rights, "Rape: Weapon of War"

IN THE 1990S, I was a teenage feminist in rural Georgia, reading riot grrrl zines and *Sassy* magazine, where indie rockers dispensing dating tips nestled column to column with Bosnian refugees and their testaments of war.[1] I was transfixed not only by the implicit connection, shadowy and unacknowledged, between what was happening to women in the Balkans and calls to Take Back the Night, but also by the mere mention of Muslim women. Beyond the confines of my own Muslim family, the Balkan conflict was the first time I could remember hearing any sustained talk of them—of what they did and what happened or could happen to them. A few years later, in college, I dumped sugar in my coffee while my Serbian classmate downed her espresso and confessed how she and her mother held hands by the television each night, praying that the United States would invade their country, praying for a war to end war, praying for what I would later learn by a more musical name: *jus ad bellum*, the right to war, the ultimate show of legitimate force. She spoke of dead uncles and the aerial bombings of medieval seaside towns, and although I could not imagine a truly just war, I could see how I might learn to desire one.

Fast-forward some years and gender securitization strategies, homonationalisms, and the repressive, deadly potential of international human rights and humanitarian regimes are key subjects in a rich vein of critical ethnic studies and queer scholarship focused broadly on examinations of governance, what makes up legitimate state violence, and knowledge production. Yet the breakup of the former Yugoslavia and later Rwanda, each couched as ethnic in causation in conjunction with a concerted if internally conflicted wave of feminist organizing that began the formal coupling of mass sexual violence and war within international law—that occasioned the entrance of rape and sexual violence in international human rights, humanitarian, and criminal law—has slipped from focus. It was then, in the wake of the Cold War, with the rise of the so-called ethnic wars, that the scope and significance of international law were reimagined. Here, for the first time since Nuremberg and Tokyo, international ad hoc tribunals were charged with the task of prosecuting war crimes, crimes against humanity, and genocide. This moment created new subjects of and subjects to international law as rape and other forms of sexualized violence were for the first time emphatically configured as enumerated violations of international, rather than national, law.

In the aftermath, as scholars and activists have noted, war and its accoutrements are understood as both a cause of rape and also an answer to it.[2] Task forces and UN resolutions proliferated as sexualized violence in conflict zones became a familiar topic of concern, study, law, and policy. Militarized humanitarianism, girded by a faith in carceral systems, became a solution to an issue perceived, as legal scholar Karen Engle writes, to involve "the worst crimes you can imagine" whose occurrence "makes wars last longer."[3] Rape and other sexualized violence became anathema under multiple theories and bodies of international law. They became international crimes, human rights violations, war crimes, and gendered, individual injuries that are in this view antithetical to "peace."

There I was, in the 1990s, with so many of "us," so many of us "of color," getting groped or worse on campus as ethnic war rape took up tenure on the nightly news. There and then the idea of rape was a door of approximate recognitions opening into a repository for so many things we could not easily express or name. And so in college I drank sugar with a splash of coffee and (almost) learned to love the bomb.

The "almost" is important. It was made possible by a hitch in the overarching tale of violence against women—an incongruence that I felt as much as thought. In retrospect, I recognize—and this book is ultimately a move more fully into that recognition—that this feeling was in some ways particular to the twentieth century's end. A feeling at the so-called end of history, after the Berlin Wall came tumbling down. A feeling formed in the thick of the US sex wars alongside what I knew and was learning about the vibrancy of Third World and women of color feminist and queer activisms. A feeling that discomfited itself into a question: what should we make of the presumptive continuity of sexualized violence as a category, of "rape" as the stuff that binds what happens on campus to what happens on the grounds of "ethnic" war?

If the concept of rape seems self-evident, the paths the word has taken to arrive at our current understanding are anything but. From the adjudication of mass rape and sexual slavery in the International Criminal Tribunals on Yugoslavia and Rwanda to state violence against indigenous women in the "Dirty Wars" in Latin America to the use of torture in US military prisons during the War on Terror to the role of Title IX in sexualized violence on university campuses, *The Work of Rape* demonstrates the wide-ranging importance of rape within contemporary sociolegal understandings of power transnationally. Using a transdisciplinary and queer historical methodology based on years of archival work, *The Work of Rape* scouts how feminist interventions in the "gender atrocities" of the 1990s-era ethnic wars have traveled across bodies of law (international and "US" domestic, criminal and civil) and social geographies.

The Work of Rape proceeds by understanding rape and sexualized violence—as well as their primary components, namely, consent, force, and coercion—as concepts and categories that are products of material histories. The ability to name and locate rape as an act and a sociolegal concept depends on power and knowledge achieved from racial, imperial, and settler colonial domination actuated through market liberalization and global racial capitalism. In other words, rape's contemporary political prominence in the United States—from #MeToo to Title IX controversies on campus—is staged on a bloodied, tumultuous, and cumulative backdrop of imperial and colonial warfare.

From this orientation, one that prioritizes decolonial, women of color, and Global South knowledge, rape and other forms of sexualized violence cannot ethically be cast as problems faced by "vulnerable women" subjugated as a group by patriarchal law and policy. Instead, *The Work of Rape* takes up how violence is socially and globally defined and distributed through the notion and naming of rape. It focuses particularly on how that recognition of rape occurs through the operation and practice of law—or how legal practice is itself a material process of theorizing both injury and evidence. How have feminist interventions—including feminist innovations in law and its practice—in the "gender atrocities" of the 1990s-era ethnic wars traveled across bodies of law (international and domestic, criminal and civil) and social geographies? How do those interventions reverberate within contemporary US engagements with gendered and sexualized violence and harassment inside the "United States" itself?

Instead of seeking to "diversify" survivor experience of what is called rape or other sexualized violence (as if these were stable or self-evident descriptors), this book takes a different tack. In the aftermath of rape's ascent into international law, *The Work of Rape* asks what work rape and its associated terms must do as it tries to hold many and conflicting forms of imperial and colonial violence across many sites, systems, and scales of law. This framing is not about how attention to sexualized violence detracts from other discrete issues or competing concerns. Instead, *The Work of Rape* asks what is uplifted, occluded, or viciously suppressed within the very definition of rape so that sexualized violence might be recognized. How does that resulting understanding of rape encourage punishing, carceral responses to it, and why do those responses feel for so many like justice?

Some answers might begin in a now familiar register of queer activism and studies—one in which gender, sex, and race, for example, do not describe fixed coordinates or settled identities but instead name concentrations and arrangements of power that change over time. From such a perspective, queer is, in Judith Butler's famous formulation, "never fully owned but always and only redeployed, twisted, queered from a prior usage and in the direction of urgent and expanding political purposes."[4] Approaching gender queerly and as a political historical category requires, as Butler aptly puts it, acknowledging that "we do not yet know all the ways it may come to signify, and we are open to new understandings of its social meanings."[5] Put to this project's purposes, we might observe that historically rape and other forms of sexualized violence (much less their attendant terms, *sexual consent, force,* or *coercion*) have had no fixed meaning—they were not and are not definitionally *obvious* but are instead sites of struggle. The terms *rape* and *sexual consent* index relationships between individuals and also between individuals and structures, especially legal ones, that seek to capture and distill the proper relationships between licit and illicit encounters and intimacies. This approach to sex and violence has implications for queer critique and racial study. Here, queerness and race contain neither fixed subjects nor objects of study but are instead inquiries into the historical and material politics of their reproduction as well as the shifting terms and affective connections that narrate those histories and emergences.[6]

From this perspective, the instantiation of rape within international legal orders and governance projects demands careful attention. Yet the rise of the "ethnic wars," demarcated from and eclipsed by the global politics of terror, is with few exceptions almost entirely neglected in activist scholarship. More pointedly, the popularization of global mass sexualized violence as a cause célèbre beginning with and extending from the Cold War's end has largely escaped the attention of scholars who seek to unravel the legacies of settler and franchise colonialism, sexuality, empire, and capital. Despite the richly detailed work of Black feminists that elucidates how rape has historically functioned as a technology of racial terror enabled by law and the state,[7] women of color feminisms and queer scholarship have only sporadically engaged the role of US race making and empire in the ascent of international criminal, human rights, and humanitarian regimes and the logics of gender and sexuality that issue from them.[8]

Meanwhile, queer of color critique and queer critiques of war have focused their attention on the Middle East and Latin America, largely sidestepping rape as an issue or analytic, and have declined to take up the 1990s wars in the former Yugoslavia and Rwanda. In other words, ethnic wars of the 1990s, the recognition of mass ethnosexual rape, and the concerted waves of feminist and other activist organizing that accompanied them are not integrated within most critical feminist, queer, and ethnic studies analyses of sexualized violence or theorizations of war. Mass rape does not enter efforts to assess the geopolitics of global governance, or analyses of racial capitalism's instantiation of what Jodi Melamed and Chandan Reddy call "differential rights orders," or the variability of applicable rights regimes "from the local to the supranational."[9] Yet Western framings and responses to the 1990s ethnic wars and the emergent post–Cold War order, distinguished by the unprecedented rise of international law as a space of justice, suture those conflicts to twenty-first-century contestations of the meaning and significance of rape and other forms of sexualized violence and therefore to discourses of race, gender, sexuality, and legitimate state violence.

The Work of Rape begins at the moment that rape and other sexualized violence become explicitly enumerated in international law: during the ethnic wars of the 1990s. This work traces the resulting legal epistemologies and effects through the War on Terror and contemporary Title IX controversies. The project's arc is an attempt to loosen the dense knot of what the long 1990s brought: the Cold War's end, the rise of "ethnic" warfare, the "victory" of global capitalism, the US embrace of multiculturalism and diversity that occurs alongside new restrictions on its most vulnerable populations,[10] and the transformations in the meanings of rape as a juridical concept and a cultural term through its engagements with an emerging new system of international law and advocacy. At this time, long-standing (albeit internally contested) multisited transnational feminist efforts to frame rape as a consequence of state inaction or state enablement (most forcefully made by Black, Third World, and indigenous feminists) begin to gain purchase in law. These efforts ultimately found a home in the language of human rights and atrocity crimes—or crimes that "take place on a large scale" and are so named as "the most serious crimes against humankind."[11] The roster of atrocity crimes includes war crimes, crimes against humanity, and genocide—the latter two recognized as occurring in and out of war. They do so, as the following chapters attest, by offering a revised universal subject of "woman" and category of "sexual violence."

Unlike prior imperial and global feminisms, these efforts are carefully, even deferentially attuned to social, national, and ethnoreligious differences among women. What knowledge about race, sexualized violence, and warfare is produced under these conditions? How does it enter into our imaginaries of sex—how we determine, how we know, what sex *is* and what good or bad or violent sex might be? How do we approach the long, diverse histories of indigenous women, women of color, Third World feminisms, and queer/trans responses to rape and other forms of sexualized violence in the age of "women's rights as human rights"? When the ongoing legacies of slavery and colonialisms are so adamantly disavowed, how do we understand the formal violation (rape as a crime against humanity, gender violence as human and civil rights violations) as an affront to what Hernán Santa Cruz of Chile, member of the drafting sub-Committee the Universal Declaration of Human Rights, called "the supreme value of the human person"?[12] How do we think about sexualized violation when the fact of the body, the evidentiary truth of the violation, received notions of believability—liberal frameworks that delineate a possessive interest in one's bodily person—were forged in fires stoked by shackles and slave bills of sale, looted lands, and their dispossessed multitudes?[13]

Through legal archival work, analysis of UN and nongovernmental organization policy reports, close readings of case, statutory, and other law, *The*

Work of Rape tracks some ways the meaning of rape and other forms of sexualized violence are produced through feminist activist and legal negotiations that traverse geographies, peoples, and bodies of law. I offer a new concept, the work of rape, and a new complimentary queer method (which I will soon discuss) for legal and cultural study of social difference, what I call *law beyond Law*. *The Work of Rape* asks how the violation and harm of rape and other forms of sexualized violence might be reconceptualized if the question of injury, harm, or evidence of such begins not with a clean journey through Anglo-American law—from coverture and seduction to sexual emancipation—but if instead those convolutions in law were placed alongside and within established and ongoing narratives of property, dispossession, and enslavement. What stories of rape and other sexualized violence emerge when they are told through the many imperial and colonial violences now reordered by the Cold War's putative end?[14] Here we might remember rape as a way to make slaves, rape as a way to make workers, rape as a way to grab land. Historicizing and privileging these contexts, I argue, shows how disavowed histories of imperial and colonial violence—which are histories of cisgendered heterosupremacy—enable the recognition of sexual injury in domestic and international law.[15]

Wars and conflicts "elsewhere," in sites like the Balkans, Rwanda, and Latin America, allowed and allow legal feminists and other activists to develop, refine, and ultimately promulgate radical overhauls in the scope and meaning of rape and other forms of sexualized violence. As rape becomes a violation of the human and is affixed to atrocity crimes in the post–Cold War management of "postsocialist," "postcolonial," "ethnic," and "genocidal" conflicts, the effects reverberate through legal and transnational feminist circuits of antisexualized violence organizing, changing the meaning and import of terms like *rape culture, consent, force,* and *coercion.* This book looks at how legal formulations of consent, force, and coercion in the US context carry in them—are in fact *possessed* by—the marks of those past efforts and struggles. To put it another way, this book argues that the legal and social meanings of rape and other forms of sexualized violence are shaped by ideas of what counts as consent and coercion, which are themselves formed through racialized geopolitical imperial and settler conflict—the materialities and imaginaries they produce. These include rape's association with torture in the Americas throughout the 1980s, with ethnoreligious warfare in the 1990s Balkans, and with Muslim terror in the new millennium. Notably, these associations all unfold within the penumbra of indigenous dispossession and other challenges to the legitimacy of the nation-state as the premier organizational unit of political, economic, and social authority. A closer focus on the primary components of rape in the Anglo-American tradition—including consent, force, and coercion—reveals what binds these far-flung sites across space and time. Fluctuations in the meaning of consent, force, and coercion do more than alter social understandings of rape. They also shift how we might approach their cultural and legal study and their conjoined relation to race, gender, sexuality, and the mass death made in the name of gendered and sexualized freedom. *The Work of Rape* thus shows how legal models of consent are removed from global changes in property regimes and the operations of settler empire, even as they are forged within them and depend on them.

The continual social and legal battle to define and redefine what consent means and what counts as force or coercion can be a symptom of the problem if rape and other forms of sexualized violence remain locked into categories of violation that depend on Anglo-American epistemological traditions of injury—ones rooted in autonomy, self-possession, or other hallmarks of individuated rights. Other kinds of lives, demands, and worldviews—other visions of good living and good sex—cannot wholly enter the terms of a debate centered on the act of rape, regardless of whether those nondominant claims are made through the language of rights or renunciations of them. Other ways of being and thinking nonetheless leave their marks in the records and inner workings of law. The method of law beyond Law follows those tracks, reviving those lives, demands, and worldviews within the terms of legal operations that include the technical aspects of law—not just the outcomes or content of legal decisions. The method of law beyond Law theorizes the making of the juridical itself and the many terms, processes, and strands of law—including the intellectual labors and theorization of harm that emanate from many locations and sources—that are necessary to its generation. In the process, the method undermines and remakes the meanings of law and its component parts.

The method recasts law, its inner workings, and its impacts in ways that at once acknowledge and resist the ravenous absorption of political possibilities in traditional juridical logics and claims. Treating law in this way allows for the insights of queer of color critique, women of color, Third World, and decolonial feminisms (and the differences between and within them) to convene in novel and unexpected ways, across categories and commitments of group, analytics, and nation. This is an account of rape as a coalescence of heterogeneous racialized and colonial histories, in law and out of it. This is an account of how those histories are lived and obscured through their fitful consolidation beneath the terms *gender, sex,* and *sexual violence* and their supportive attendants: consent, coercion, force, and welcomeness. This is an account of how the histories, logics, and structures of many forms and histories of empire and colonial violence—including cis-white-heterosupremacy—that are at least nominally forsworn under liberalism nonetheless persist, even at times in the terms and language of left liberation. Heterogeneous histories and epistemologies shape the micro- and macro-politics of rape. In turn, they shape the distribution of global resources, rights, and violences according to whose lives and which stories about sexualized violence are credited and valued and how varied juridical operations hasten or foreclose that valuation. This is the work of rape.

#MeToo / From Rape Culture to Structural Misogyny

In 2019, as reports of Daesh soldiers imprisoning Yazidi women as "sex slaves" flooded the news,[16] "homegrown" US sexualized violence was once again in the spotlight.[17] Feminism—often cast as a campaign to end violence, especially sexualized violence against women—found itself in a moment of cultural ascendance. From Hollywood's adoption of Black activist Tarana Burke's #MeToo to Title IX campus controversies, the contours of sexualized violation and impropriety, often couched as an impassioned rejection of rape culture, were undergoing spectacular and public reworking.[18] Originating in certain wings of 1970s US feminism, rape culture turned attention to the "general cultural beliefs supporting men's violence against women"[19] to counter entrenched explanations of rape as natural, biological, or instinctual, and therefore inevitable.[20] In the intervening years, liberation efforts that have gathered beneath the term have been tireless and many. Rape culture has provided a framework that shifts the motivations of intimate violence beyond men's instinctual need for sex, changes the meaning of rape from a stain on honor or damage to the property of men, publicizes its frequencies and impact, and insists on its gravity—demanding that allegations be taken seriously. At the same time, the notion of rape culture—which increasingly attempts to accommodate and theorize global sexualized violence through its unifying flexibility—can ultimately be stultifying.

In many ways, #MeToo—a many-headed phenomena that contains divergent experiences and theorizations of sexualized violence—has taken the foundational premises of rape culture and run with them. From Harvey Weinstein to Sherman Alexie to the manager in the corner office, men in power, long accustomed to exerting influence and wealth for stealth sexual advantage, are now open to public excoriation. For mass media publics, now dramatically exposed to the long work of feminists to transform how gendered and sexualized violation is recognized and understood, the simple presence of "consent" is no longer the last word on rape, nor does continued contact—sexual or otherwise—with the accused automatically disprove or invalidate the charge or experience of rape. "Social media," as queer theorist Juana María Rodríguez writes, "has changed almost everything we associate with testimony."[21]

If this is true socially, it is also increasingly true legally. Attention to rape culture—cast broadly as social pushback against sexualized violence—has become a basis for theorizing and imagining new relationships to legal systems and structures. As legal feminist Catharine A. MacKinnon, who cleared paths in US and international law with her theorizations of sex discrimination, writes "#MeToo moves the culture beneath the law of sexual abuse . . . early indications are that some conventional systemic legal processes are shifting too" as US courts begin, however tentatively, "to take explicit account of the cultural shift in what is 'reasonable' to expect of a survivor."[22] In her view, the #MeToo movement "is accomplishing what sexual harassment law to date has not. . . . Structural misogyny, along with sexualized racism and class inequalities, is being publicly and pervasively challenged by women's voices." Women, she writes, "have been saying these things forever," but now "power is paying attention."[23] What relationship between sex and violence is envisioned here? To whom exactly is power paying attention?

MacKinnon's claim—pithy and direct—rehearses and slightly revamps the truism that when women are brave, when they speak out and voice their suffering at the hands of men, justice invariably arrives—often with a siren, a sentence, and cellblock. But it takes more work, she suggests, than speech to tackle structural misogyny. It requires a movement: sustained engagement with power across multiple sites, from sex discrimination law to protests around the world. As she writes, "Sexual-harassment law prepared the ground, but #MeToo, Time's Up, and similar mobilizations around the world—including #NiUnaMenos in Argentina, #BalanceTonPorc in France, #TheFirstTimeI GotHarassed in Egypt, #WithYou in Japan, and #PremeiroAssedio in Brazil among them—are shifting gender hierarchy's tectonic plates."[24] This language, its seeming breath of inclusive solidarity, is inspiring and even seductive—it seems to acknowledge what historian Estelle Freedman calls "the centrality of race to the political history of rape."[25] What exactly are rape and race in that political history?[26]

For MacKinnon, structural misogyny—notwithstanding the requisite mentions of "sexualized racism" and "class inequalities"—places the stereotype of the "lying slut" and "shifting the gender hierarch[y]" as key plot points in the unfolding sociolegal drama.[27] This is an old story and a driver behind liberal feminist rape reform efforts of the 1970s and 1980s that hinge on the oft-recited "discrepancy between female experience and the law's definition of rape."[28] In this view, the violence of sex is gendered, and the role of law is ultimately to reflect the gendered reality of sex and correct for the subordination of women. In this view, the more rape law addresses the category or idea of "women" or "gender," the more just it becomes. In this account, feminist lawmaking and feminist organizing function symbiotically and dynamically—each fostering the emancipatory potentials of the other. But there are other ways of understanding and staging the prevalence of gendered and sexualized violence and shifting its tectonic plates. There are other spaces to locate its harms, describe its contours, and propose redress.

Work in the radical traditions of Black and women of color feminism, queer of color critique, and decolonial feminisms, for instance, has long challenged and engaged the state as the guarantor of justice while eschewing a narrow gender frame as the best way to describe sexualized violation. Writing in 1978, Black feminist Angela Davis insists that racism must be central to any analysis of sexualized violence: racism, she writes, is "nourished" by sexual coercion.[29] For Davis, the specter of the Black male rapist and the ongoing entitlement of white men to Black women's bodies are an inheritance of a property system dating back to US slave days—a system of terror. "Lynching," she writes, "in turn complemented by the systematic rape of Black women became an essential ingredient of the strategy of terror which guaranteed the overexploitation of Black labor and, after the betrayal of the Reconstruction, the political domination of Black people as a whole. . . . The crisis dimensions of sexual violence constitute one of the facets of a deep-going crisis of capitalism."[30] More recently, Muscogee scholar and MacArthur Fellow Sarah Deer has characterized rape and other forms of sexualized violence against indigenous women as the product of legal relation wherein US federal jurisdiction strips tribes of political sovereignty. Such rape, she avers, "is a fundamental result of colonialism, a history of violence reaching back centuries."[31]

Trans activists have also framed rape and sexualized violence in ways that complicate rape culture and its relationship to structural misogyny. In a 2014 report prepared by the Center for Gender and Sexuality Law at Columbia Law School, Chase Strangio, staff attorney with the American Civil Liberties Union, notes how antisexual violence legislation, namely, the Prison Rape Elimination Act (2003), has "been used to restrict the gender expression of people in custody under the guise of ending sexual assault."[32] Strangio describes how he "represented a transgender woman in a New York men's prison who was disciplined after reporting a sexual assault perpetrated against her. The officials argued that her gender non-conformity was evidence that she had consented to the rape. Meanwhile, all corrections agencies continue to prohibit consensual sexual contact or touching of any kind."[33] Finally, regarding the rape of the Yazidi in northern Iraq, legal scholar Lama Abu-Odeh refuses both racist explanations that blame Islamic rape culture for the violence against the Yazidi as well as the imposition of Western "anti-imperialist" frameworks by elite "public intellectuals" that prevent local activists (or simply people) on the ground from protesting gendered and sexualized violence for fear of being cast as "the unwitting handmaiden[s] of western imperialist projects" or more sinisterly as "native informant[s]."[34] As Abu-Odeh writes, "There is an undeniable affinity between the anti-imperialist line 'made in the USA' and the local political Islamist and nationalist positions that are antagonistic to the politics of gender and sexuality."[35]

People of color, indigenous, and queer and trans feminists and global activists, it seems, have been saying *these* things forever. To hear and heed them does a number on a thin notion of rape culture that underlies and enables an antidote to "structural misogyny" premised on transposable accounts of gender/sex.[36] What Davis, Deer, Strangio, and Abu-Odeh describe and what MacKinnon offers are divergent, incompatible accounts of the violation known as rape. The rape of the "lying slut," where the problem is framed as one of social and legal believability, differs not only in degree but in kind from the rape of a slave, tribal citizen, prisoner, or one who resides in the crosshairs of weaponized gender politics and Islamophobia. This recognition in turn affects, as Abu-Odeh elaborates, what and how people who agitate for gender and sexual justice are understood as agitating for and against. Rape culture—and the systemic analyses it enables—can become synonymous with Muslim or "other" cultures, a problem of groups or peoples that locates those who would condemn gendered and sexualized violence in the unenviable position of either feeding racist or orientalist thinking or ignoring sexualized violence. Distilling the act of rape to a question of the norms or attitudes of various social milieus can degenerate quickly into colonizing or imperial gestures that cast entire regions as "rape prone," as a variety of feminists have charged in relation to Western reporting on rape in Africa, India, and the Middle East.[37] In the cases described by Davis, Deer, Strangio, and Abu-Odeh, the ability to be the rights-bearing subject of law, to be considered fully present in the conceptual bounds of the human or simply recognized as someone with something to contribute, is absented or strained.

Collectively, Davis, Deer, and Strangio offer particular critical commentary on the notion of rape culture, universalizing accounts of gender (like MacKinnon's structural misogyny), and their relationship to law and institutional oversight. While the changes MacKinnon lauds—the social redefinition of what proves or refutes a charge of rape emblematized in the eponymous mandate to "believe women"—are the fruit of long, hard, feminist struggle, the heralded liberation of rape from a phallogocentric worldview nonetheless sparks anxiety, unease, and anger in some circles, and not simply those of men's rights activists and incels. Some men of color, queers, trans people, and incarcerated people now find themselves in the glare of what Chandan Reddy might call a "sexual freedom [that] . . . powerfully disallows a reckoning with its own conditions of possibility."[38] This is a disavowal that redeems "the very state that . . . global sexual and racial violences have built."[39] In other words, what is staged as separate—war rape, as opposed to debates about affirmative consent on campus, for example—or conversely collapsed, so that any rape anywhere at any time is best explained through the framework of "structural misogyny" or "rape culture," is in fact connected in a particular way: through disparate global struggles to socially and legally define and interpret the offense and its harm.

The cultural shifts that MacKinnon praises, the ones that rework the operations of sex, gender, and law, do not automatically or inevitably address the kinds of sexualized harms elucidated by Davis, Deer, Strangio, and Abu-Odeh. What these authors gesture toward is something more expansive. Together, they demonstrate how the differential ability to name rape and have it addressed make plain the material politics of feminist knowledge. Together they show how the officially recognized parameters of sexualized violence—and MacKinnon's structural misogyny—are shaped and policed by the literal and epistemic control of land and bodies. Only certain accounts of what rape is can be credited. Debates over the terms that seem to signal sexual safety, sexual health, and good sex and that constitute the "reasonableness" of the survivor under law—words like *consent, coercion, welcomeness,* and *enthusiastic consent*—are not obvious. They are polyvalent and discordant; they contain and cover the histories of race, empire, cis-heterosupremacy, and colonialism, which are histories of material exploitation, dispossession, attempted annihilation, and control. These contestations are made starkly evident in the debates over rape proper and in the constellation of sexualized violations that emanates from them. They include debates that now grip US college campuses about sexual harassment—the limits of what can be said and done to whom—and what speech or conduct creates an actionable hostile environment.

The question then becomes *how* to talk about what kinds of violence shape our understandings of what sex or the sexual (good or bad) is or isn't. In other words, the question becomes how to talk about the kinds of rape that Davis, Deer, and Strangio describe in ways that break the stranglehold of certain feminist framings of sexualized violence—to attempt to recognize and address sexualized violence beyond aggregate stories of individual encounters with individual men, who collectively make the world "bad for women" and, at least rhetorically, for others who are cast as sexually vulnerable or subordinate (i.e., children and occasionally men from "rape-prone" regions or cultures). The questions become how to do it without casting women of color, indigenous, or queer and trans knowledge production as identitarian, monolithic, or inevitably progressive contributions to leftist thought and action. To ask this question is not to suggest that women of color, queers, and the indigenous are presently barred from entering the capacious narratives of #MeToo. The problem is not simply a question of individual relationships, personalities, best intentions, or goodwill.

The problem is one of thought and of law—of the sociolegal conceptualization of the individuating injury of sexualized violence. It is a problem of evidence, of relegating the harm to categories of sex or gender that are presumed to be transparent in meaning. The problem is also one of affect and desire—of wishing for a movement to end sexualized violence that is enacted through the massed figure of the violated "woman," now the legal subject of human rights, which requires for its pilgrim's progress a tale of commensuration, of exchangeable, commodity-like harms: a rape for a rape, in peace or at war, coed to border crosser, "free" citizen to settler colonized subject—a push toward a standardization of coercion like a garment that anyone can wear.[40] Rape as a concept offers a fiction of coherence. Yet the very idea of sexual freedom—here, a world without rape or other forms of sexualized violation—cannot help but involve itself in racial and colonial world orderings, their attendant arrangements of reproduction, territorial and resource acquisition, labor, and social space.

What would it take to forgo the mainstream centering of "me" in the ongoing march of "too"? How could we instead consider what it would take for all of "us" to reckon with the global dispersion and occurrence of sexualized violence in its many forms, rationales, and motivations and as part of historical, uneven, and contradictory exploitations and expropriations? From these coordinates, legal scholars might well ask in this age of human rights, when rape is an affront to the value of humanness, the following question: What is the harm or wrong of rape? Activist scholarship might do the same.

The Work of Rape and Queer Critique

In the place of rape culture, this book offers a new theoretical concept: the work of rape. The work of rape directs attention to the legal, geopolitical, economic, and cultural contexts that post–Cold War US domestic and international efforts to combat rape and sexualized violence may enable and that, in turn, create the meaning and terms of their recognition. The work of rape foregrounds how the footing certain feminisms have gained in national and international institutions are predicated on women of color and indigenous feminist and other activisms. These various kinds of activisms are often critical of local manifestations of gendered and sexualized violence and of neocolonial, imperial, and economic policies that further such exploitation. Instead of assessing or assigning the causes and effects of sexualized violence to culture or opportunistic militarisms alone,[41] the work of rape is an onto-epistemological project. It examines how women of color and indigenous feminist and other activism and justice forums exist not only or inevitably through a parasitic or oppressive relation to elite legal feminisms but also through misapprehensions and failed commensurability required by structures of law. We can witness these interplays in contestations over the meaning of force, consent, and coercion—the interpretive frameworks that narrate harm and enable the recognition of injury—and how these concepts are produced through evidentiary accretion and contextual collapse.

War is no metaphor, although it now passes for such. The battlefield is no longer a battlefield, or rather the battlefield is the office, the grocery store, the university, the playground, the doctor's office. These and the limitless reaches of the internet are all the same: battlefields where women of color, indigenous people, and queer/trans folk perhaps hurt worse but ultimately hurt in some quintessentially "womanly" way. Under this telling, the mere introduction of women of color, queers, and the indigenous as categorical and invariably "leftist" or "progressive" additions cannot alter its temporal logic—#TimesUp. Inclusion does not reorient the meaning and harm of the violation. The included may only invariably, nebulously, "have it worse" in some way that involves "social structures" and an immiserating "history."[42] In this comparative and additive framework, the structuring logics of racial capital, premised as they are on globalized dispossession and exploitation, sexualized or otherwise, nonetheless remain.[43] The task then becomes thinking about how and when certain forms of violence register as "sexualized" ones and what the relationship might be between that recognition and ideas of redress, accountability, and justice that invariably follow. These ways might touch and overlie, but they are not consummately absorbed by the narrative of the gendered human body, the one whose freedoms, however threatened or attenuated, might still be consolidated through a certain language of law—where, for example, the presence of sexual consent or other indications of self-possession or autonomy presumes coincidence with self-fulfillment and liberation.

Stressing incommensurability or difference would move beyond the inclusionary aspirations of dominant #MeToo narratives where race or other forms of social difference exist merely as amplifiers of distress. Thinking about difference as it is articulated within women of color feminisms and trans/queer of color critique is instructive. In those traditions, difference is not oppositional and static but "a practice that holds in suspension various, mutually exclusive structures of values."[44] Approaching difference in this way keeps the socialities that result from population divisions in close contact with the creation of economic value and exploitation. This framing sets sexualized violence within something like Édouard Glissant's right to opacity, which would seem to exist at a hard angle to the protected classes of civil or human rights law that submerge struggles in meaning beneath an air of transparent, categorical belonging.

The work of rape centers, supplements, and redeploys work in critical ethnic studies, queer critique, and women of color feminisms through an engagement with feminist legal epistemologies that have shaped some of the terms of their inquiries in the wake of the Cold War. Throughout the 1990s, with the advent of mass ethnosexualized violence in the Balkans and later Rwanda and the putative end of socialism, new systems of international law emerge as newly authoritative sites of justice.[45] At this time, mass war rape, or more precisely mass ethnoreligious war rape, helped occasion a veritable revolution in international law. Transnational feminist organizing—understood here as an uneasy and contradictory amalgam of feminisms, from international elite legal feminists to local, grassroots groups and analytics, explicitly feminist or otherwise—helped spur these transformations.[46] At this moment of mass rape during "ethnic" conflict and capitalism's triumph, "women's rights" first became widely recognized as human rights, and sexualized violence was first codified in emergent international legal instruments as a violation of what it means to be the human subject of international law. At this moment, the United States seized unexampled geopolitical clout as the world's lone superpower. Yet these instantiations of sexualized violence as central to liberalism as a project of US empire have not been analyzed in queer critiques of racial capitalism or allied scholarship.

The remarkable feminist influence and presence in international law throughout the 1990s has found attention in feminist legal and related scholarship, including feminist international relations and security studies. Particularly insightful work has constellated around the term *governance feminism*. For feminist legal theorists Janet Halley, Prabha Kotiswaran, Rachel Rebouché, and Hila Shamir, governance feminism is "an overarching term" that embraces "any form of state, state-like, or state affiliated power"—including those called "state feminism, carceral feminisms, femocrats, female policy entrepreneurs, the 'special advisors on gender violence' who dot the international legal landscape"—that is "capable of being influenced and guided by feminists and feminist ideas."[47] With an avowedly Foucauldian influence, governance feminism is also "every form in which feminists and feminist ideas exert a governing will within human affairs" and also "human-inflected processes like knowledge formation, technology and even the weather."[48] Theoretical breadth aside, the notion of governance feminism begins with a particular set of coordinates: "the classic intrafeminist struggle between a dominance feminist legal project and its socialist/leftist/postmodern-feminist opposition."[49] Dominance feminism—most closely associated with MacKinnon—"is a theory of how the eroticization of dominance and submission creates gender, creates woman and man in the social form in which we know them."[50]

What I am concerned with here is how value is created and extracted through transnational feminist interactions and packaged as a "legal feminist idea" in ways that the relationship of "feminism" to "governance" or "the state" or even the "law-like" apparatuses of nonstate governance might elide. The work of rape interrogates the material and racialized conditions and knowledges that submerge or enable the recognition of fervent debate—that lean on or crowd out long-standing and ongoing feminist or other activist modes of thinking or being that may or may not operate within the ideological or onto-epistemological commitments that legal feminists typically recognize as "legal" or even "feminist."[51] Engagements with issues connected to "feminism," "gender," and "sexuality"—even ones that might appear easily classifiable as dominance theory—are better theorized through and integrated within other sites of struggle, including racial, antiauthoritarian, antinationalisms, antiwar, or decolonial ones.[52] The heuristic of "governance feminism" can gloss these distinctions and pit dominance feminisms against "the rest" when the factors that might enable or frustrate dominance or radical feminist principles are vastly and more queerly complex than adherence to or rejection of a vision of men dominating women through sex, as chapter 1's discussion of the sex wars and the entrance of rape into international law in the context of eth-nonationalisms explores. Likewise, work in feminist international relations, which broadly considers the rationales for and root causes of wartime rape—nascently through the lens of feminist political economy—has not primarily concerned itself with the subjects and insights of queer and critical ethnic studies or what I call the work of rape.[53] Racial capitalism and the queer en-gines that power it—the insights of queer of color critique in particular—remain out of frame.[54] I am interested, then, in the generation of onto-epistemologies around sexualized violence and how, when, and by whom they are assumed to cohere (or are corralled into coherence) beneath the sign of "feminism" through global material struggles over the ever-unfolding meaning and scope of freedom and emancipation.

The Work of Rape asks what happens when queer and allied scholarship, including Third World and women of color and decolonial feminisms and other activisms, are brought to bear on the long 1990s. When feminist efforts in US civil rights and liberal forums are brought through racial capitalism and empire into novel and dynamic conversations with international law, what contestations surrounding global racial and sexual politics, woven with what possibilities—what violent possibilities, never pure—come into view? From and through queer critique and other activist scholarship, *The Work of Rape* offers a transnational genealogy of rape and law in the aftermath of the Cold War, when violations of "women's rights" were configured as mass crimes and mass violations of human rights against the backdrop of the new wars, the so-called ethnic conflicts in the former Yugoslavia and Rwanda.

Queer of color critique and queer diaspora's materialist inquiries into gen-der, race, indigeneity, and sexuality and the generation of knowledges about them emphasize the instability of "difference."[55] Queer critique asks how people come to understand themselves with, through, and against the insti-tutions, structures of thought, and histories and locations that they inherit or in which they otherwise find themselves. Those places where rule cannot describe or capture life—for example, where discrimination paradigms fail to account for the range of what people experience as injustice—are sites that might (partially and not inevitably) yield "alternative representational domains and practices for addressing the voids in our historical conscious-ness (in other words, a consciousness riven with structurally produced voids)."[56] Yet queer of color critique's defining explorations of sexuality, race, and political economy cohere through an absence. The reconsolidation of international law through the "ethnic" wars as a regulatory device for ap-propriate arrangements of racial "pluralism," gender, and sexuality is missing, and so is an exploration of how they index appropriate alignments to capitalism and property that exceed the single nation-state frame. As Chandan Reddy writes, sexuality "frames, redivides, or seeks to offer synthetic 'meaning'" and in the process "simultaneously conserv[es] and revis[es] the relations and histories of force of both US globalism and racial capitalism."[57] This requires an account of how sex becomes a part of human rights and humanitarian discourse through mass sexualized violence during "ethnic" warfare—the moment of contemporary international law's formal consolidation. The imbrications of human rights law with humanitarian law and international criminal law—what had historically been distinct, if related, bodies of law—has yet to be adequately interrogated in critical ethnic studies or queer critique as a process and not a juridical given, although the results of these entwinements are routinely assessed. My recourse to queer scholarship and methodologies is an effort to resituate queer of color, US-based women of color feminist, and decolonial feminist scholarship in global political spaces and histories often absent in these projects.[58] It is also an insistence that feminist analyses of rape and antirape activism be attuned to the shifting, heterogeneous formations of sexuality often connected to queer and trans of color critique, such as trans subjects, femmes, or other nondominant sexual subjects and errant pleasures.

The work of rape, then, concerns itself with new legal and social articulations of gendered and sexualized freedom, born through global geopolitical reorderings of capital, race, and sex at the end of the twentieth century. Here, I view the call for such freedoms not as strategic alibis or guises through which unpalatable agendas are unilaterally imposed by the state or the international order of them but as a part of "ever-expanding crisis[es] of confusions and conflicts around the ethics and assemblages of liberal knowledge and power."[59] The ambiguity and elasticity of what counts as freedom position it as ever elusive and exceedingly plural. Freedom so figured (or unfigured) is the foundational rationale for the existence, practices, and methods of liberal government and international governance. These escalating scales of freedom and violence—from individual to state, state to international order, individual woman to women as a global group, solitary prejudice to genocide—follow the irregular paths and assemblages of gender, race, and sexuality as they are articulated and rearticulated as critical nodes of state and suprastate justice. As Michel Foucault writes, the liberal state is the consumer and producer of freedom. It "can only function as a number of freedoms actually exist: freedom of the market, freedom to buy and sell, the free exercise of property rights, freedom of discussion, possible freedom of expression, and so on. The new governmental reason needs freedom therefore, the new art of government consumes freedom. It consumes freedom, which means it must produce it. It must produce it, it must organize it."[60] Mimi Thi Nguyen encapsulates Foucault's insight, deeming freedom "an actual relation between governors and governed" that is "precisely the story of liberalism as empire."[61]

For Neda Atanasoski, such a production of freedom, of liberalism as empire, ties absolutely to the international deployment of diversity—as global humanism—at the Cold War's end, where the ascent of "ethnic" warfare (and later global terror) stands in firm contradistinction to US governance. In her words, "the racialization of ideological and religious formations conceived of as antithetical to the flourishing of human diversity, proliferating 'regimes of terror' that have replaced communism, at once reaffirm older notions of humanity and introduce new ones."[62] From this perspective, the ability to frame the conflicts following the collapse of the two superpower world orders as "ethnic" was no knee-jerk reaction to unprecedented events. It instead built on historical efforts by the United States to position itself as the watchdog of democracy, the bastion of a variegated freedom, and otherwise distinguish itself from the stain of European colonialism and the drab uniformity of Soviet control. As Atanasoski explains:

> Developing in response to the juridical gains of the civil rights movement, the liberation struggles in the Global South, and the threat of communism, racial multiculturalism isolated the possibility of human uplift within the boundaries of the U.S.-led "free world," while homogeneity became associated with the suppression of human difference in the Communist "unfree world." Coding the U.S.S.R. and the Eastern Bloc as ethnically homogeneous, even if only ambiguously European, enabled U.S. foreign policy to portray Soviet foreign interests as expansionist and "imperialist." In contrast, the United States' self-understanding as a racially diverse nation, with the paradigm of multiculturalism taking the place of early Cold War civil rights, buttressed its logic of "containing" the Communist threat in the Third World by distancing U.S. military interventionism from an association with European colonialism.[63]

Reentering this long history through the work of rape, with a mind cast toward the twenty-first-century maelstroms of war rape and campus sex, opens spaces for new connections and engagements to emerge. Staging contemporary sexualized controversies through the concept of the work of rape allows connections between present contestations over the bounds of legitimate state violence and the meaning of good sex (and good gender, good race, etc.) so often framed as either national psychodramas or "men versus women" to resonate with the not-so-distant, transnational controversies of the recent war-torn past. Transnational feminisms (which I take to include the "second world"),[64] women of color feminisms, queer of color critique, and other activist scholarship can now meet at a moment when a new complex of international law and governance emerges to manage "ethnic violence" distinguished by mass ethnosexual rape, the world's latest threat.

This staging cuts against individualized responses to and framings of sexualized violence that risk "establishing a wide chasm between the (experience of) empowerment and an actual capacity to shape the terms of political, social, or economic life."[65] It does so by paying attention to how meanings of consent and coercion emerge, as I argue, through racialized framings of the problem of global sexualized violence. As rape and other forms of sexualized violence become crimes against humanity and violations of human rights, they amend what it means to be the human subject of international law. Such a human subject, in cultural theorist Sylvia Wynter's estimation, exemplifies "our present ethnoclass (i.e., Western bourgeois) conception of the human, which overrepresents itself as if it were the human itself."[66] Central to these maneuvers is the entrenchment and extension of the autonomous individual who is "not just any single human being but a particular way to understand and inhabit human being—a subjectivity—in which the individual understands himself to be free when he acts without influence from others."[67] Janet Jakobsen, writing in the US context, describes how "the imbrication of Protestant values and the production of value . . . make sexual relations a central part of US policy both domestically and internationally. . . . [S]ex is intimately tied to the ethics of capitalism and, ultimately, to war."[68] Jakobsen explains: "Just as the discourse of sexual freedom focuses on autonomous individuals, so also the discourse of national sovereignty is organized around the idea of autonomous nations."[69] The alleged autonomy of individual and nation thus becomes "not only the ideology of subjectivity under capitalism but the ascription of both value and citizenship to that subject under the law, including (or perhaps especially) the law of the sovereign nation."[70]

What the work of rape also demonstrates is how visions of sexual autonomy formally activated by elite legal feminists under international legal regimes in the 1990s help produce an uneven order of states. New systems for criminalizing war rape as war crimes, crimes against humanity, and even genocide provide a check on state sovereignty and autonomy, constraining how states might permissibly choose to manage their populations. Building on

Jakobsen's compelling formulation, if such sexual ordering produces autonomous subjectivities, then bad sex or illicit sex produces relations to be shunned because they disorder the conditions necessary for labor and capital's continuance. This is not to condone war rape or other forms of violation but to press against framework of rights, civil or human, that are rooted in individual frameworks of freedom and fail to recognize historically produced and variegated collective vulnerabilities. In the postsocialist era, under the new system of international law, the recognition and production of "bad sex" transpires unevenly under liberal and human rights regimes that depend on what critical ethnic studies scholar Randall Williams calls "the divided world," or a world yet riven by colonialisms. As Williams writes, "Human rights have increasingly come to define 'the political' in this age of advanced capitalist globalization."[71] In his estimation, the "postwar re-formation of international institutions" that inaugurated the formal project of human rights "did not constitute a break with the historical structures of colonial violence but instead was part and parcel of an imperialist-directed reorganization of relations within and between contemporary state and social formations: the colonial, the neocolonial, and the neoimperial."[72]

After the Cold War, expansions in the meaning and social significance of sexualized violence reorient and rework the boundary between sexual consent and coercion as a means of demarcating peace and terror. The meanings of consent and coercion emerge through racialized framings of the problem of global sexualized violence and particularly through the figuring of rape and other sexualized violence as atrocity crimes within international law. From antinationalist Balkan understandings of rape in warfare to indigenous or postcolonial activisms in the Americas, wildly varying feminist understandings of sexualized violence were differently mobilized in the campaign to establish rape as a verifiable violation of what it means to be human—for rape to become a violation of human rights, a crime against humanity, a war crime, and a kind of genocide.

From these disparate contexts and experiences, rape and sexual violence emerge as negotiated terms, recognizable in part by their definitional components, which generally include what it means to be forced to have sex, what constitutes consent to sex, and what sexual coercion looks like. The push-pull between frameworks of consent and coercion is a part of the fractious and difficult work of identifying what "counts" as rape, other sexualized violence, and even sex itself.[73] Coercion frameworks—tested in part on the grounds of racialized war—are often presented as a corrective to contract theory that would render rape and other sexualized violence a problem of consent. Here, consent is taken be assent to the actions taking place without further examination of context. The meanings of consent and coercion emerge, I argue, through racialized framings of the problem of global sexualized violence—exploitative and expropriating contexts that are paradoxically (but productively) disavowed through the very act of "contextualizing" the problems these contexts present to frameworks of individual sexual consent. Mass war rape, for example, presses hard against individual asseverations of consent as an appropriate metric for diagnosing the presence or absence of sexualized violence. But the discussion of consent and coercion (not to mention its application in law) often assumes artificially delimited fields of what counts as "sexual." In this way, sexual injury is already sundered from formulations that do not solely locate the wound on autonomous, individual bodies.

The changing contours of sexual consent and coercion, I argue, reshape the world. They affect what counts as legitimate warfare. They create at-risk populations and geographies subject to new and intensified forms of governance in the name of public health and reproductive freedom. They contour the social and legal meaning of race (or simply "difference") by revamping the limits of state sovereignty in a "postsocialist" order. Contestations over the parameters of sexual consent and coercion in turn rework the meaning and operations of empire and neocolonialism in a moment of US geopolitical ascendency. By formally setting sexualized violence as external and not foundational to the concomitant splay of global capital, it becomes a problem that the righteous investments of capital and the judicious application of political and military power might mitigate, if not solve outright. It is in this underacknowledged relational context and history that the current preoccupation with sexual harassment and rape unfolds. International law and governance, legal theory, and scholarship, produced partly by elite feminist attorneys through their encounters with transnational feminist activisms, are thus metanarratives and material practices that help structure relations between states, individuals, and the international order of states. Law and the terms of law—including its articulation within and through feminist legal academia in concert with transnational organizing networks—is in many ways an undertheorized archive and architecture of power.[74]

What this means for international and domestic governance, rights, and populations—for how power operates through concepts like gender, race, sexuality, and nation—requires a method that takes into account legal developments in the articulations of consent, force, and coercion. These developments must be treated not only as discrete occurrences, but as malleable and contingent processes that are themselves dependent on other legal processes and theorizations that at first blush may seem unconnected to antisexualized violence law and activisms. This analytic, I argue, gives us something to say about the inclusionary impasse of certain strains of #MeToo. It is a gesture toward a theory of sexualized violence that does not assume a coherent global feminist subject, pit social groups against each other in a hierarchy of comparative suffering that presupposes those groups as ahistorical and discrete, or align any particular form of feminism, queerness, or social activism with unmediated progress. This requires a method for the cultural study of law that emphasizes what falls away as much as what remains. This method must consider, as Williams succinctly puts it, what is "negated and refused in order for the liberal model of rights to emerge as the privileged ideological frame through which excessive cruelty" was and may be "conceived and interpreted,"[75] the thinking and work that can only "count" aslant.

Those political possibilities can be difficult to see when rape is so often framed in the contractual/transactional terms of consent. If the story of rape has thus far remained largely portrayed as atomized negotiations for sex overwritten by rage or misunderstanding—or, in the case of war rape prosecutions, a problem of a certain type of governance system (or lack thereof)—the work of rape is a radical replotting. It is a rearrangement of plot in deference to critiques of historical time. It is a new vantage from which to consider how law works, from which to probe the coherency of the legal subject and the subjectivities, or ways of understanding and situating oneself in the world, that such a subject helps engender. I think of the work of rape as an effort to rearrange or even derange plot in all its many senses—the ground, the story, the plan, or intrigue. This plotting is a heuristic for keeping abstractions of gendered sexuality and theory grounded in rape's intimacies with property and law and their instrumentality to racist, settler colonial, imperial, and slaveholding orders—of keeping rape, through its genocidal and dispossessive iterations, roughly tethered to expropriations of resources, lives, and land. Of keeping changing legal models of consent not solely as isolated considerations of individual will or desire, but dependent on changes in property regimes and relations. Otherwise, rape is, in essence, a deceitful act, an act of "individual" violation that supports collective lies, a way of claiming possession within and across multiple sites for what is never one's "own." To apprehend the work of rape is to apprehend the lie. Zeroing in on the work of rape lets us perceive how efforts to create legally recognizable sexual harms through the standardization of concepts like consent and coercion render disparate instances of sexualized violence commodity-like and interchangeable, echoing the violation's centrality to property regimes. By following how the meaning of rape and sexualized violence is produced through feminist activist and legal negotiations that range across geographies, peoples, and bodies of law, this project considers how the concept of women's rights as human rights forms a connective tissue—a global medium of exchange—that is neither simply repressive nor a site of unqualified liberation. To consider these often-contradictory effects, I develop a method that reconceptualizes the meaning, scope, and impact of law—recognizing it as an archive of queer kinships, of unacknowledged limits, bans, and productions. The work of rape is about bordering, ordering. The method, what I call law beyond Law, kicks at the fence.

Thinking *law beyond Law*

With the 1975 publication of *Against Our Will*, Susan Brownmiller's remake of rape from an instinctual act to a crime of violence morphed into a phrase that begat a million feminist think pieces and became a battle cry: "Rape is about power, not sex."[76] But a genealogy of rape inaugurated by queer, trans, and women of color writers, scholars, and activists tells a more complicated story. What falls within the ambit of sexuality, good or bad—what is, in fact, *sexual*—is certainly about power, as legal scholar Katherine Franke and others have observed. Writing in the case of the police assault of Abner Louima, Franke defines the sexual as less a static descriptor of certain acts, body parts, or events and instead as "a particularly efficient and dangerous conduit with which to exercise power."[77] Building on this work, Jasbir Puar notes that "'the sexual' is always already inscribed" within regimes of power—be they necropolitical, biopolitical or otherwise—in ways that "implicat[e] corporeal conquest, colonial domination, and death."[78]

The Work of Rape provides a transnational genealogy of rape and sexual violence as salient terms and concepts in international humanitarian, criminal, human rights law and selected sites of US domestic law through attention to the racialized legacies that append feminist and legal theorizations of sex, gender, and violence locally, internationally, and transnationally.[79] These genealogies—which contain but are not reducible to traditional accounts of legal precedent—emerge only by reading across the multiple mediums, practices, and locations that converge to lift the concepts of rape and sexual violence to international legal attention, shaping its discursive potentials. These include war theory and securitization practices; historical and contemporary popular accounts of the disintegration of the former Yugoslavia and Rwanda at and across local, international, and transnational scales; US/Western feminist organizing and theorizations of race, sexuality, gender, violence, and the state; transnational feminist commitments and organizing networks; (academic) legal treatments of rape and sexual violence as torture and as human rights; the placement of rape and sexual violence in humanitarian law as mass crimes; the resulting convolutions in how we conceptualize consent at home and abroad; the invagination of the neoliberal state by nongovernmental organizations and auxiliary institutions; and the racialization of Islam in and outside of the Balkans.

The list is long and tortured by design. It is an attempt to illustrate how a narrow focus on rape, a seemingly self-evident violation that a lagging rape law must rush to correct, cannot account for what underlies it. Too close of a focus on law that spans only the surface of feminist movement efforts—such as a narrative that presents each ruling or statute as a discrete event—belies foundational and ongoing interrelations. Such a focus elides the concentrated, multiscalar feminist and other activist ambitions that source from overlapping legal, geopolitical, and theoretical locations. To put the proposition slightly differently, a fixed focus on the bounded rule, statute, or judicial decision (or even a flat reliance on the legal concepts that animate them, like consent, coercion, agency, or autonomy) can obscure how the creation of good or bad sex, especially impermissible or bad sex, has value. Sex has political, geopolitical, and economic value—differential value across people and places and times. And sex has since the ethnic wars become a key facet of the international management of states and neoliberal economies in very particular ways.

As Sharon Holland writes, "There is no raceless course of desire"; even this sentiment might be enhanced by a focus on settler colonialism and the making of desire or the erotic within law and law-like systems of governance—of how borders and property allocations foster certain proximities and distances that "desire" glosses over, leaving those less salutary dimensions to labor at a remove beneath other names.[80] Sex, good or bad, has value, value is always about desire; pleasure is gleaned from the fields of violence, of race, class, and gendered power—it does not exist in isolation from them. The work of rape is the generation of value—value that is produced in part through the structural intimacies created through collisions between what is and is not able to be named sexual violence through demands for state responsibility and international modes of redress. What shape that state responsibility now takes—how impermissible sexualized violence is defined, when its occurrence spurs legal or militaristic action—is a negotiation of political and economic value at the core.[81] But this vantage can be lost in traditional feminist legal approaches to sexualized violence. This vantage can also be diminished in activist scholarship, including certain feminist and queer ones, that accept law's pronouncements about what it does and does not do or otherwise fail to examine law's technical inner workings—the conduits of power that at once create and complicate divisions between the local, regional, transnational, or global.

Juridical categories are contested configurations of language and practice that frequently constitute and support specific notions of the state but do not inevitably align or harmonize in any easily digestible totality. Across and within national and international legal systems, the juridical realm is, like the state itself, noncohesive and at times inchoate—it is nothing without the people who create, interpret, implement, and rework it. So, too, the composition of the elite themselves—their partial alignments with institutional, state, and juridical authority, varying across international, transnational, and local scales—must be considered, even if it is rarely noted. Omissions of these sorts obscure crucial dimensions of how state power and international governance work to facilitate and convert "gender progress" to less desirable ends, including the economic exploitation of countries or regions deemed sexually "backward" or otherwise "unsafe." They also tend to downplay how deeply those conflicts and controversies "elsewhere" live in the center of so much of the Global North's understanding of the appropriate moral, ethical, and legal demarcations of sex into permissible/pleasurable and illicit/harmful. Because domestic law so immediately governs us, it is easy to lose sight of how legal norms and meanings concerning sexualized violence are produced not only through national or local law but through interactions across global borders. Given these developments, large-scale and small, the task at hand is, as Donna Haraway writes, "to tell big-enough stories without determinism, teleology, and plan."[82]

The Work of Rape develops a queer method that bridges theories and operations of international law, governance, and power. It draws from feminist legal scholarship's attention to institution building and legal technics as well as activist scholarship's theorizations of transnationalism, statecraft, racial capitalism, historical social difference, and subjectivity. I call this method law beyond Law. The method is an approach to studies of law and identity that views law not simply as a formal, transparent vehicle of state and institutional authority. Through this method, law is understood as a transnational archive of attachments and intimacies whose force draws in part from the secretive relations of its contents, the coded proximities that coil in the legal theories, terms of art, mechanics, and processes that underlie the decision or rule, the pronouncement. The method directs attention to the making and inner operations of law—the human and nonhuman relations and connections required to theorize harm within the preexisting strictures of available structures and theories of violation. Situating gendered and other injuries in this complex of meaning-making disrupts the presumed force and coherence of law as well as what Wendy Brown calls "liberal solipsism" or "the radical decontextualization of the subject characteristic of liberal discourse that is key to the fictional sovereign individualism of liberalism."[83] It does so by placing the concept of grievance or injury, in this case sexualized injury, within the onto-epistemologies and structures that make it cognizable as individual violation.

In contrast to law beyond Law, capital-*L* "Law" approaches artificially bolster the purpose and power of Law, amplifying its normalizing and disciplinary effects as a social regulator. Largely aiming for the empowerment and redress of the individual, these approaches isolate the making of legal theory and law to the province of the legal elite. This shapes what, in the present instance, can and cannot fall within the realm of sex and sexualized violence by creating their terms and meanings through a thin and isolated history of Western gender that, among other things, downplays or denies its foundational and ongoing settler colonialism. Instead, law beyond Law emphasizes how people who resist oppressive conditions and create (multiple, competing) knowledge about their situations are in fact theorizing harm. The method also emphasizes how (and how often) their work participates in or otherwise becomes part of *legal* theorizations of harm.

The most trenchant cultural critiques of race and sexuality within law aspire to a practice of what Siobhan Somerville calls looking "sideways" or interpreting legal opinions and lawmaking in their historical contexts. In "Queer Loving," Somerville interrogates ideologies of race and sexual orientation from within the historicized juridical production of racial and sexual formations.[84] By reading the US Supreme Court decision *Loving v. Virginia*—which forbids state prohibitions of interracial marriage—alongside the contemporaneous legal history of homosexuality and transformations in federal policy on immigration and naturalization (a.k.a. she reads "sideways"),[85] Somerville offers an account of race, sexuality, and nation as legally and culturally intertwined. This method of reading law eschews the much-critiqued traditional reliance on formal legal precedent availed by judges and legal practitioners to ground and legitimate the legal reasoning marshaled in support of their present determinations. Instead, Somerville's method favors a historically specific analysis that refuses analogical thinking—the notion that "race" might be like "gender," which in turn might be like "sexuality"—for the purposes of extending legal protection. Not only do race-gender-sexuality analogies promote the fiction that the originating unit of comparison—in this case, race—is now essentially immune to discrimination or other issues encompassed in the purview of civil rights legislation, but analogizing also, as Puar writes, "relieves mainstream gays, lesbians, and queers from any accountability to anti-racist agendas, produces whiteness as a queer norm (and straightness as a racial norm), and fosters anti-intersectional analyses that posit sexual identity as 'like' or 'parallel' to race."[86] On a more practical level, legal reliance on analogy has also been roundly criticized by legal scholars, including MacKinnon, who caution against a narrowing of the legal recognition of sexism that can result from defining its injury within the limited strictures of recognized civil rights violations.[87]

Reading sideways counters an aggressive reliance on precedent as the preeminent mode of legal reasoning by periodizing statutes and opinions within the historical currents of their time. Legal and trans studies theorist Dean Spade has also argued against the uncritical celebration of rights, noting that rights guarantees and their administrative and legislative enforcement produce inequities by design.[88] Yet cultural studies of the law still tend to treat the statutes or the legal opinions at issue as fairly discrete objects of analysis—their vitality as legal artifacts bounded by the official language in which they are finally promulgated. Even as law is inserted, read back into its historical moment, the historical process of its creation—the inner workings of strategy and process, these resolutely legal processes—are sidelined, not portrayed as forms of power or typically incorporated into analyses of the making of race or other forms of social historical difference.

My method builds on both Somerville's and Spade's insights by placing the historical contexts of legal decision making and administration in conjunction with the doctrinal, theoretical, and procedural production of law to emphasize law beyond Law. This method brings the insights of queer critique, allied scholarship on transnational race making, and feminist legal studies' attention to how law works in more explicit contact.[89] This method infuses analysis of legal processes and concepts that produce law into any attempt to assess the meaning and impact of law. Such concepts include doctrines of privacy and autonomy but also theories of punishment, liability, and jurisdiction that implicate larger histories and crucially other subjects than, in this instance, the juridical treatment of rape. Legal processes also encompass the minutiae of law—the procedures that shape an internal narrative of law, including the technical crafting of precedent, which depends on multiple strands of thematically disparate, historically situated administrative and other law.

With this in mind, I direct considerable energies toward situating the work of legal scholars in relation to the work of humanities scholars and nonlegal feminist activists, treating the sum of these encounters as essentially a part of lawmaking. Here, legal academic production and practice are not transparent accounts of what law is, was, or will be. They form a neglected but meaningful site of analysis because they contain the traces or marks of engagements that cannot be wholly represented within the language and practice of law. I therefore view legal practice and academic production as the sum of the efforts, affects, circumstances, and activisms or social relations and engagements that are distilled into the legal argument or thought. In this spirit, I turn toward ancillary forms of legal knowledge, including journal articles, talks, white papers, position papers, case and statutory law, and conference attendance records and reports. My method examines legal scholarship in the context of authors' participation in legal and extralegal processes—including activist networks and organizing. In doing so, it makes the process and production of law and law-like spaces geared toward the address of historical social "difference" into an archive and relation of study bound to any discussion of what the law does or what it is. In this account, liberal and human rights law is not just a project premised on individual rights but a conflicted process that must account for the structure of legal arguments. As such, law beyond Law attenuates tendencies to enshrine US law, legal practice, and conceptual genealogies as global templates, while acknowledging the undeniable effects of US law on international legal feminisms and the crafting of international law as a carceral project. In this way, the method joins scholarship that cautions against overendowing and overdetermining the heft and expanse of law, overestimating or prescribing the area, degree, and kind of influence it may exert.

This method is no reclamation of law or queer liberalism that justifies legal protections for the few at the expense of the many. It is instead a way to think through law's effects in ways that don't presume an outcome, good or bad, or pin stable legal meaning to the particular issue a single law or set of laws might address. It seeks what can be naturalized in discussions of civil or human rights from any location, politics, or intellectual formation that does not query the transnational racial, gendered, and sexualized and other politics of the organizational and institutional knowledge understood to describe and evince its harms.[90] This method requires thinking about not only the differential order of rights—or the hierarchies of rights and their applications across national, regional, and international registers—but also the processes, activisms, knowledges, and logics that form and connect them, that disrupt clean articulations of those scales. The method appeals then, as the following chapters show, to the promise of transnational analysis and work in the queer diasporic tradition, where the transnational is "not merely multinational, but . . . an analytic or methodology that denaturalizes the forms of social, subjective, and political organization implied by the nation-state form."[91] In this way, the method builds on queer scholarship that performs, as Gayatri Gopinath writes, "a queer incursion" that "instantiates alternative cartographies and spatial logics that allow for other histories of global affiliation and affinity to emerge."[92]

At stake in this effort is not the form of immediate institutional recourse available for those who experience sexualized violence. Rather, law beyond Law considers what breadth of knowledge and experience will be consulted and considered in current public and legal debates about the meaning and significance of sexualized violence, broadly, and rape, sexual assault, and sexual harassment more narrowly. What is the legitimate or valid context in which discrete legal issues can be framed and subsequently evaluated? As Kyla Wazana Tompkins writes, what conceptual configuring of the circular relations between selves and social worlds allow us to "recognize our bodies as vulnerable to each other in ways that are terrible—that is, full of terror—and, at other times, politically productive"?[93]

My motivations here run alongside Robert Reid-Pharr's insistence on a "post-humanist archival practice" that does not cede discursive, material, or institutional ground to a totalizing humanist metaphysic but instead considers "the multiple ways that the intellectual protocols of slavery and colonization have structured increasingly complex and novel discourses of human subjectivity" and the "intellectual insurgencies" that undertake that work.[94] In other words, I view law, the state, and the international order of states not from the perspective of sovereignty or legitimacy but precisely as sites that evince "a complex problem of power."[95] Following this line of reasoning, law is no cogent "deliverable," and the subject of law is no blank or coherent agent exercising free will. Both are amalgamations of the concepts and processes of their conjoined epistemic and bureaucratic inner workings in an uneven world—together, a fretful incoherence.

The Work of Rape and *law beyond Law*

The conceptual trajectory of rape in the Anglo-American tradition—from crime of property, to crime against honor, to gender violence and a potential affront to sex equality or autonomy principles, to a violation of human rights and at times genocide—is a case study in the incoherence of law and its subject. But only if we view that trajectory as marking changes in human subjectivity, geopolitics, and property and labor arrangements that are otherwise diminished and obscured when changes in interpretations of rights or crimes are posited to be self-evidently "on the books." For example, as rape and sexual violence become atrocity crimes through "ethnic" conflict—and are statutorily defined or litigated as war crimes, crimes against humanity, and genocide—they transform from individual to collective violations. As formal armed conflicts abate into zones of instability, mass rape and other forms of sexualized violence also migrate, becoming concerns that persist both in and out of war.[96] This movement is facilitated and made recognizable by shifts in international legal literature terminology—which initially designate the problem of gender and sexualized violence in armed conflict as "rape," then "sexual violence," then "sexual slavery" and finally "gender violence." These name changes are predicated on a complex interplay of local, international, and transnational feminist activisms; legal feminist activisms; and the larger international legal and global response to the "new wars."[97]

The transformations of content and scope that accompany this changing nomenclature reorder and reemphasize different aspects of the wide range of violations that may occur in the orbit of the sexual. An emphasis on "rape" in warfare, for instance, marks certain acts and aspects of the term—under Anglo-American legal traditions, what constitutes consent, what signals compulsion or force, whether anal or other penetration will be considered rape—as subject to public reconfiguration and debate. "Sexual violence" encompasses and foregrounds recognition of nonpenetrative acts as sexual violations, including forced public nudity.[98] "Sexual slavery" accounts for prolonged control and physical restraint, a potential theft of labor, and repeated sexual violation.[99] "Gender violence" expands the purview of "women's human rights" to encompass reproductive violence such as forced pregnancy, forced abortion, and forced or underage marriage.[100] Gender violence also attempts to acknowledge male vulnerability to sexual violence.[101] Mutable theorizations of rape and sexual violence, as well as the content and meaning of war, thus unfold as commentators and tribunals interpret the language (statutory or otherwise) that puts rape and sexual violence within their purview. Tribunals and courts issue judgments and decisions that depend on the work of legal and nonlegal experts to structure charges and theorize evidence from the lives of the locals, the people who work and live on the grounds of war.

These terminological shifts, largely unmarked in law and its supplementary literatures, transpire unevenly and should not be understood as marking discrete historical episodes, events, or studied intentions. Instead, these shifts feed and are in turn fed by further transformations in the host of factors that conspired to bring wartime rape and sexual violence to attention in the early 1990s—changes in how we understand warfare, gender, sexuality, state violence, and more recently the politics of terror. Moreover, these shifts explicitly carve out gendered sexuality as a domain for international humanitarian law and other military matters, providing formal legal avenues that international sexual rights advocates and Global South and decolonial feminists also avail for a number of purposes and to a variety of ends.

The method of law beyond Law highlights the processes, mechanics, and conceptual underpinnings that give legal life to the grievances of civil or human rights claims, connecting them in ways that vaunt and reenvision the terrain of (liberal) individualism. This occurs not only through the uptake of equality paradigms enacted through "diversity" or "multiculturalism" but by availing the mechanisms and structures of law and legal thought that must be summoned to forward them and that operate unevenly in an uneven or, in Williams's evocative term, "divided" world. Analogy, autonomy, contract, doctrines of responsibility, jurisdiction, and the legitimate use of violence shape the definition and recognition of rape and other forms of sexualized violence. This in turn affects the social meanings and arrangements of gender, sex, race, and sexuality. The structures and inner workings of law also affect how states may be deemed responsible to their publics and how the international order of states is understood to be responsible to humanity. These operations remake "private" and "public" spaces by changing understandings of war and risk, as the following chapters explore, and therefore remake how people live and experience "freedom."

The structures, internal processes, and conceptual scaffolding of law point to unexpected connections of power and capital between nation-states, regions, and peoples that are enlivened through international law and its epistemic structures of harm, injury, and evidence that circulate legal knowledge and ideas. Neglecting them, I suggest, inadvertently contributes to the process by which "history transforms documents into monuments" by brushing past the ways that even law contains stories that revamp or undermine its presumed authority.[102] The "legal kinships" and affinities that scholars trace by following solely, for example, the legal position on the issue rather than the embedded histories of the technical arguments marshaled to discuss them (and the labor arrangements and institutional locations of those who make the arguments) inadvertently disavow a host of relationships, of kinships, that exceed standard accountings.[103]

Using law beyond Law holds open a transnational queer space between a number of disciplinary and methodological approaches to violence. These include writing that elaborates the political flexibility of gender-based freedom advocacy and the underbelly of liberal strategies that fuse the language of human rights, sexual and reproductive freedom, and gender equality;[104] explorations of race, property, and labor inaugurated by Cedric Robinson beneath the banner of racial capitalism and carried through in work on the racial roots of neoliberalism as a counter to post–World War II freedom movements, decolonization, and the ongoing labors of settler dispossession;[105] legal and sociolegal scholarship on Title IX, human trafficking, war rape, and theories of sexual consent and coercion;[106] queer and trans theory's complex revelations in desire, kinship, and solidarity, which are also concerned with empire and "racial capitalism," if not always recognized as such;[107] and scholarship that interrogates the sprawl of the surveillance state through the state's embattled relationship to racialized Islam.[108] The method holds that space to offer a queer geopolitics of empire, one where any account of the "standard architecture" of empire must take up negotiations and overhauls in force, consent, and coercion that transpire as sexualized violence and ethnic warfare meet at the Cold War's end.[109]

The method is also an attempt to give critical attention to liberal and internationalist feminisms as they exist across national and class divides and not just to extract the repressive effects of their alignments with ever-encroaching security states. I want to mark how subscribers to these feminisms (or those portrayed as subscribing to them) experience them (as constrained choice, as liberatory) and how their language and practice may imperfectly, haltingly, provide opportunities for other motivations or worldviews to take root. This approach does not discount the social fact of uneven distributions of power typified by mass disenfranchisement from political institutions—like the United Nations and the nation-state itself. Instead, it seeks to open seemingly entrenched or congealed apparatuses to the possibility of transformations that provide more than hegemonic reinforcements, to see what may be seized, when it may be seized, and by whom. The method of law beyond Law is an effort to remedy how treatments of international human rights and humanitarian law can telescope international law and governance with Global North state policy and compound the collapse by focusing on local response to the homogeneous thrust of Law.

Reading law beyond Law as method retheorizes and reorients the conceptual and procedural inner workings of law and what we think of as law itself in an effort consider how histories of colonialism, imperialism, and militarisms not only foment its concepts and operations (including the concepts of sexual consent and coercion) but continue to contour their meaning and color their work. The terms *consent* and *coercion* are negotiated through historical contestations of sociolegal concepts like force, fraud, autonomy, and self-possession, requiring attention to the social translation of what counts as sexual violence as it informs legal terms of art and process. Some of this is definitional—what suffices, for example, as evidence of consent or coercion. Some is procedural, administrative, and even conceptual, where the idea of violation is bound to theories of harm that implicate larger histories and subjects rather than to sexualized violence alone.

This method shows how the work of rape is desire work in intimate and public properties exceeding human action and intention. By this I mean that the legal recognition of rape is not simply recognition of an individual or even mass violation. It is a structuring of what forms of sexual desire are licit—what forms desire may take without prompting state interference or cultural condemnation. It is also a pivot in a much broader system that in turn endorses and entrenches certain ways of thinking about law and certain theories and operations of law that exceed the delimited issue of rape. It is a pivot in the work of global racial capitalism.

In other words, if Black, brown, and indigenous experiences are "left out," merely iterating that these rapes are somehow "worse" or that these bodies are simply "more vulnerable" does not engage the structures of thought that underlie legal and social ways of thinking and speaking about sexualized violence. Recognizing this is a start, but not an end. It is better to follow how the concepts of consent and coercion become commodity-like, exchangeable as evidence of gendered vulnerability, in political and legal speech. With the advent of rape as a violation of international criminal, humanitarian, and human rights law, notions of consent and coercion can and do undergird the international order of states through the language of human rights and humanitarianism while facilitating indigenous dispossession, militarized interventions, and racial capital flows—echoes of the property logics that initially structured the Anglo-American recognition of the crime.[110] This contractual framing allows arguments about the impermissibility of sexualized violence to stay locked in the initial transaction, framing violation as simply a bad negotiation, misrecognition, or mostly one-off compulsion. This casts the concept of sexualized violence as an issue of consent, force, or coercion—an imposition on the "free will" of the self-actuated rights-bearing subject—and leads to debates familiar to feminists, including the sex war–era grapplings about the abstracted possibility of sexual agency under conditions of patriarchy.

In feminist circles and mass publics, subtleties have often been blanketed by the demand to "believe women." In some queer antiracist circles, they have not.[111] Crucially, consent and coercion are not simply "differentially experienced on the ground," but they are also concepts that take the experiences of the indigenous, vulnerable domestic populations, and the war-raped of the Global South and use them to advance an idea of violence against women and form legal terms of art, like *consent*, that traverse social and legal contexts and bodies of law. In this way, the history of state and judicial engagement with antisexualized violence activisms may be more productively traced through an embedded and context-dependent genealogy of what sexualized violence means—what work it does—than a simple mapping of legal decisions or precedent or a push for recognizing, however well-meaning, the prevalence of sexualized violence in the lives of "all women." The work of rape and the method of *law beyond Law* destabilize progressive notions of history, time, and social group formation by recognizing, for example, how high-order international human rights and criminal violations like genocide—which can push against the standard of consent as being the most relevant indicator of sexualized violence—reverberate in ongoing debates on Title IX, a civil rights issue. In short, the making of antisexual violence law can open into vistas of law and governance beyond the singular issue of rape and sexual violence in ways that defy straightforward narrativization of the progress of women's rights and that complicate critiques of historical progress that skirt close attention to how the law works. Attention to the making of antisexual violence law also opens up how we think about law and justice and inclusion in law by asking that we reconsider what law is and exactly what it does. The following sections illustrate this.

Rape as Reproduction, Rape as Genocide / Dead Labor and *law beyond Law*

Here is a way we often discuss law and social justice: law will give it to you, or it will not. In each case these declarations conceptually sever justice from law—justice is something that simply can or cannot happen in this place called law. The dislocation of law from justice reifies each as categories that are mostly self-evident and isolated; they cannot touch. Yet through this separation, justice happens. An idea of justice emerges in relation to the work of law that shifts and changes and accommodates and in turn shifts, changes, and accommodates what justice is—even as we assert what it is not. As Lisa Lowe observes, the language of justice and ability to imagine it is entangled in the history of colonialism; the language of justice is inherited.[112] Thinking about law and justice relationally and as colonial inheritance reframes the significance and possibilities of the 1990s advent of rape and sexualized violence as atrocity crimes—war crimes, crimes against humanity, and genocide—in the grip of ethnic war. It provides another plot point in the narrative of rape.

This relational thinking, coupled with an attention to law beyond Law as method, can tell us something, for example, about genocide and the possibilities for justice that accrue or disperse through the heavy presence of its formal charge or the unmarked logics that persist in its absence—that largely cannot be officially, legally apprehended in that name, in part because international law turns on voluntary compliance and valorizes state sovereignty. The 1948 UN Convention on the Prevention and Punishment of the Crime of Genocide defines *genocide* as acts "committed with intent to destroy, in whole or in part, a national ethnic, racial or religious group." Genocidal acts as enumerated include "killing members of the group," "causing serious bodily or mental harm to group members," and "deliberately inflicting on the group conditions of life calculated to bring about its physical destruction in whole or in part." The convention also defines genocide as a form of reproductive violence, including acts that "impos[e] measures intended to prevent births within the group" and the "forcib[le] transfe[r] of children of the group to another group."[113] In the midst of the 1990s ethnic wars, rape as genocide emerged as a privileged way of thinking about race and sex and gender and violence—a corrective to the critiques long made against radical or dominance feminists like MacKinnon or Andrea Dworkin, whose totalizing views of gender made little space for thinking through other historical forms of social difference. How do these changes in law shape what justice can and cannot mean? As a method, law beyond Law clears space to think about genocide by looking at how it is named or not named and not only in legal decisions or pronouncements. The method also directs us to consider legal technologies and terms of art—those epistemic and procedural inner workings that give words like *consent* and *coercion* legal meaning and social force. By looking at how law theorizes the harm or wrong of rape—as an incursion, a besmirching of autonomy or self-possession, as an affront to equality principles, or, in the case of rape as genocide, as animus-driven group destruction—the meanings and utility of consent and coercion as concepts that promote or frustrate "justice" come into relief.

To demonstrate the method of law beyond Law, I follow it in concert with theoretical models developed in queer of color and transgender critique and consider the relationships between property/land, genocide, and rape.

Rather than look at charges of "genocidal rape" as a discrete category, I place rape as genocide in relation to broader claims about the nature of rape as a violation and the primacy of consent to its diagnosis. Specifically, I look at the legal charge of rape by deception—a legal form of rape no longer widely recognized. Rape by deception is exactly what it sounds like—a usually penetrative sex act obtained under false pretenses. In locations where it is prohibited, this charge has attached itself to race jumpers, trans men, and butch women. Interestingly, it has recently emerged at the center of a set of legal debates that seek to determine on what grounds rape should be considered a legal wrong. Rape by deception is thought to offer a conceptual paradox for those who contend that rape's infringements of autonomy—conceived mostly, but not exclusively, as individual decision-making and the manifestation of free will—are the rationale for its criminalization. The thinking goes: how can rape by deception not be uniformly outlawed if the rationale for condemning rape in the first place is an autonomy violation? This positioning holds the notion of choice or welcomeness to a sexual encounter as indicators of autonomy at arm's length from queer work on the contradictions and complexities of affect and desire.[114] Rape by deception and rape as genocide are kept apart, theorized separately, but there are connections between them that law beyond Law opens to view, honing in on shifts in the meanings of consent and coercion as commodity-like, as reproductive technologies that designate permissible and impermissible forms of intimacies and population control—ones that can merit military campaigns in the name of justice, as sites of capitalist expansion.

What ties rape as genocide and rape by deception together are not only notions of wrongs or harms that justify juridical attention or oversight but also how debates about consent and coercion are mechanisms that collapse and connect what we might loosely call sexualized injury across time, location, and type or kind. Famously, Karl Marx has the following to say about dead labor: "Capital is dead labour, that, vampire-like, only lives by sucking living labour, and lives the more, the more labour it sucks."[115] For Marx, dead labor is work ossified, congealed into a machine, a piece of property—a commodity. I understand legal definitions of rape and the legal recognition of rape as akin to dead labor, as commodities—things that embody and obscure the social relations of their productions, objectify and attempt to consolidate ideas about sexual violence. Efforts to create legally recognizable sexual harms by standardizing concepts like consent and coercion render disparate cases of sexualized violence—and the affective attachments and forms of care that drive antisexualized violence organizing—commodity-like and interchangeable. Harassment in the classroom, sexualized torture in a black site prison, and rape on this or that battlefield are conceptually connected, marked by a lack of consent and the presence of force or coercion, proffering a capacious concept of sexualized violence that collapses these sites of violence and the variations in them,[116] summoning the consequences of global capitalism and securitized democracy to these recognized sites of sexualized violence. The commodity-like concept of rape extends the rationale for militarized securitization and humanitarian logics and initiatives beyond the site of war—quelling thinking and furthering a murderous episteme through attempts to enact a unified social justice agenda: a world without rape.[117] With the homogenization of rape and other forms of sexualized violence, perpetual wranglings over the boundaries between consent and coercion or definitions of force or welcomeness are battles over the reach and spread of state power, capital, and the parameters of appropriate intimacies: little pivots in the plot, in the relationship between law and justice. In this way, the fascination in legal circles with the conceptual difficulties that rape by deception poses to regimes of consent or autonomy might be better understood as negotiations in the production of social value, which I understand as a form of reproductive labor. This is the real deception of rape and its racialized juridical entanglements, one that is dramatized in recent treatments of the legal category of rape by deception proper. The advent and designation of genocidal rape itself can obscure how rape law, exemplified by controversies over the concept of rape by deception, can operate ruthlessly, genocidally, in the service of a settler and cis-hetero championing of gender justice.

Rape by Deception and Rape as Genocide /
Race, Kinship, and the Commodity Form

To position rape by deception and rape as genocide in proximity requires something beyond the sex wars or #MeToo to account for the social significance and legal genealogies of rape. How do we think about rape, genocide, capitalism, law, and justice together in this moment? How do we do this thinking not to correct course per se but more in the spirit of Adorno's negative dialectic, which does not "posit an alternative to the contradictions that score contemporary capitalism" but instead enacts a reach toward "the possibility of overcoming those contradictions through overcoming the conditions of capitalism"?[118] A start might follow when and how rape is figured as an individual affront to the possessive individual and when it also becomes a proxy for geographies of peace and terror—the only form of "gender-based" violence capable of threatening international security.

In his 2013 *Yale Law Review* article, "The Riddle of Rape by Deception and the Myth of Sexual Autonomy," Jed Rubenfeld begins with an account of a 2010 rape conviction in Jerusalem. In the *State of Israel v. Kashour*, an Arab man is convicted of rape in Jerusalem "not for forcing sex on his victim, but for posing as a 'Jewish bachelor' with a 'serious romantic' interest in her." Rubenfeld quotes the opinion: "If [the complainant] had not thought the accused was a Jewish bachelor interested in a serious romantic relationship, she would not have co-operated with him. . . . The court is obliged to protect the public interest from sophisticated, smooth-tongued and sweet-talking criminals who can deceive innocent victims at an unbearable price—the sanctity of their bodies and souls."[119] Rubenfeld presents the core problem of this case as one of dishonesty. In that way, the problem it presents is essentially like laws and pronouncements made in places from Tennessee to Massachusetts to Canada that express some understanding that sex procured dishonestly should be conceptualized as rape because it vitiates consent. For Rubenfeld, the *Kashour* case, although admittedly "politically charged," is an example of the philosophical problem that rape by deception or fraud presents for current formulations of rape law that do not uniformly prohibit it. He asks: if "rape law today cannot rest on principles of female defilement, . . . how then does [law] explain why sexual assault is different from other assaults? If not defilement, what is the special violation that rape inflicts?"[120]

Rubenfeld ultimately argues against sexual autonomy as "rape law's central principle" and against understanding rape as "unconsented to sex." If rape by deception is in fact, as most jurisdictions would have it, not rape at all, then autonomy can't be the norm at stake—liberal notions of autonomy simply cannot be squared with the absence of the necessary preconditions to achieve valid consent. Instead, he favors of a model of rape as a violation of a person's "fundamental right to self-possession" and in this way he views rape as more akin to violations like "sexual slavery" and "torture." For Rubenfeld, force—and lots of it—is required to dispossess a person from their body, and those are the conditions under which he would recognize the occurrence of rape.

The article spurred a number of critiques, rejoinders, and clarifications in legal academia—all of which can be read as part of ongoing legal and intellectual projects on how to best conceptualize and address rape and other sexualized violence through liberal law's foundational values, concepts like autonomy, equality, dignity, liberty, and self-possession. The legal scholar Deborah

Tuerkheimer's response reconceptualizes rape as a problem of sexual agency, rooted in group subordination rather than individual choice or will, and in this way retains the primacy of consent.[121] Other defenses or reworkings of sexual autonomy as an organizing principle have since emerged.[122] In Joseph Fischel's articulation, for example, the absence of "explicitly conditioned sex" becomes the benchmark for charges of rape by deception, a standard thought to function as a bulwark against an unbridled "undemocratic sexual hedonism."[123] None of these theorizations or solutions critically address how the "deception" of the paradigmatic case—*Kashour*—is deeply and obviously tied to gendered and racialized sexual contexts that arise out of a particular settler colonial context and imbue concepts like "coercion" with social and legal meaning.

In *Kashour*, the struggle in Palestine—a genocidal and settler one for land ownership and use—underlies and shapes the meaning and import of the deception at issue. In other words, the region's ongoing political ethnoreligious conflict is not incidental to the meaning of rape the *Kashour* court proposes. The full meaning of the deception as credible deception must be understood as part of a racialized history of property dispute. In Rubenfeld's argument, the material conditions that make the deception meaningful, particular, and persuadable to the court are routed through an argument of abstract principle—fraud versus consent—that is the hallmark of capitalist enterprise. Rubenfeld asks how the wrong of rape can be grounded in an affront to autonomy when we/society do not categorically forbid any infringements of it. This framing enables Rubenfeld to argue against sexual autonomy as "rape law's central principle" and against understanding rape as "unconsented-to sex"; in these ways, he takes a position on the meaning and the scope of "rape"—what it could or should mean.[124]

What this example makes clear is the urgent need for other routes of thinking about rape and the kinds of political, social, and cultural work that thinking about and working to end rape does and enables. This kind of thinking might not easily resolve the question of what rape law's central principle is or should be—but this is the wrong first question. What a focus on the work of rape does provide is another angle for thinking through how violence is socially created and distributed. Ideas, including legal ideas, and debates about sexualized violence and legal mechanisms to combat it can be integral to those processes of recognition and disavowal. The assemblage of rape's meaning is largely neglected in queer of color and allied critique as well as within legal scholarship that presumes rape is something that already exists—that we all already know what it is—and law simply has to name it or place it in the correct framework or strain of analysis. Rubenfeld's recourse to self-possession—his understanding that rape should be categorically understood to require extreme amounts of force, enough to "dispossess a woman of her body" in a manner akin to slavery or torture—belies the historic and lived interrelations of those categories, separating rape and other forms of sexualized violence from racialized violences that are (by some definitions, in the case of torture) undertaken and supported by the state, even as it binds them in the obfuscating intimacies of analogy. Genocidal logics are folded in abstraction: fraud, self-possession, autonomy, sexual democracy. The state is kept safe, at good remove—the blindfold of justice does not slip.

If in *Kashour* a "commonsense" understanding of indigenous/settler or ethnoreligious antagonism provides scaffolding over which "objectively" believable or persuasive understandings of sexual consent, desire, or welcomeness might form, an earlier case of rape by deception in Israel/Palestine also shows how integral normative gender presentation is to those concepts. In 2003, Hen Alkobi was found guilty of attempted rape by deception. The conviction was based, as legal scholar Aeyal Gross describes it, "on a set of facts describing the intimate relations between Alkobi, a young man who had been born with female genitalia but lived as a man at least some of the time, and a number of younger girls."[125] As the opinion put it, "In a case in which relations of love are established, and the 'consent' of one side is won without the disclosure of this essential fact, there is a violation of the partner's autonomy, and the situation cannot be described as 'free consent.'"[126] For Gross, the Alkobi case and *Kashour* show how "seeking to protect women from what is conceived of as sexual injury, by criminalizing sexual intercourse that is allegedly not fully consensual" participates in "how the gender-national order is preserved against boundary crossing by the criminal law rules governing rape by deception regarding the perpetrator's identity."[127] The Alkobi case, like others in the United Kingdom and the United States, feeds into understandings of gender-nonconforming people as abnormal and dangerous. As trans studies theorist Toby Beauchamp writes, "Gender nonconformity . . . itself indicates the likelihood of dangerous behavior, [which rationalizes] both policing and panic by imagining that a gender-nonconforming individual fundamentally has something to hide. This [understanding]—and the surveillance practices mobilized through its logic—helps construct the gender-nonconforming figure as an inherently deceptive object of state and public scrutiny."[128] For Beauchamp, there is a structuring deceit, a "perceived deception underlying transgressive gender presentation."[129] By these distorted lights, Alkobi is the embodiment of fraud or deception: his face is a bad bargain, his body is a false contract.

The accepted legal definition of genocide requires the presence of a mental element (intent to destroy) and a physical element (act designed to bring about that destruction).[130] If this legal definition occupies itself with the intentional, concerted destruction of racial, ethnic, and religious groups, a legion of feminist, queer, trans, and critical ethnic studies scholars have hardly let that definition go by without comment. Dylan Rodríguez frames racial and colonial genocide as a structuring logic that exceeds the event or events that produce a "mind-boggling body count," viewing them as "but one fragment of a larger historical regime that requires the perpetual social neutralization (if not actual elimination) of targeted populations as (white, patriarchal) modernity's *premise of historical-material continuity.*"[131] In contrast, Rodriguez writes that society must be addressed through "a genocide analytic as well as through focused critiques of neoliberalism's cultural and economic structures: the logics of social neutralization (civil death, land expropriation, white supremacist curricular enforcement) always demonstrate the *capacity* (if not the actually existing political will and institutional inclination) to effectively exterminate people from social spaces and wipe them out of the social text."[132] Other postcolonial, critical ethnic, queer, Black, and genocide studies scholars, including W. E. B. Du Bois, Patrick Wolfe, Achille Mbembe, Andrea Smith, and Scott Morgensen, offer expansive definitions of genocide that eschew the temporal limitations and identity-based motivations of the World War II model. Instead, these scholars favor historically and economically attuned accounts of how, through race, indigeneity, and sexuality, law and governance regimes make mass death.[133]

To my mind, the transgender rape by deception cases expose a thinking that underlies and enables mass death, one that is obscured by structures of law and legal thought. These cases show the importance of gender, gender identity, and sexuality not only, as Gross argues, to the operations of the nation. They also demonstrate how debates in law about individual consent to sex—what can and cannot be consented to, and how to gauge it—can displace and enact genocidal logics that cannot be named as such. But they are genocidal nonetheless: they foreclose queer kinships, desires, and intimacies and in turn structure social and property arrangements. These logics are echoes of empire in excess of the nation-state and are produced through a number of sites that are often obscured "because empire is seen as an extension of nation-states, not as another way . . . of organizing a polity."[134] Structures of analogy and commodity, hand in hand, work in law to homogenize thought about the meaning and significance of "sexualized violence," of consent, force, and coercion. This work clears space for capital, distributions of property, life chances, and liberalism as empire that at once further and surpass the bounds of the nation-state. These operations of law alter the relations between what will be private or public in and among states. This is the work that confirms what may be secreted away and what may be interfered with and known. In other words, feelings of coercion implicate modes of belonging predicated on land claims that depend on state-supported racial, ethnoreligious, settler, and gendered orderings.

Positioning rape as deception alongside rape as genocide is an attempt to "relocate what counts as knowledge and its fields of force."[135] As *Ha'aretz* reports, "Alkobi claimed the minors lodged their complaints because of parental pressure—the parents were apprehensive that their daughters would be stigmatized as lesbians, and so instructed them to submit charges of rape."[136] Later, "one of the complainants had sent a letter to the court in which she withdrew the rape charges, and said that she felt genuine feelings of love for Alkobi."[137]

Rather than imagine rape by deception as simply a chance to reconsider how we evaluate the import of something called "consent"—as means to afford both "women's autonomy rights" and "trans privacy rights" the appropriate deference and respect as Fischel and much of the legal literature frame it—the method of law beyond Law instead shows consent itself as reimagined and reified through such queer and transphobic moments of surveillance. The wavering lines between consent and coercion can themselves be a part of how "gender deviance is produced, coded, and monitored not only in these spectacular moments, but also in the everyday."[138] The idea that such sex can potentially vitiate consent is a boundary issue that shapes not only what consent can mean. These sex disputes also support the fiction of rights and law as premier sites of achieving a thing called justice. What debates about legal standards, consent, and how to achieve an appropriate balance between "women's autonomy rights" and "trans privacy rights" best illustrate is the enduring need to constantly imagine race, gender, and sexualized violence as not only exceptional, mostly random acts but as acts that reinvigorate the political order. Modifications and modulations in how courts view issues of consent and coercion (e.g., through theories of autonomy or privacy) might alter the relationship of the nation and its peoples to rights but nonetheless preserve the primacy of rights (as well as the categories of people whose interests are allegedly opposed) and the state as sites of authoritative justice. Debates that take up as imperative a need to "philosophically" align the wrong of rape in a way that makes sense to Rubenfeld and other legal scholars is not a way to square law with and an endlessly deferred, although fully formed, "justice" but a way to alter the relation of law to the very concept of justice in ways that ignore the work of rape. Meanwhile, critical queer, feminist, and ethnic studies work that cedes discussion of the full dimensions of law to others loses spaces of inquiry that underlie and overlap the iterations of liberation they seek to address. The work of rape is world-making work. And there are many worlds, awful and awe-ful, to be made.

Chapter Summaries

The first chapter, "The US Sex Wars Meet the Ethnic Wars," maps the transnational, international, and site-specific feminist networks that enabled transformations—however internally contested—in the meaning of rape and sexual violence during the conflict in the former Yugoslavia and later Rwanda. By retreading and reconfiguring the heated 1980s-era US sex war debates on the workings of gender, sex, and violence, divisive feminist theorizations and dialogues surrounding "genocidal rape" enabled the conflicts in the former Yugoslavia and Rwanda to transform human rights, humanitarian, and international governance discourse. The feminist legal and sociocultural gendering of sexual violence within a complex of ethnoreligious difference propelled recognition of the war-raped not only as violated persons but as violated populations—suitable for focused international law and governance campaigns in the name of gendered human rights and, more recently, human security initiatives. Changes in the naming of rape and sexual violence—as well as its reconceptualization from an individual to a mass crime—are indicative of an ongoing racialization process that produces the war-raped as a population to be internationally managed and governed and the states that cannot manage them as inferior, failed states in need of external governance. I call this theoretical concept *the racialization of mass rape*.

The next two chapters look at how legal feminist and political theorizations of state sovereignty and responsibility have often rendered militarized, mass sexualized violence against some groups largely invisible. These chapters continue to elevate the submerged and often fractious theoretical work of feminist theory and activism that rarely leaves a mark in the domain of law proper. These chapters also delve more deeply into how the work of rape and the method of law beyond Law augment contemporary work in transnational feminisms and queer critique. The second chapter, "States of War, Men as State," analyzes the differences in how some feminist attorneys (many of whom were involved in creating the tribunals in Rwanda and the former Yugoslavia) represented 1980s-era military- and state-backed violence against women, particularly indigenous women, in Latin America in their own legal, scholarly, and activist work. I consider how transnationally produced feminist and US/international feminist legal knowledge of mass sexualized violence depends on largely unacknowledged and silenced, but not silent, conceptualizations of race, indigeneity, and what I call the *sexual state form*. I use the term *sexual state form* to reference the imagined character of the state whose actions become the subject of legal feminist thought and action through their attempts to theorize sexualized legal harm. I examine that feminist work to understand how the meaning of consent and coercion—as well as the legal frameworks for evaluating and recognizing sexualized violence—are subtly shaped by imagined sexual state forms: dictators torture; multicultural states in distress commit genocide; and rogue ethnoreligious actors sow terror.

The third chapter, "My Own Private Genocide," asks that we read the current iterations of Islamophobia in tandem with the 1990s racialized massification of sexual violence by revisiting recent US law and policy on torture. Specifically, I situate provisions of the US Military Commissions Act of 2006 that narrow definitions of rape, sexual assault, and torture for the newly created category of "unlawful enemy combatants" within the narrative of how individuals became liable for some violations of international human rights and humanitarian law. Transnational feminisms, I suggest, had a role to play. Critical historicization of these issues is necessary, I argue, in understanding how habeas corpus and other legal rights—including protections from sexualized violence—were in this moment denied to War on Terror detainees and used to justify militarized interventions that further wealth extraction (oil) and wealth creation (military expenditures and arms trading) in the Middle East.

The fourth chapter, "Two Title IXs," begins with the 2013 reauthorization of the Violence against Women Act (VAWA). This legislation contains provisions that affect how Title IX of the Civil Rights Act (the federal law prohibiting sexual discrimination in federally funded education) is administered. The 2013 VAWA also contains its own Title IX, subtitled "Safety for Indian Women." Title IX of VAWA recognizes tribal criminal jurisdiction over domestic intimate violence regardless of their Indian or non-Indian status, provided that tribes ensure certain enumerated due process protections. I use the coincidental titling of the VAWA's provisions regarding tribal authority and the Civil Rights Act's prohibitions on sex discrimination as an invitation to think about the versions of consent, sovereignty, property, gender, gender identity, and authority that circulate beneath the banner of "violence against women." I turn to campus protest as a way to think through these connections.

This book closes with a meditation on rape and rights. The expansiveness and unruliness of life, but also of law and its effects, leads me to a final question: How do we address and name sexualized violence when the work of rape is multidirectional, continually unfolding—a testament to the multifaceted impossibility of repair? Reading June Jordan's 1978 "Poem about My Rights" with the work of rape in mind, the epilogue charts an approach to sexualized violence that emphasizes transformative justice and the abolitionist, decolonial, and anti-imperialist feminist visions of liberation that point a way forward.

ONE

The US Sex Wars
Meet the Ethnic Wars

SINCE THE EARLY 1990S, wartime sexual violence horror stories have become headline mainstays, particularly in reference to what UNICEF has described as Africa's ongoing "rape epidemic"[1] and, more recently, the Daesh rape of ethnic Yazidi women.[2] From the Congo to the Middle East, reports of armed militias sexually assaulting women and children as an organized strategy of war have spawned international attention and condemnation, including calls for armed intervention. Yet the trouble, the UN suggests, does not just concern armed combatants' use of rape as a weapon. The latest threats involve the "spread" of rape and sexual violence in civilian populations that have survived—or are currently surviving—armed conflict or civil war.[3] These rapes are often cast as part of a genocidal targeting of ethnoreligious or racial minority groups, like the Yazidi in Iraq or the Hutu in the Congo by Rwandan, Ugandan, and Burundian forces. In such accounts, rape and sexual violence are intimate outgrowths of rampant social and political instability, thereby presaging—if not already indicating—wholesale social collapse. As UNICEF deputy executive director Hilde Johnson explained, "When societies collapse there seems to be a license to rape in some of these countries. That's why we call it epidemic proportions—it takes a life of its own."[4]

Framing sexual violence as a premeditated weapon and fatal social contagion has further mainstreamed a recently popular lexicon of rape, including the phrases *mass rape*, *war rape*, and *genocidal rape*.[5] Far from trendy or inconsequential shifts in nomenclature, these designations signal slight, yet significant, shifts in the conceptualization of rape and other forms of sexualized violence. No longer ignored, downplayed, or solely portrayed as the essentially private violations of individual victims, sexualized violations in and around conflict zones are increasingly characterized as public, collective injuries mandating nothing short of concerted global response. A failed state is now often a rape state, in a state of rape, riven with sexualized violence—its recognition, culminating in external governance or consecrated in bombs, a feminist victory.

Contemporary accounts of wartime rape and sexual violence arise from formative and heated debates involving the 1990s armed struggles in the former Yugoslavia and Rwanda. As the first major armed conflict in a post–Cold War era, violence in the Balkans set the prototype for the "new wars"—conflicts characterized by the "fragmentation and decentralization of the state" and ostensibly galvanized by the ancient feuds of ethnic enclaves.[6] If the splintering of the former Yugoslavia piqued the theory, the deterioration of the Rwandan state, represented as a mortal clash between Tutsi and Hutu people,[7] hardened the "new wars" into "fact." These struggles ignited popular and legal furor over how to address ongoing and extreme violence, including the prevalence of wartime rape. By the next decade, the UN had formally acknowledged rape and other forms of sexual violence as a collective security interest.[8] The 2008 UN Security Council Resolution 1820, to give just one example, condemns the use of sexual violence as a tool of war while recognizing that "rape and other forms of sexual violence can constitute war crimes, crimes against humanity or a constitutive act with respect to genocide."[9]

In the early 1990s, when the first reports of mass rape in a disintegrating Yugoslavia began to register on the international radar, there were no tribunals or international criminal forums where mass armed violence, much less rape and sexualized violence in conflict, could be routinely addressed. The International Criminal Court (ICC) did not yet exist. Rape's place within international law was also far from settled. In humanitarian law and the laws of war—which include the Geneva Conventions and various other treaties, laws, and established legal customs—the status of rape and other forms of sexualized violence was murky at best. International human rights law hardly provided a more welcoming forum. Yet within several years, freedom from rape would be ensconced in the pantheon of human rights and enshrined as a violation of international humanitarian and criminal law. Rape would also be prosecuted as war crimes, crimes against humanity, and even genocide.[10] Ultimately, gender would also be statutorily defined for the first time—in binary terms, to boot—in an international legal instrument. The ability of individuals (but not necessarily corporations) to be tried for some violations of international law would also solidify. How and why did these conflicts propel rape and other forms of sexualized violence to this position of relative international legal and cultural prominence? How did the association of rape and sexualized violence with mass crimes, including genocide, change the meaning of and response to those violations—and to what effects?

In what follows, I explore how the divisive, transnationally mobile feminist theorizations and dialogues surrounding mass rape, war rape, and genocidal rape enabled the conflict in the former Yugoslavia and, later, Rwanda to transform human rights, humanitarian, and international governance discourse. I suggest that these debates reworked and reconfigured the heated 1980s and 1990s US sex war debates on the workings of gender, sex, state power, race, and violence. In the process, they revitalized forms of radical and dominance feminisms that so heavily marked not only contemporary international legal feminist thought and action but also (as I discuss in chapter 4) US understandings of the meaning and significance of sexualized violence. The resulting legal shifts in the naming of rape and other forms sexualized violence—their reconceptualization from a typically individual assault between friends or strangers to a mass crime like genocide perpetrated or enabled by the breakdown of state governance—are indicative of what I call the racialization of mass rape. This racialization (of a category as much as a people) is an ongoing process that produces the war-raped as a population to be internationally managed and governed and the states or regions that cannot manage them as inferior, failed states or places in need of external governance (if not militarized humanitarian intervention) in the name of freedom. At the same time, the conditions of rape under war have become part of a more general story about sex and what sexual consent and coercion can and should mean.

Crucially, the process by which the mass war-raped and sexually violated enter international law and policy is neither solely a feminist victory nor a cautionary tale of US radical feminism gone global. This is an account of displacements—among other things, of the forestalled promise of US racial and gender justice, of what makes up the appropriate recalibration and deference to "differences," of the centrality of states to warfare and the civilian's place in it, of the meaning of intimacy under structures of force and coercion, and of the scope and significance of human rights and "justice" in a moment when the world was down a superpower and capitalism prepared for a victory march across the erstwhile Soviet bloc. This is an account of the US sex wars as part of the onto-epistemological projects of racial capitalism, empire, and neocolonialism.

The US sex wars were a series of bitter political and cultural battles over the relationships among sexuality, sex, gender, and violence. Controversies raged in feminist and broader US culture over the place of "sex" in society, including the regulation of pornography, the scope of legal protections for LGBTQIA+ people, the funding of allegedly obscene art, and the contents of safe-sex education.[11] Although the sex wars are often recounted as past battles over "truths" about "men and women, sex and power, aggressivity and passivity,"[12] this view depends on which bodies of scholarship and activism enter the genealogy of the sex wars. In particular, this view depends on whether radical, dominance, and liberal feminisms are or are not understood as racial projects at the root. Furthermore, it depends on whether analyses of the US sex wars, which were in Catharine MacKinnon's and Andrea Dworkin's hands tied to legal debates over the meaning of the US civil right to be free of sex discrimination, follow how that concept has been subsequently articulated in international human rights and related law.[13] As legal theorist Janet Halley has analyzed, during the so-called ethnic wars of the 1990s, radical feminist precepts migrated to the realm of international humanitarian and criminal law, where in their address of wartime rape, elite legal feminists like Rhonda Copelon and Catharine MacKinnon promoted an understanding of law rooted in gender difference. Halley describes this radical or structural feminist project as entailing the creation of "a new universe of wrong," where "the wrongs women suffer in time of war must be classified separately from the wrongs men suffer in time of war."[14]

Meanwhile, for decades, activists and scholars have abundantly denounced the imperial, racial, class, and colonial operations that can lurk in the many calls to "save women" from violence, including sexualized violence and pornographic sex, or have examined how presumed gendered and sexual vulnerabilities have been mobilized to justify repressive, militarized state social and economic policy.[15] Scholars have used multiple methodologies, among them queer of color critique, to theorize how the terms of sexual propriety and the extension of sexual and gendered freedoms have affected global deliveries and distributions of violence abroad.[16] In this chapter, I bring case law and legal feminist scholarship detailing the inclusion of rape and other forms of sexualized violence within international law into conversation with Black and other women of color feminist critiques of radical feminist essentialism (where gender liberation is a war between two sexes) and dominance feminism (where the relation of violence between those two sexes is in fact sex itself). Radical, dominance, and certain liberal feminist views, battle-scarred by the criticisms of Global South and women of color feminisms, I argue, helped nurture and in turn were sustained and "resolved" by the rise of so-called identity-based conflict as emblematic of post-Soviet warfare. Within certain international law and policy spheres, radical, dominance, and aligned liberal feminisms were resuscitated through their engagement with genocidal rape.

Resituating the sex wars within these historical currents helps mark the enhanced focus on rape in armed conflict as part of a particular geopolitical and historical moment: the end of the Cold War. The repositioning helps show how some of the primary drivers of radical feminisms at the putative "end" of the sex wars, including MacKinnon, absorbed and redeployed critiques of dominance feminism as too straight, too middle class, too "American," and too white through an explicit engagement with an emaciated version of transnational feminist organizing. Geographical and ethnoreligious differences between women in this way displace substantive engagement with histories of decolonial and US Black and other women of color feminisms or with local feminists and allied activisms outside of US territories. At a moment when rights (human and civil) are extended as anchors of capitalist models of "freedom" and "choice," women's "human rights"—figured as intimate, private, sexual—become key to reimagining freedom and property and thus become explicitly matters of global public concern. In other words, Third World, women of color, and other criticisms of dominance feminism did not simply fail to "register" with elite legal feminisms.[17] They were known and repurposed, and they still leave their marks.

As rape under certain conditions became recognized as a crime against humanity, as it became recognized as an act that could trigger a charge of war crimes or even genocide, the theorization of what popularly and legally constituted rape changed. As rape entered the universe of atrocity crimes, it became a feature of population abuse, of mass civilian exploitation, and not solely—or even some would argue, primarily—about the maltreatment of individual women.[18] Correspondingly, the juridical concept of sexual violation began to tilt from a model heavily weighted toward individual choice or consent to one cognizant of collective coercion in the context of mass ethnic war rape.[19] To be sure, these conceptual shifts were indebted to elite legal feminisms and the interplay between dominance and liberal feminisms. But they were also spurred and shaped by structures of international law (the legal elements and definition of, for example, crimes against humanity), local and transnational feminist organizing and other activisms that exceeded liberal legal and state conceptualizations of authority, and the geopolitical and economic upheaval of "ethnic" war in the ashes of Soviet empire. The resulting changes in the conceptual and legal relationship between states, war, and sexual consent anticipated and encouraged the gendering and sexualization of contemporary human rights controversies and international governance and securitization strategies, as well as the militarization of humanitarianism.[20] In this way, the war-raped enter a process of figuration as racialized populations who are not only in need of individual state attention but require collective international assistance for a guided entrance—at times with planes, with bombs, the full-dress parade—into the postsocialist era.

Rape at the End of History

What we may be witnessing is not just the end of the Cold War, or the passing of a particular period of postwar history, but the end of history as such: that is, the end point of mankind's ideological evolution and the universalization of Western liberal democracy as the final form of human government. —FRANCIS FUKUYAMA, *The End of History*

I begin with Francis Fukuyama's much-critiqued notion of the "end of history" not to rehabilitate it but to set a mood—to recall the sorts of totalizing pronouncements that accompanied the collapse of the Soviet empire that staged liberal democracy as desirable and inevitable. What was rape's place in "the universalization of Western liberal democracy," at history's imagined end? At first, perhaps not much. In a law journal article published in October 1991, legal feminists Hilary Charlesworth, Christine Chinkin, and Shelly Wright noted the "immunity of international law to feminist analysis" despite decades of concerted effort.[21] But the terrain had already begun to shift.[22]

In 1991, the violent disintegration of the Socialist Federal Republic of Yugoslavia, a country cobbled together from six regional republics and two autonomous provinces in the aftermath of World War II, took up tenure in international headlines and nightly news.[23] The death spasms of the Cold

War had left the West bereft of a clear and visible threat to its component national securities—the clarifying categories of capitalism and communism in spectacular collapse. The brutal splintering of the former Yugoslavia and subsequent communal upheaval in Africa and the Middle East gestured toward the nascent new world imaginary: a globe divided and at risk. Zones of peace and stability were no longer vulnerable to siege by calculating Soviet forces but by the irrational or spillover menaces of violence-prone areas of the Global South.[24]

The Balkan peninsula, Europe's "backyard" and buffer against Asia, the Middle East, and Africa,[25] would loom large in emerging articulations of global peace and security. As an unaligned nation both of and not of Europe, the Balkan people had the constitutional mystique of both "otherness" and "inevitability," figuratively embodied as ethnically inbred and prone to "traditional justice executed through blood feud"—a tendency exacerbated by their alleged and perpetual inability to maintain anything but an unstable political climate, rife with ethnic antagonisms.[26] At their most reductive, narratives of the collapse of Yugoslavia pit Serbian aggressors against Bosnian and Herzegovinian and Croatian resistance, staging Serbian military-backed ambitions for a contiguous, ethnically pure state territory as resolutely genocidal in every sense (moral, ethical, and legal) of the word.[27] Dubravka Žarkov, in a study of the "media war" that precipitated and encouraged the decline of the Yugoslav state, discusses the rise of *ethnic* as a descriptor of a war that had once been known as "civil." Žarkov writes: "What made the ethnic component recognizable to Yugoslav citizens, and those familiar with the country, was the growing nationalism of different groups throughout the 1980s. As a political force nationalism had appeared earlier, as both a bottom-up (in 1968 in Kosovo) and a top-down (in 1971 in Croatia) movement. But the term 'ethnic war' was to a great extent part and parcel of Eurocentric, Orientalist, and Balkanist perceptions of the Balkans—both within and outside it—that slowly but surely became the main frame of reference for Yugoslav disintegration."[28] The turn toward "ethnic" conflict was further exacerbated by the post–World War II struggles of communist elites, which had been organized along republican-ethnic lines. Thus Žarkov suggests, "Political processes leading to the war had already produced ethnicity as the main carrier of political power, as the most significant social category, and as the most privileged identity, resulting in decentralization without democratization, and finally, in the creation of ethnodemocracies."[29] To deem violence in the former Yugoslavia as ethnic in origin is then to dismiss the political reality of the region: that "these wars were the creation of modern, urban elites; that they occurred in relatively open and cosmopolitan society; and that they were a direct response to the very strength of economic and political trends of liberalization in the country."[30] To call the violence "ethnic," as a number of Balkan feminists have written, is to erase the solidarity and antiwar initiatives that occurred across ethnic boundaries.[31]

Reports of sexual violence and the emergence of mass rape as news-hour mainstays coincided with and helped fortify a vocabulary of "ethnic conflict," "ethnic cleansing," and "genocide" that would come to characterize the conflict. In summer 1992, reports by British journalist Ed Vulliamy exposed the existence and conditions of Serbian-run camps in Prijedor, northwestern Bosnia and Herzegovina, where prisoners and nonethnic Serbs targeted for removal from the local area were housed (Logor Trnopoljie) or sent to be killed (Logor Omarska and Logor Keraterm).[32] By August 1992, Vulliamy and US *Newsday* journalist Roy Gutman transmitted the brutal details of mass sexual violence against Bosnian Muslim and Croat women at the "rape camps" of Foča, a medieval fortress town on the Drina River in eastern Bosnia.[33] The Serbian military practice of *etničko čišćenje* (ethnic cleansing)— "the systematic and forced removal of members of an ethnic group from their communities to change the ethnic composition of a region"—would become the focus of international alarm.[34] Ethnic cleansing would resonate with (when not interpreted as part and parcel of) the preexisting international discourse of genocide.[35]

By late summer 1992, the bloodshed in the fragmenting Yugoslavia was globally broadcast as nearly reducible to the historical presence of ethnoreligious antagonisms, prompting former UK prime minister Margaret Thatcher to denounce the West's and then prime minister John Major's failure to intervene with a cutting indictment: "I never thought I'd see another holocaust in my life."[36] Reports—one titled "Does the World Still Recognize a Holocaust?"—of Bosnian Muslims and Croats subsequently falling "upon each other in spasms of their own ethnic cleansing" paradoxically sealed the comparison between the Serbs and the Nazis while casting the Balkans as a zone of violence descending into chaos and in dire need of allied/Western intervention.[37] With no extant international legal apparatus to address alleged violations of international humanitarian law, calls for military intervention escalated on pace with demands that the UN convene an ad hoc tribunal to administer justice and help regulate a collapsing region.[38]

These calls only intensified in urgency after April 1994, when long-simmering turmoil in Rwanda erupted into unrestrained bloodshed and mass ethnosexual violence, seeming to confirm warnings from the UN that future ethnic conflicts—beyond, but also in Europe—loomed large. In 1993, José María Mendiluce, former special envoy of the UN High Commissioner for Refugees in the former Yugoslavia, had warned that "cynical politicians" could stoke ethnic antagonisms almost anywhere: "The rest of Europe is not immune to this kind of manipulation. It could happen in Britain or France or Germany or Spain."[39] Just one year earlier, in 1992, experts feared that the Serbs' aggressive hold on Kosovo could drag Albania, Turkey, and even Greece into the front lines.[40] Some even suggested that the seeds of World War III had been sown in the Balkans.

Ethnicity was also not the sole or primary category of social, political, and economic organization in Rwanda. Yet when the killings began in April 1994, ethnic warfare and mass ethnosexual violence were immediately available as mutually productive frames that overwrote the desultory effects of structural adjustment, property shortages, larger regional instabilities, and the failure of the Arusha Accords.[41] The reduction of the conflict to ethnic infighting downplayed "the complexity of pre-colonial ethnic ascriptions" and relations.[42] It also obscured "how the centralisation of the state led to a harsh centralised regime in which access to the highest courts of power was based on Tutsi aristocratic clan membership."[43] Other factors, like class, occupation, and regional location—critical and organizing aspects of political, social, and economic life—that contributed to the bloodshed also vanished beneath the alleged evidence of yet another new war.[44]

The horror of these conflicts was compounded not only by the lack of international mechanisms to address the "new" wars but by the specter of mass (ethnoreligious) rape as a glimpse into the future of armed struggle—a future that, as feminists around the world argued, was also haunted by the unacknowledged and ongoing past of sexualized and gendered abuse. Prior to the conflicts in the former Yugoslavia and Rwanda, rapes during conflict were not considered strategic or systemic acts of gendered sexual violence. They were portrayed as isolated, individual violations of "family honour and rights,"[45] absorbed under other "grave offences,"[46] or viewed as "outrage[s] against personal dignity."[47] The statutes of the International Military Tribunal at Nuremberg and the International Military Tribunal for the Far East at Tokyo did not reference rape or other forms of sexualized violence.[48]

During the 1990s, however, the status of rape and sexual violence in international law transformed. At the dawn of the 1990s, no independent, permanent international criminal court existed, yet international consensus demanded that war crimes in the former Yugoslavia and Rwanda—as well as charges of genocide and crimes against humanity—be addressed. In these fevered climates, on May 25, 1993, the UN Security Council adopted the Statute of the International Tribunal for the Prosecution of Persons Responsible for Serious Violations of International Humanitarian Law Committed in the Territory of the Former Yugoslavia since 1991 (the founding statute of the International Criminal Tribunal for the Former Yugoslavia [ICTY]). The formation of a second ad hoc tribunal, the International Criminal Tribunal for Rwanda (ICTR), was formally established on November 8, 1994. Ad hoc tribunals are special courts granted jurisdiction over a limited set of broadly defined domestic and international crimes in specific postconflict locations for a limited time.[49] The ICTY and ICTR were empowered to investigate crimes against humanity, genocide, war crimes, and violations of the Geneva Convention (which regulate wartime conduct and concern in part the acts by warring parties that contravene the obligation to protect citizens in war).[50] In convening these tribunals, the UN premiered its first war crimes courts and established the first international war crimes ad hoc tribunals since those at Nuremberg and Tokyo. The new tribunals were legal breakthroughs. Their statutes staked the terrain of contemporary international humanitarian criminal law via a reordering and consolidation of several strands and systems of international public law.[51] The ad hoc tribunals' configurations of law and punishment were further engaged and formalized in 1998, when the Rome Statute established the world's first permanent international criminal court—a court of last resort that would preside over war crimes, genocide, crimes against humanity, and crimes of aggression committed by nationals of a signatory state or if they took place on the territory of one of its member states. The reach of the International Criminal Court (ICC), however, is hardly even or absolute; because the Rome Statute is a treaty, "only states that expressly consent to be bound by it are even nominally governed by it."[52]

What international legitimacy the UN lent to the ICTY only fanned the acclaim that greeted the statute's inclusion of rape in its jurisdiction. Significantly, the founding statutes for the ICTY and the ICTR were the first to portray rape not merely as a violation or outrage against personal dignity or the like.[53] Instead, the ad hoc tribunals enumerate rape as a crime against humanity and thus as an atrocity crime.[54] Atrocity crimes, which "take place on a large scale," are so named as "the most serious crimes against humankind" due to the belief that "the acts associated with them affect the core dignity of human beings."[55] These serious violations of international law are a class of legal crimes directed against protected populations (including civilians) or individuals.[56] They include genocide (which can occur in and out of war and concerns acts committed with intent to destroy, in whole or in part, a national, ethnical, racial or religious group), crimes against humanity (which denote widespread or systematic attacks against civilian populations in times of war or peace), ethnic cleansing, certain war crimes (which delimit permissible conduct in warfare), and emergently, some acts of terror.[57] By defining rape and other forms of sexualized violation as crimes against humanity, the ICTY statute marked the explicit inclusion of rape as a violent crime within international humanitarian and criminal law.[58] Mindful of ICTY precedent, the ICTR statute's Article 3 also recognizes rape as a crime against humanity.[59] In addition, as feminist legal scholar Doris Buss writes, "Both the Rwandan and Yugoslav tribunals issued early judgments ruling that, in the case of Rwanda, rape could constitute genocide (*Prosecutor v. Akayesu*), and in Yugoslavia (*Prosecutor v. Delalić*), that rape would be effectively 'read in' to provisions where it was not specifically listed, such as grave breaches of the Geneva Conventions and war crimes."[60] Building on this work, the 1998 Rome Statute, which founded the permanent ICC, became the first international treaty to empower the prosecution of not only rape but a broader array of gendered and sexualized crimes, including sexual slavery, enforced prostitution, forced pregnancy, enforced sterilization, or any other form of sexual violence of comparable gravity as crimes against humanity or war crimes.[61] The Rome Statute, however, does not explicitly name rape as genocide, which, as the next sections discuss, has allowed the full impact of feminist controversies around the meaning and significance of genocidal rape to slip from view.

When Women's Rights Became Human Rights /
The Rise of International Criminal Law

The address of rape and other forms of sexualized violence at this moment might seem to be the inevitably desired result and address of an easily named and identifiable problem. The emergence of sexualized violence as cause for redoubled international legal concern, much less its definitional scope and application, was not an inevitable unfolding of law. As the UN Security Council contemplated and then drafted the founding charters of the ICTY and the ICTR, feminists around the world made a global push to address rape in the former Yugoslavia through international law and to secure rape and other forms of sexual violence as crimes subject to the jurisdiction of the tribunals and later the ICC. By January 15, 1993, the *New York Times* already understood the militarily ordered rapes of Muslim women by Bosnian Serbs to be "a legal test" for international law, one that potentially authorized a "war crimes tribunal on rape" or even a permanent international criminal tribunal to "consider charges against Serbian soldiers."[62] Feminist organizing was front and center; the article reported on the efforts of the Ad Hoc Women's Coalition against War Crimes in the Former Yugoslavia, a group of women's advocacy groups and human rights groups "seeking legal avenues to stop the assaults and to prosecute those responsible as war criminals." Notably, the *New York Times* documented the group's multiple sites of legal engagement:

> In addition to pressing the United Nations to create a tribunal to try such crimes in the former Yugoslavia and other Balkan Nations, lawyers working with the women's coalition are exploring the idea of helping individual women file complaints under the Convention Against Torture, a treaty signed by Yugoslavia before its breakup in 1991. They said they were also considering the possibility of filing civil or criminal charges against wrongdoers when they come to the United States, using the concept of universal jurisdiction, which holds that certain crimes against humanity may be tried anywhere.[63]

One way to understand this description of feminist advocacy is relatively straightforward. If "in the past, rape as a tactical form of warfare has really been overlooked," as director of the Women's Rights Project of Human Rights Watch Dorothy Roberts observed in 1993,[64] then availing every possible entrance into international law and therefore (imagined) redress is simply the strategic path forward, a way of recognizing what is self-evident but has thus far fallen outside of legal purview.[65]

In the aftermath, here is another way: the conceptual massing of rape and sexual violence under war conditions not only places "women's rights" on the international legal map, it puts them in the heart of state violence—at the shadowy crux of what stands as legitimate violence and what surpasses the scope and means of the acceptable use of force. It places violence against women alongside the most severe forms of illegitimate state violence—atrocity crimes that include crimes against humanity, war crimes, and genocide. It does so through strategic engagement with multiple bodies of law that converge to produce the idea of rape as a violation of many stripes: of what it means to be human (international human rights), of appropriate war conduct (international humanitarian law), and as an atrocity crime (international criminal law). These each affect the legal meaning of rape and the social imaginary of what rape and sexualized violence might be. In turn, the consideration of rape and sexualized violence as ethnic cleansing, crimes against humanity, or genocide transforms the contours of those violations. Situating rape within those legal concepts also transforms the meaning of the discrete, if overlapping, bodies of law that house them, and therefore the workings of international governance on the post–Cold War terrain. The ways that rape and sexualized violence might map onto bodies of international law and the specific violations enumerated therein (like genocide or torture) depended and depend on feminists theorizing the relationships between sex and violence—of force, sexual consent, and sexual coercion. In other words, feminist theorizations of rape are essential for understanding the workings of postwar governance. In particular, elite legal feminists brought the legacy of the sex wars (and women of color criticisms of dominance feminism in particular) to bear on the meaning of rape during the 1990s' "ethnic wars" through direct engagement with local feminist takes on rape in the Balkans, which were fraught and imbricated with older histories of cooperation and conflict between various iterations of feminism and the socialist state.

From pronationalist women in the throes of war (including Bosnian and Croatian women's groups Kareta, Tresnjevka, Biser, and Bedem Ijubavi) to internationalist legal feminist elites (including Rhonda Copelon, Catharine MacKinnon, Valerie Oosterveld, and Patricia Viseur Sellers) to feminists in a variety of locations who were suspicious of nationalist predilections (including numerous on-site antiwar feminists such as Djurdja Knezevic, the Zagreb Women's Lobby, Bosnia's Medica Zenica, Belgrade's Žene u crnom or "Women in Black," and the US-based NGO MADRE), feminists of many orientations and beliefs railed against sexual violence during the war.[66] At a time when women's rights were far from assured within international human rights agendas, a number of elite legal feminists consciously framed rape and sexual violence in and outside of conflict zones within ongoing campaigns to help enshrine "violence against women" (a concept with its own feminist history) in an international human rights framework while they pushed for the creation of ad hoc tribunals and even a permanent international criminal court as forums of redress.[67] The phrase "violence against women" hints at the elasticity of what constitutes abuse—if not necessarily what constitutes "women"—and suggests evolving feminist strategies on how best to name what they sought to address. Securing mass rape in conflict zones as part of the platform to frame women's rights as human rights allowed rape to index other gendered sexual violations occurring in and out of conflict.[68]

Unsurprisingly, the potential breadth of "violence against women," and the insistence that such violence exceeds declarations of war, led many states to resist feminist attempts to classify violence against women within the scope of international human rights. Relegating rape, marriage practices, abortion, and other feminist issues to the realm of the family and sexuality allows states to publicly promote "women's rights" while nonetheless refusing to intervene or permit external intervention in the personal matters of the private sphere.[69] As the rapes in the former Yugoslavia came to be represented as part of Serbian state-coordinated ethnic cleansing of Bosnian Muslims and Croats, however, the public-private divide became increasingly untenable to those seeking to exclude violence against women from the reach of international human rights law. With the splintering of the former Yugoslavia, the "gender war" motif assumed a new, literalized urgency. As reports of mass rape began to trickle into mainstream media, the notion of a "war on women" gained traction, as did the notion of gender war crimes. The June 1993 World Conference on Human Rights in Vienna—the first such conference since the end of the Cold War—was, in Copelon's words, a "watershed" that capped years of feminist organizing around violence against women.[70] The conference not only located such violence squarely within the international human rights agenda but also initiated the process of integrating rights to be free of that violence within all strata of the international legal system.[71]

In Copelon's account, objections to the feminist agenda were ultimately vanquished by the participation of women from the disintegrating Yugoslavia. "That women were being raped systematically in Bosnia—just hours from the site of the Conference—prevailed over objections to incorporating gender violence as a human rights problem."[72] Firsthand stories of rape camps and military orders to rape belied the notion that rape was solely a private matter beyond the scope of international law, overcoming those who did not believe that "sexual subordination in the home" should be absorbed into the human rights frame.[73] That those called to testify were primarily Bosnian and Croatian Muslim women who had suffered sexual violence only strengthened feminist appeals. Ethnoreligious "difference" helped surmount the "archly patriarchal and religious" (as some feminists named them) opponents to the establishment women's rights as human rights: the Holy See and a bloc of countries that follow some iteration of Islamic law.[74]

With accounts of former friends and neighbors inflicting rapes, sexual humiliation, and forced detention on women as part of an organized military operation in the disintegrating Yugoslavia, feminists found paradigmatic examples of a range of sexual and intimate violence that exploded liberal articulations of the public-private divide. That such violence was popularly considered part of an ethnic conflict—in which Muslim women suffered in the crosshairs of their ethnoreligious affiliation and their gender—placed violence against women firmly in a human rights frame. In this way, the response of international criminal law to rape and sexualized violence was prompted by a critical discursive move by legal feminists: the gendering of sexual violence within a matrix of ethnoreligious difference for which the conflicts in the former Yugoslavia and Rwanda worked as ideological templates. This figuring had effects that reverberated far beyond the issue of rape in wartime.

The ideological imprint of these human rights struggles manifested, for example, within international criminal law proper. In addition to encompassing a greater array of sexual violence within its judicial charge, the Rome Statute organized the administrative functions of the ICC in an effort to heighten what the literature refers to as "gender sensitivity." The Rome Statute and other rules pertaining to the ICC mandate the "fair representation of female and male judges" and require that "States Parties shall take into account the need to include judges with legal expertise on specific issues, including but not limited to, sexual violence, and violence against women or children."[75] Article 43(6) of the Rome Statute mandates that the registry, the entity responsible for the "non-judicial aspects of the administration and servicing of the Court," create a Victims and Witnesses Unit, where staff with expertise in trauma and sexual violence assist victims and witnesses who appear before the court and even make travel arrangements for them. Article 43(6) also established a trust fund to provide reparations and assistance to victims and their families in rebuilding their communities.

Notably, such "gender-sensitive" addenda are accompanied by and enacted through a delimited notion of gender. The Rome Statute is the first international criminal law treaty to define gender, which it does as "two sexes, male and female, within the context of society," adding, "the term 'gender' does not indicate any meaning different from the above."[76] Accompanying this codification of the gender binary are the formalized recognition that individuals or nonstate actors may be liable for atrocity crimes and the exclusion of corporations from being considered individuals for the purposes of the statute—a turn in international criminal liability that I discuss in greater detail in chapter 3. For now, I mark a confluence. In the storms that accompanied the collapse of the Soviet order and the advent of the ethnic wars, international law emerged as a preeminent space of "justice." The Cold War's end also brought with it a series of debates over the meaning of gender, the aptness of individual liability for some violations of international law, and the very definitions of genocide, crimes against humanity, and war crimes. It is in this context that new legal conceptualizations of rape and other forms of sexualized violence were also forged. These emerged as feminists in the former Yugoslavia and beyond brought their own understandings and genealogies of feminism and rape—the relationships between, for example, sex, the state, social historical difference (racial or ethnoreligious identity, in particular), and harm—to bear on the issue of wartime sexualized violence. And bear they did. The meaning and import of rape and other forms of sexualized violence were shaped by the strictures of international law, and they ultimately shaped that law as feminists mobilized human rights forums to affect international humanitarian and criminal purviews. All told, feminist efforts to render rape a mass or atrocity crime changed the sociolegal meaning of sex and sexualized violence by rearticulating the relationships among force, consent, and coercion. This process transformed the relationships among individuals, groups, and the protections to be guaranteed by functioning states in the new world order. This transition was accomplished in part by some radical feminists' conflation of the coercive circumstances of mass rape during war with more general theories of the domination of women by men—a view of gender and sex that, as Janet Halley observes, has often been fairly uncritically (if unevenly) absorbed by sectors of the international legal community who view such analysis as the professional, unified opinion of legal feminists.[77] But legal feminisms, like every other iteration, are just that: plural. They are subject to the inheritance of the clashes that preceded them.

US Sex Wars Meet the Ethnic Wars

In the 1960s, US radical feminism emerged as a political movement that reimagined Karl Marx, Friedrich Engels, and Sigmund Freud to make a case that a sexual class system lay at the root of social inequity.[78] Catharine MacKinnon summarized the problem as follows: "Men may dominate and women must submit and this relation is sexual—in fact, is sex."[79] MacKinnon's particular strand of radical feminism, known as dominance theory, offers a version of feminism that is symptomatic of long-standing debates within the movement over the role of sexuality in liberation and its relationship to race, gender, class, and violence. It is an example of how some strands of the radical feminist analysis of gender could largely constrain liberatory politics to particular practices—namely, the need for all women to evaluate their oppression as gender oppression, to parse and privilege gender from and against any matrix of racial, sexual, economic, or other motivations that might hurt or promote them and then value this core analytic of gender oppression as the most pressing site for solidarity.

The question of who is the subject of feminism and what one must do to be a proper feminist sparked the internecine disputes that wracked the

US feminist movement in the 1970s, setting the stage for the subsequent sex wars and the fights over pornography and appropriate sexuality that later convulsed US feminisms and culture.[80] Throughout the 1960s and 1970s, as civil rights, decolonization, and counterculture movements converged and gained force, US feminists struggled to find common ground. Fervor erupted over same-sex sexual desire with some camps equating lesbianism—particularly butch-femme roles—as reproducing masculine sexual oppression, while others advanced lesbianism as the ultimate path to liberation. Equally loaded debates emerged around issues of race and class in tandem with an increasing tendency for liberal feminists to position antirape and battering strategies in alliance with a classist, racially oppressive US criminal justice system.[81]

In what follows, I consider the legacies and contestations of radical and dominance feminism through the US sex wars and their aftermath. Here I trace how the concept of sex discrimination in US law and attending debates about the relationships among race, gender, and sex among US legal feminists contributed to the rise of a "global" feminist interest in war rape and violence against women. If, as elite legal feminists explicitly averred, the strategy throughout the 1990s was to install rape as a violation of human rights and other iterations of international law, in the case of the "ethnic wars," rape would be framed through and as existing, canonical violations, including mass atrocity crimes like genocide and crimes against humanity, which depend on the maltreatment of protected groups or mass injury. For radical legal feminists attempting to affect the trajectory of the ad hoc tribunals and the Rome Statute, this was an opportunity to promote women as a legally recognized and protected group by gendering mass sexualized violence and representing it as ethnoreligiously motivated. This framing forestalled engagement with the substance of US women of color critiques of universalizing feminism, fusing sex wars–era debates that understood sex as an antagonism between "the sexes" with the "blood feuds" of ethnoreligious difference in the Balkans—a framework that was later transposed onto Rwanda as evidence of the (sexualized) danger of the new wars.

The current international fixation on violence against women, gender violence, and sexual violence has arisen in part from the self-conscious grappling with questions of difference by Western mainstream feminists. In response to critiques of class and racial insularity, some feminists vigorously advanced violence against women as an organizing principle for international feminist action as an expansive gesture—an often earnest, if not always easy, means of moving beyond the narrow politics of self-interest, of which they had too often been accused.[82] As feminist messaging began to coalesce around violence against women, the public emphasis on sexual danger came at the expense of a comprehensive press for sexual freedom and economic equality, bolstering conservative political frameworks that emphasized sexual danger over sexual pleasure.[83]

Notwithstanding fractious internal politics and controversies over what exactly constituted "women's issues," and even the category of "women," US feminists of the 1960s and 1970s mainstreamed the call for freedom from rape and sexual violence as issues of paramount public concern by portraying women and children's lack of protection from male encroachment as part of an escalating "gender war."[84] The metaphor of war helped drive a popular sexual panic—of which the fight against pornography, as I will discuss, was one front—that conceptually grouped women and children as mutually, lethally endangered. Mass war rape in the former Yugoslavia and Rwanda would literalize the gender war, figuring wartime as an unwaveringly sexually coercive environment and retrofitting MacKinnon's dominance theory in representations of wartime mass rape and other sexual violence.

In April 2010, at the Nobel Women's Initiative's International Gender Justice dialogue, MacKinnon summarized her take on the direction of international rape law and the concept of gender crime: "Sex crimes are gender based. That means they happen because of the social meaning of sex—being a woman or man in social context.... Everyone who is raped is harmed individually, but rape itself is an attack on a woman because she is a member of the group women, targeted and defined for this specific violation as such."[85] MacKinnon presses the case for violence against women as degradations of women's human rights by forging a direct connection to her domestic efforts to ensure robust analyses and civil prosecutions of acts of sex discrimination—prejudicial treatment of a person based solely on the person's sex. Her conceptualization of sex discrimination expressly casts women as a group oppressed by virtue of their sex and sees violence against women as a violation of basic equality guarantees foundational to any understanding of international human rights. Claims of equal citizenship between men and women, she concludes, "must encompass what women need to be human, including a right not to be sexually violated and silenced."[86]

In MacKinnon's account, violence and victim are easily recognizable, transcendent labels: violence is the act of rape; the victim is woman (or, later, one who occupies the "feminine" position). Universalizing women as a category and rape as an act places both terms on a theoretically pristine plane, untouched by sociohistorical context or competing, interrelated iterations of violence. Critiques of this kind—anchored by an insistence on specific material and historical contexts in which gender and race gain cultural meaning—were not the first leveled at MacKinnon.[87] Legal feminist Angela Harris has argued that dominance feminism is the annihilation of particular histories—particularly Black women's relationship to sex under slavery and to the state after emancipation—in exchange for an imagined future free of rape. In the February 1990 issue of the *Stanford Law Review*, Harris, while recognizing the rich traditions of Black and other women of color feminisms in other disciplines, nonetheless notes that "in feminist legal theory, however, the move away from univocal toward multivocal theories of women's experience and feminism has been slower than in other areas."[88] This observation appears in Harris's foundational article, "Race and Essentialism in Feminist Legal Theory," which uses Black feminist writings in literature and other disciplines to unravel the place or nonplace of Black women in MacKinnon's dominance theory. MacKinnon, Harris observes, "assumes, as does the dominant culture, that there is an essential 'woman' beneath the realities of differences between women."[89] To the point: "In her search for what is essential womanhood, however, MacKinnon rediscovers white womanhood and introduces it as universal truth. In dominance theory, black women are white women, only more so."[90]

Within contemporary feminist scholarship, the idea that sex wars–era disputes have significant afterlives runs counter to the generally accepted wisdom that "within the academy there is no doubt that the so-called pro-sex position has 'won.'"[91] A 2016 special issue of *Signs: Journal of Women in Culture and Society* makes that claim, adding that "groups such as Women against Pornography and theorists like Andrea Dworkin and Catharine MacKinnon come in for more derision than devotion among both feminist professors and their students"[92]—pornography is everywhere and genderqueer is here to stay. At the same time, special issue editor Suzanna Danuta Walters cautions against drawing hard lines or casting the issues at stake—of violence, sex, representation, pleasure, and danger—as competing, "ossified" worldviews.[93] Today, she writes, "young activists demanding changes in universities' handling of sexual assault are not simply litigious 'carceral feminists' parroting the likes of Catharine MacKinnon (indeed, most of them wouldn't have a clue who she is!) but are often the same folks marching in SlutWalks and pushing for genderqueer freedom and polyamorous perversity."[94] For Walters, this positioning suggests a difference between "then" and "now" that can be eclipsed by the "battlefield" metaphor of the sex wars. She concludes, "It is long past time to move away from war metaphors and, more importantly, from the kind of excessive polarization and 'calling out' that seems to characterize too much feminist debate, particularly debate that takes place on the intimate and fraught space of the body, of desire, of pleasure, of violation."[95] For Walters, "Sex (and porn, and sex work, and just about everything) is a feminist issue, but it is not, truly, a battle or war."[96] What remains in this telling is a certain vision of the sex wars and its aftermaths—one that undoubtedly contours "contemporary discussions around sexual pleasures and dangers."[97] But this telling does not position feminist epistemologies generated from the sex wars as central to war, governance, and the idea of state responsibility to its publics in the aftermath of the Cold War. Nor does it understand the continuance of those feminist epistemologies as efforts to contend with racial critiques from Global South and women of color feminists based in the United States through the apprehension of Balkan feminists on the ground, dwelling at the site of war. The "emancipatory visions of sexual freedom so crucial to feminism's future"[98] do not, in this framework, account for rape and its work.

Meanwhile, within existing legal scholarship, critical commentaries on the inclusion of rape within international criminal law overwhelmingly train a narrow lens on its absorption of radical or structural feminist precepts. Elaborating this development as part of a larger project of governance feminism, or the uptake of feminist ideals into law and law-like institutions, Halley describes a form of legal activism that is striking not only in its commitments to a structural analysis of gender-based oppression but also in the "performed consensus" of the elite legal feminists "insiders" seeking to shape international criminal law. Halley tracks the genesis of this iteration of governance feminism's ideological stance from the radical US feminist protagonists and positionings of the 1970s and 1980s:

> Just as G[overnance] Feminism learned to walk the halls of power—now dressed not in the butch street clothes of the marginal radical feminists of yesteryear but in power suits from Neiman Marcus—its consensus ideology became as radical and as structuralist as anything we ever got from Mary Daly, Adrienne Rich, or Andrea Dworkin. And—except for some very alarmed and entrenched resistance from the Holy See and States that use Islamic law as a source of law—mainstream international lawyers accepted G[overnance] Feminists as authoritative on the badness of rape and the need for many specific reforms to end the impunity of rapists.[99]

For Halley, the issue is the ultimately uncanny uniformity and coherence of the legal feminist agenda surrounding wartime rape, which "evolved over the course of the 1990s without producing a literature of internal dissent."[100] Rape's relationship to genocide was the exception—a problematic that "agitated" legal feminists in the early 1990s,[101] as they debated whether an emphasis on genocidal rape threatened to eclipse the harm of rapes that occur in and out of war, in and out of genocide.[102]

Early and sharply diverging legal feminist perspectives on whether to pursue the prosecution of rape as genocide are positioned largely as a historical pit stop or skirmish on the road to a "performed consensus" of radical legal feminists involved in drafting the 1998 Rome Statute. The productive interplay between racialized and gendered warfare—between the political frameworks of "genocidal" and "gynocidal" conflict—are evacuated in this narrative. In other words, the genocidal rape debates seem less a conflict between feminist universalism and feminist particularism than a comment on how radical legal feminism, particularly dominance feminism—marked by the sex wars, in a moment when US multicultural diversity becomes an emblem of freedom—needed the semblance of difference between women to remedy and rehabilitate gender/sex itself as *a* if not *the* premier category of social historical difference. The positioning of international humanitarian law on rape and sexual violence as either successfully or nearly fatally invested in radical feminist ideologies conceals the transnational routes of knowledge production about war rape and sexual violence, as well as the labile impact of "US" thought and policy within the international realm. Consequently, such framings do not acknowledge how global geopolitical engagements and the racial histories of feminisms reshape earlier radical feminist views on rape and sexual violence through encounters with mass war rape and ethnic conflict—not to mention how the pitched and sexualized rhetoric of "violence against women" turned "international human rights" turned "war crime," "crime against humanity," and "genocide" functions in a world distinguished by many racist histories of imperial and colonial occupation, marked economic disparities, and global militarisms.

Feminist efforts—particularly elite legal ones—to ensconce rape within international humanitarian and international criminal law depended upon the conceptualization of rape as "mass," and even "ethnoreligiously motivated" or "genocidal," at a moment when (as I elaborate in chapter 3) the meaning of war itself was undergoing profound redefinition. As economic relationships in and between states faltered at the Cold War's end, the ultimate conviviality between rape and international law was enabled by such reorderings of global power and property actuated through the diversity logics of multiculturalism. If Cold War cartography sorted states and regions into free and unfree based on their proximity or distance to socialism, "multiculturalism as a value system and mode of knowledge about the world . . . demands that individuals declare their faith in a global humanity made manifest in normative articulations of racial, religious, and cultural diversity enshrined as individual juridical rights."[103] More than a question of the difficulties of addressing race and gender together—a framework that describes the locus of much work in legal feminisms and international relations—the absorption of rape within international law bolstered and extended a worldview, enacted through the social and economic vision of freedom proffered by the world's remaining superpower. Liberal subjectivity in the aftermath of the Cold War putatively required certain arrangements of sexuality, which in turn depended on specific modes of governance; governments could not commit (or, more accurately, could not be framed as committing) genocide or crimes against humanity, crimes that international law recognized as occurring in and out of war.

The sex wars figured prominently in this new world order. Debates within US academic and legal academic feminism, conceptually and materially entwined with global activist organizing and international law's place in it, enabled legal feminists like MacKinnon to move past US women of color criticisms by engaging global and geographical differences among women. MacKinnon did this in part by routing developments in the US civil law of sex discrimination through coterminous methodological developments and inquiries in nonlegal academic thought, including women's studies.

As Jennifer Nash writes, by 1994, the National Women's Studies Association was on a search for a feminism that spoke a "'common language,' to borrow Adrienne Rich's oft-cited phrase." This longed-for feminism required "a grammar centered on the 'global' and imagined the transnational as a remedy for racial exclusivity that had long plagued both the organization and the discipline."[104] For Nash, the interest in transnationalism had "*institutional* reasons," from "racist violence" at national conference gatherings in 1990 to "the efforts of nongovernmental organizations to foreground gender inequities as questions of human rights."[105] Indeed, since the 1970s and in the wake of the UN's Decade for Women (1976–85), transnational activist and professional international feminist networks had blossomed, bolstered by the concurrent invagination of the state by NGOs, and the explosion of UN-hosted conferences in the 1990s,[106] including the Fourth World Conference on Women in Beijing in 1995 and the UN World Conference in Human Rights in Vienna in 1993. Nash's invocation of human rights gestures toward an important, if easily glossed point: feminist knowledges are shaped not only by feminist scholarship and activism but also by law and by law as an academic enterprise. As a professional discipline, law and legal academia can be—and were in the case of rape and legal feminisms in the wake of the Cold War—a place for ideas and arguments to unify as a strategy for affecting international law and governance outcomes.[107] The strategies and structures of law and legal thinking in turn alter the terrain on which broader iterations of feminist academic and activist work take place. The efforts of legal feminisms and other activists, unmistakable if unacknowledged in Nash's description, provide a clue to where, why, and how the theoretical coordinates of US radical feminism and dominance feminism make an international, if not a transnational, turn. Understanding US legal feminism's "transnational turn" as a reckoning with US race relations helps explain how the projects of radical and dominance feminism would come to walk the halls of power. The expansion of the US concept of sex discrimination to include sexual assault and harassment is a part of this story.

Until the mid-1980s, sex discrimination as a legal concept—one primarily housed in civil right/antidiscrimination law—had not been widely recognized or theorized to encompass sexual assault or issues related to sexual reproduction.[108] It took two Black women, Mechelle Vinson and Lillian Garland, taking their respective complaints regarding sexual harassment and pregnancy leave to the US Supreme Court in 1986 and 1987 for "sexual" issues to become a matter of sex discrimination. For MacKinnon, the racial identity of these women is significant. In 1991, in response to persistent criticisms of dominance feminism's inability to account for "differences" among women, MacKinnon published "From Practice to Theory, or What Is a White Woman Anyway?"[109] The article criticizes "theory" and valorizes "practice." Because the Black women plaintiffs in foundational sex discrimination cases won their suits, MacKinnon recognizes Black women as instrumental in changing the meaning of sex discrimination by "insisting that actual social practices that subordinated them as women be theoretically recognized as impermissible sex-based discrimination under law."[110] This practical approach, she believes, not only recognizes Black women, but can also rehabilitate what she views as the degraded pain of white womanhood. In MacKinnon's hands, the denial of white oppression is "a particularly sensitive indicator of the degree to which women, as such, are despised."[111] Too much attention to theorizing about race and gender and not enough attention to practice elides the conditions of oppression that connect all women.

MacKinnon frames her response in a fear-laden misreading of much of deconstructionist or postmodern discourse. In her hands, it amounts to elites "deconstruct[ing] power relations by shifting their markers around in [their] head"; they and their practices are woefully out of touch, a game of fantasy and equivalencies touching nothing of what "women experience"—devastatingly unreal.[112] At the same time, in asking after white women, MacKinnon does not positively engage with women of color or specifically Black feminist scholarship. She names Black plaintiffs who availed the legal mechanism of sex discrimination as the "experience" that counts, as the practice that trumps the theory. The labor of Black feminist academic intellectual work is purely theoretical.[113]

Angela Harris, on the other hand (and whose work MacKinnon cites in this writing), asks "only that we make our categories explicitly tentative, relational, and unstable, and that to do so is all the more important in a discipline like law, where abstraction and 'frozen' categories are the norm. Avoiding gender essentialism need not mean the Holocaust and a corncob are the same."[114] But then "another Holocaust" arrived, one in which Bosnian Muslim women were victims who were racialized as white and cosmopolitan—and thus worthy of human redemption.[115] In university contexts as well, Jennifer Suchland notes that transnational feminist studies had positioned postcolonial and Third World feminisms as emblematic of "global women" while "the former second world" is not "read as a difference."[116] Yet Bosnian Muslims were also, as I will discuss later, "ethnic" or "different" in ways that could both bolster a radical feminist project marred in particular by Black feminist critique and contribute to new postsocialist global racial orderings. This positioning as white and other enabled the emergence of mass ethnoreligious rape in the Balkans. Mass rape in war would subsequently bolster and expand the meaning of discrimination or exploitation "on the basis of sex" in ways that fed ongoing feminist agitations in US civil and international human rights domains.

MacKinnon's beleaguered white woman, now the cosmopolitan subject of ethnic cleansing, and Nash's nod to human rights bring me to a pair of somewhat obvious but easily obscured points. The first: feminist legal studies cannot be placed in feminist studies without also noting its relationship to law and legal thought—a field "that remains formally dominated by a modernist political idiom."[117] This is important because feminist legal studies could not make what Suchland describes as the "critical shift in language and epistemology from the international to the transnational in feminist scholarship" that occurred unevenly, and not without its own controversies, throughout the 1990s.[118] At the very least, in preserving international law and governance as premier sites of feminist engagement or "governance feminism," legal feminist knowledge obtained by eschewing the determinism of fixed geographies in analyses of power or engaging with Third World, indigenous feminist, or other struggles against regimes of the state almost inevitably undergoes translation into the professional idioms, categories, and processes of international law, which presume an organization of sovereign states.

The second point: gendered human rights concepts feed and have historically been fed by US civil rights concepts. The elaboration of US sex discrimination through human rights law needs an account of the sex wars. As the next section explores, this requires renewed attention to how some of the sex wars' most prominent participants (like MacKinnon) took the substance of their engagement with pornography as a violation of women's civil and human rights beyond US borders, setting these concerns at the heart of human rights debates and controversies that were themselves entangled in the push for the establishment of ad hoc tribunals and an international criminal court. This is not to say that international law or all legal feminists adopt or adopted MacKinnon's formulation of dominance feminism and its views on sex, or to set MacKinnon as that law's sole architect. It is instead to emphasize the epistemological effects of sex wars–era debates on post–Cold War theorizations of rape and other forms of sexualized violence. In other words, at the Cold War's end, legal feminisms, including radical and dominance-based ones, were able to mobilize human rights—and international law more broadly— and develop a "common language" through idioms of genocide, torture, war crimes, and crimes against humanity even as the appeal of radical and dominance feminism mostly waned in other disciplines and venues. If atrocity crimes became the common language, sex discrimination as theorized in US civil law and litigated in US courts, embroiled in the politics of US racial histories, was in many ways a mother tongue. The turn to international law is an alteration and continuation of these lineages. Through them, versions of radical feminism's well documented conviviality with "law and order" approaches to social problems are made manifest through legal feminist attention to mass (ethnic) rape, which animates and creates racial formations.

In these ways, international human rights—and its attendant and constitutive bodies of law, including humanitarian and criminal law—became a critical site for the rehabilitation and rearticulation of radical and dominance feminism in the aftermath of its encounters with US women of color feminisms. Mass war rape in the former Yugoslavia and Rwanda literalized the gender war. Elite legal feminist tactics of framing "war"—and particularly so-called ethnic war—as an unwaveringly sexually coercive environment in turn retrofitted MacKinnon's dominance theory within representations of wartime ethnoreligious mass rape and other forms of sexualized violence. Global feminist contact updated the radical and dominance feminist project, inviting it into international law and governance, in the process changing not only the terms of what elite feminist politics might mean but also the definitional contours and social significance of rape and sexual violence.

The Genocidal Rape Debates, Pornography, and US Racial Legacies

In the midst of Balkan dissolution, an association with certain versions of a US racial "past" helped propel rape and sexual violence into the orbit of international law. Mass rape, narrated to echo US–style race wars, would profoundly affect multiple strands of international law and usher women's rights into the sphere of human rights proper. International reports, with their emphasis on the rapes of Muslim women at the hands of Serbs, circulated in Croatia throughout the conflict, bringing US feminist and social criticism to bear on the Croatian view of rape. As Dubravka Žarkov documents, Croatian newspaper articles published during the height of the conflict routinely link sexual domination to racial domination, whereby individual perpetrators became stand-ins for larger regional histories. The Croatian paper *Danas*, for example, ran a lengthy article, "Europe Is Raped Again," by Muradif Kulenović, which begins by categorizing rape as "an act of power, revenge, and humiliation. All the evil in the human genome." The article further classifies rape as "an issue of power and male domination over women" and "explicitly credit[s] feminism for this analysis."[119]

These lessons of feminism are articulated through US racial and gendered histories—a significant framing that often passes without remark in the literature. The *Danas* article quotes Eldridge Cleaver, who calls rape a "dialogue between races" and the "'rebellion' of a black man against the white master via the 'desecration of his women.'"[120] These ways of thinking about rape and race—ways that were to some extent mirrored by legal discourse and strategy—bring the specific sexual and racial histories of US slavery to bear on Croatian analyses of gender in the context of ethnoreligious violence.[121]

Elite legal feminist engagements and uptake of local Balkan feminisms also brought US racial understanding of violence to meet postsocialist ones. MacKinnon's international work depended on selective engagement with certain feminists: those in the former Yugoslavia who understood rape and warfare in nationalist frameworks that complimented post–Cold War political framings of the conflict as "ethnic war." These are the feminists whose nationalism—or whose attention to historical power differences in the disintegrating Yugoslavia became framed as "nationalistic"—refracted the US understanding and experience of race as "race war."[122] "Patriotic" women's collectives in Bosnia and Croatia such as Kerata, Tresnjevka, Biser, and Bedem Ijubavi, urged consideration of mass rape in the former Yugoslavia not only as war crimes and human rights violations but as genocidal acts, part and parcel of a concerted Serbian campaign of ethnic cleansing waged against Croatian and Bosnian Muslim people generally and Croatian and Bosnian Muslim women specifically.[123] To insist that rape as a weapon of war could occur on any side, they argued, obscured and trivialized the genocidal nature of these particular rapes.

In 1992, MacKinnon became one of the first, most vocal legal supporters of linking wartime rapes to genocide, after being retained to represent several women's groups (including Kareta) in Croatia and Bosnia and Herzegovina seeking legal redress for mass sexual violence. That redress eventuated in a complex of cases in US federal courts, culminating in *Kadic v. Karadzic* (1995).[124] After weathering years of criticism for her totalizing view of women, MacKinnon proffered a formulation of rape as genocide that aimed to account for women's group affiliation as both ethnic other and as women. For MacKinnon and others, rapes in the former Yugoslavia were "part of an ethnic war of aggression being misrepresented as a civil war"—a situation that left Bosnian Muslim and Croatian women doubly imperiled: at risk of rape in the way that all women are at risk, but also in danger of ethnoreligious targeted rape that expressly sought their extermination.[125] To shore up the connection she made between human rights, rape, and genocide, MacKinnon compared rape in the Balkans to the Holocaust: "These rapes are to everyday rape what the Holocaust was to everyday anti-Semitism. Without everyday anti-Semitism a Holocaust is impossible, but anyone who has lived through a pogrom knows the difference."[126]

In retaining the notion of a global class of women bound by mutual susceptibilities to male sexual dominance, MacKinnon revived an old sex war controversy: pornography as an engine of violence against women. In an infamous and much circulated article titled "Turning Rape into Pornography: Postmodern Genocide,"[127] published in the July/August 1993 edition of *Ms.* magazine, one of the most widely circulated US feminist magazines of the time, MacKinnon reiterated an analysis of pornography as the cause of sexual domination generally and the perpetration of genocidal sexual violence in the former Yugoslavia specifically. MacKinnon labeled pornography "a tool of genocide," arguing that the fall of communism had resulted in the country's saturation with sexually explicit, dehumanizing images of women. Sexual war criminals, she argued, "learned to rape" from the "motivator and instructional manual" of pornography.[128] With this charge, she linked the conscious use of sexually explicit media directly to the alleged uniqueness of the mass sexual violence that occurred in the former Yugoslavia. Pornography became irreducibly coupled with the singularity of the paradigmatic new war: "In the conscious and open use of pornography, in making pornography of atrocities, in the sophisticated use of pornography as war propaganda, this is perhaps the first truly modern war."[129] In this way, radical feminist understandings of what it means to be a woman transform through contact with ethnoreligious difference produced and maintained in relation to deadly violence of war.

The formulation of genocidal rape carries with it further traces of US sex wars' feminist debates. By prosecuting genocidal rape, MacKinnon sidesteps charges of exclusivity and allegations of speaking for others that had plagued earlier discussions of sexuality and race within feminist and legal feminist circles. Her involvement in the conflict may be viewed and promoted as not only solicited but reflective of the views of her clients—women who witnessed and experienced the devastation firsthand. In the *Ms.* article, MacKinnon presents genocidal rape as foregrounding the differences between women, even as their shared susceptibility to male violence knits them together in global sisterhood. Thus the plight of US porn star Linda "Lovelace" Boreman can preface discussions of pornography that ineluctably segue into descriptions of sexual violence in the former Yugoslavia. MacKinnon writes as if this connection were a well-known, historical truth: "Gloria Steinem reworded the essence of the disbelief and blame Lovelace encountered as amounting to asking her, 'What in your background led you to a concentration camp?' If this was ever only an analogy, it isn't anymore."[130] In the context of atrocity and armed struggles, questions of consent, pleasure, and agency and US racial history that had agitated feminists during the sex wars could be tacitly (if not explicitly) understood as moot. Activists in the region, however, countered that "the publicity given to the [*Ms.*] article contributed to further stirring up the ethnic animosities and to polarizing the women's movement in the former Yugoslavia."[131]

While Dworkin and MacKinnon championed the uniqueness of genocidal rape, others (notably feminist attorneys Rhonda Copelon and Hilary Charlesworth) cautioned against distinguishing any iteration of rape as "worse than or not comparable to other forms of rape in war or peace."[132] For these feminists, the exaggerated distinctiveness of genocidal rape masks the brutality of nongenocidal rape and hinders efforts to recognize and address persecutions based on gender in and out of war.[133] Copelon defines genocidal rape in expansive terms, downplaying fixations on war and specific ethnoreligious and national balances of power to emphasize that genocidal rape can occur on all sides, in and out of war. She joins others who critique concepts of ethnoreligious nationalism that in the Balkan context tend to view all Muslim women as raped women and preclude recognition of women's capacity to be war criminals themselves.[134] Copelon and MacKinnon agreed that all questions of genocidal rape aside, the political—and legal—import of these mass rapes concerned women as a global group. On this view, mass rape and sexual violence in the former Yugoslavia were not only genocidal due to the ethnoreligious targeting of particular women but also independently tantamount to "femicide" or "gynocide"—a crime against women en masse as a globally "subordinated group."[135]

Bosnian nonnationalist feminists note, however, that MacKinnon's and Copelon's competing theorizations of genocidal rape each ignored the political histories invoked by the contesting powers in the embattled countries themselves.[136] In the postsocialist nation, feminists' uptake of genocidal rape affected their approach to the war and their political and social viability in the fractured Yugoslavia.[137] Feminism in the Balkans was cast at times as "Western" and "antistate," and yet later, as the nation disintegrated, was championed as part of ethnonationalist projects.[138] As Jalena Batinic writes, "The antifeminist discourse, well-known in the socialist tradition of the former Yugoslavia, was reshaped to fit the nationalist context, and simultaneously found a new impetus. Ironically, the same women that were labeled 'the enemy of the state,' 'procapitalists' and 'pro-Western' elements under communism, became under state-nationalism—'Marxist feminists,' 'communist profiteers' and 'Yugo-nostalgics'—the enemies of their nation-state."[139] Western feminists who ignored the history of the countries—particularly the historical interplay between socialism, feminism, and secularism—arguably did little more than advance particular nationalist projects through their assessment of genocidal rape. Some critics, including Balkan feminist Vesna Kesic, relying on detailed historical assessments of postsocialist Yugoslavia, also questioned the pivotal role that pornography played during the conflict, including the very existence of such media in military campaigns.[140] In the fracturing Yugoslavia, antiwar feminist collectives—including Belgrade's Women in Black and the Zagreb Women's Lobby—railed against warmongering appropriations of sexual violence, wherein "raped women become flags waved by the warring parties."[141]

While legal feminist scholarship tends to frame the genocidal rape debate as a contest between the Copelon/Charlesworth and MacKinnon/Dworkin frameworks, placing legal feminisms in the context of the US sex wars and understanding them as contests over the place of race in feminist accounts of sex shifts the grounds of analysis. Tracking the revival of sex wars logics in the treatments of wartime rape in international law alters the terrain, too, of how we perceive local nonlegal feminisms and other activisms. Centering legal feminisms within the 1990s "transnational turn" in academic feminism helps show one way that "geographic travel" comes to stand in for epistemic transformation[142]—or, as Sandra Soto writes, "the ease with which the transnational turn can slip into a desire for multicultural/multinational difference."[143] In US legal academia, for example, some feminists (including Black and other feminists of color) praised MacKinnon's "intersectional" attention to the ethnoreligious identities of the raped women and through her formulation of genocidal rape.[144] Yet the substance of her engagement evacuates the material histories of reproduction, property, and labor within the former Yugoslavia and within the context of US slavery.

For MacKinnon "ethnic rape" is, like pornography, a cultural expression of gendered rage. In 1993, Mackinnon distinguished ethnic rape from rape under US slavery even as she portrayed them both as gendered projects of cultural transmission:

> Most distinctively, it is rape for reproduction as ethnic liquidation: Croatian and Muslim women are raped to help make a Serbian state by making Serbian babies. This is ethnic rape. If this were racial rape, it would be pure pollution, the children regarded as dirty and contaminated: their mothers' babies as in the American South under slavery, Black babies. Because it is ethnic rape, the children are regarded as clean and purified: their fathers' babies, Serbian babies, as clean as anyone with a woman's blood in them and on them can be.[145]

Here, geopolitical histories of property, labor, slavery, and empire are evacuated through attention to differences among women, the cleaving of ethnicity and race, in order to place "reproduction as ethnic liquidation"—the ultimate iteration of sex as domination—within the bounds of genocide. The structure of recognized international violations of law (genocide, with its group-based harms) scaffolds the meaning of rape. This structure of group endangerment requires a version of history that distances the concept of mass rape from contemporary US racial (not to mention settler) relations—a move that relegates the concept of mass sexualized violence against Black women or other groups in the United States to a distant past by tethering it to the reproductive economy of US slavery.

Presenting women as a global class in this way, as a rejoinder to Marx, is an utterly pornographic reworking of the Marxist tradition. The concept of gender as sexual antagonism, as Wendy Brown argues, "reinscrib[es] and exploi[ts] the power of the code [of totalizing male domination] even while denouncing its contents."[146] Here there is not only the relentless heterosexuality of dominance feminism—framed in a narrow, cis-centered vision of reproductive autonomy seemingly required by legal definitions of genocide—but also the attempt to harness slavery and the post–Cold War destruction of economic collectivism as evidence of a theory of gender as sexual antagonism. The genocidally raped—where genocidal rape signifies forced reproductive labor across ethnoreligious lines or a damage so severe that the raped are rejected by their culture and ejected from its reproductive economy[147]— become key to the value work of diversity in the divided world of human rights. In the process, the multiple economies of carceral feminisms—prisons, policing, border control, mental health regimes that describe certain feminist orientations that appeal to the violence of the state as the solution to gender and sexual problems—don a more worldly military-industrial guise.

So considered, genocidal rape debates are not a form of particularism but reworkings of what universalism could mean in the face of vast difference. In both Copelon/Charlesworth's and MacKinnon/Dworkin's framings, militarized rape and sexual violence as a tactic of ethnic cleansing or genocide still functions as a stark, if not the starkest, example of the sexual vulnerability of all women. The underlying view of women as a group united through shared sexual vulnerability is not contravened by the genocidal rape debates but enhanced by the bare acknowledgment of ethnoreligious difference—itself a cipher, in this context, for the illiberal, undemocratic, and oppressed. These feminist epistemologies—embedded within the structures and jurisdictions of international criminal law, requiring the suppression of racial histories of slavery, labor, and property—inaugurate what I call the racialization of mass rape.

The Racialization of Mass Rape

I use the term *racialization of mass rape* to reference the collusions of feminism and efforts to combat state-sanctioned sexual violence in humanitarian policy making, global securitization strategies, and militarisms that interact to effectuate and maintain pathologized nationalities, geographic regions, and peoples subject to predatory capitalist accumulation. Here, apprehending rape as a weapon of war not only transforms the tactics of war (understood as ethnic or genocidal conflict) to include military campaigns of rape and sexual violence (understood mostly as violence against women) but also overhauls the scope and sociocultural meaning of rape and sexual violence through an encounter with ethnoreligious violence.

I follow Jasbir Puar in understanding racialization as a process that "informs the very distinctions between life and death, wealth and poverty, health and illness, fertility and morbidity, security and insecurity, living and dying" through "specific social processes and formations" that are not "necessarily or only tied to what has been historically theorized as race."[148] Racialization in this way encompasses not only what the biological body "looks like" or "can do" but also can include the more diffuse process of its disassembly into "the subhuman and the human-as-information"—the interactions of bodily traits, gestures, movements and descriptions with the "numbers and facts that matter," such as Social Security numbers, records of criminal activity, country of origin, visa status, and place of residence.[149] The result is a fluid assortment of populations that blur and overlap as much as they delineate, producing subjects that may be defined by applying multiple analytics—some of which combine to produce what we experience as, for example, race and sex. Puar's assessment breaks positivist analyses that extract race from historical sociopolitical, cultural, religious, and economic contexts to figure race as a settled identity that only needs to be better represented or included in legal and cultural realms for racial justice to be served.

The racialization of mass rape is accomplished in part through a reconceptualization of rape and sexual violence. This entails not only maneuvering rape from an individual offense to an atrocity crime (as war crimes and crimes against humanity or as constitutive acts of genocide). It also entails analyzing rape's inception within an emerging international legal system that is calibrated to ensure a social order premised on capitalist expansion through the global extension of rights. Rape could come to be regarded as a mass crime, I argue, through changes in legal regimes of proof that concern the relationship between and meaning of sexual consent and coercion during ethnoreligious warfare as a way to shore up the difference between US multicultural democracy and improper, illiberal modes of population management and control. Could the multicultural new world order, for example, allow charges of wartime rape as genocide—a charge shadowed by the Holocaust, the bloodbath of US racial history, and the unbearable whiteness of much of US legal feminisms—to be defeated through individual avowals of sexual consent? In other words, the creation of a legal subject of mass sexual injury necessitates transformations in the definitional relationships between sexual consent and sexual coercion as the charge of rape becomes attached to mass crimes and charges of systematic group persecution—as rape comes to describe not just violated persons but violated populations that surpass traditional racial demarcations. Here, US civil law debuts and models some legal theorizations that prefigure feminist arguments in international law, reflected in some of the resulting jurisprudence.

While the 1998 ICTR case *Prosecutor v. Akayesu* resulted in the first formal charge of wartime rape as a constitutive act of genocide in international criminal law, the first case to allege wartime rape as genocidal (albeit as a civil charge) occurred in US federal courts. In spring 1993, MacKinnon, on behalf of patriotic women's groups in Croatia and Bosnia and Herzegovina, filed a civil action against Radovan Karadžić for his alleged participation in and instigation of a campaign to eliminate non-Serbs in Bosnia and Herzegovina— this is *Kadic v. Karadzic*, which I take up again in chapter 3. MacKinnon characterized the proceeding as an attempt to seek "relief specifically for injuries of genocidal sexual atrocities perpetrated as a result of Karadžić's policy of ethnic cleansing in collaboration with Slobodan Milošević's administration in Belgrade, Serbia."[150] *Kadic v. Karadzic* prefigures the debates in the international arena, supplying a template for international jurisprudence of what arguments could find purchase in a reputable domestic court. Questions involving the nature of consent, the limits of state sovereignty in effectively guaranteeing human rights, and the notion of sexual assault as a collective and individual offense find legal articulation in this suit and do so through ethnoreligious charges of gendered sexual violence—including rape, forced prostitution, forced impregnation, torture, and summary execution—as part of a genocidal war.[151] In June 1995, the appellate court found that Radovan Karadžić's planning and ordering of "a campaign of murder, rape, forced impregnation, and other forms of torture designed to destroy the religious and ethnic groups of Bosnian Muslims and Bosnian Croats clearly state a violation of the international law norm proscribing genocide."[152]

Decided three years after *Kadic*, the 1998 ICTR case *Prosecutor v. Akayesu* was the first tribunal case to engage the matrix of rape, sexual violence, and genocide within international law, settling them within the bounds of permissible future treatment in international legal jurisprudence. For his alleged failure to summon assistance or otherwise attempt to quell the violence against the Tutsi population, the ICTR pronounced Jean-Paul Akayesu, mayor of the Taba commune, guilty of a number of charges, including genocide (with rape specified as an instrument of genocide) and crimes against humanity (with rape a specific allegation). In a move unprecedented within the international legal arena, the ICTR explicitly defined rape—solely in conjunction with the charge of a crime against humanity and not as an element of genocide—as "a physical invasion of a sexual nature, committed on a person under circumstances which are coercive."[153] Analogizing rape to torture by assessing rape as the sexualized malicious intent of its perpetrators, the ICTR specified rape to be "a form of aggression" that defies the standard, purely descriptive catalogs of objects and body parts common to legal definitions of rape. The ruling insists "that the central elements of rape cannot be captured in a mechanical description."[154]

The association of rape with genocide and war transformed the debate around consent and the problem of coercion. *Akayesu* decoupled the traditional linking of coercion and force, stating that "coercive circumstances need not be evidenced by a show of physical force [and can instead] . . . be inherent in circumstances like armed conflict or military presence of threatening forces on an ethnic basis."[155] By understanding rape as the default designation of the coercive circumstances inherent in (ethnoreligious) wartime conflict, *Kadic* and *Akayesu* provide legal models that effectively dislocate the primacy of individual consent from the definitional heart of rape by focusing on the presence of social coercion—an element many domestic courts had not previously found to be present without a demonstrable, often physical, show of resistance.[156] For rapes "proven inflicted as part of war, genocide, or crimes against humanity," *Akayesu* thus defined rape "in terms of its function in collective crimes."[157] For MacKinnon, this is correct standard for *all* rape, in and out of war. "Most rapes," she writes, "go unreported because most women know they will not get justices; state rape is a more appropriate description of their experiences, with rape ineffectively addressed to a discriminatory degree."[158] MacKinnon lauded *Kadic* and *Akayesu*, greeting them as landmark decisions that "arguably for the first time" accurately recognized the true plight of the rape survivor by defining rape "in law as what it is in life."[159]

Despite some (albeit contested) evidence that sexual abuse does not serve the same function in every violent conflict, nor is it present in the same degree,[160] *Akayesu* advanced a portrait of rape and sexual violence as endemic to the necessarily coercive context of wartime sex, embedding the "commonsense" notion of cross-ethnic sexual encounters as anomalous.[161] This emphasis on the inherently coercive circumstances of violent war couched as ethnic conflict can segue ineluctably into dominance theory claims on sexuality, activating and reinvigorating the animating logic of the gender war in which women-as-group are perpetually at the mercy of men. This revamping and revivifying of the radical feminist "dangerous (hetero)sex" motif consolidates the project of global sisterhood by reifying, but ultimately subordinating, women's ethnoreligious affiliation through an assertion of women's human rights.[162] This in turn serves the trend of seeking international criminal solutions to global sexual problems. As feminists turned violence against women into an international human rights campaign, rape and sexual violence became visible as analogs of ethnic conflict and genocide. Ethnoreligious antagonisms—framed as the mark of difference between women—allowed arguments for women as a globally endangered group to piggyback on analyses of genocide that had already separated women into ethnoreligious enclaves.

Focusing on sexual consent and coercion shows how the recognition and charge of mass rape as a crime against humanity or genocide is a racialized crime. It is racialized by structures of international law through the commodification of rape, law's ability to produce social and historical value through wholesale denial of the political and economic relations that render these particular rapes legible and make them mass. Mass sexualized violence in Rwanda, in a context where women actively and aggressively perpetrated and incited genocidal violence against women,[163] can serve as evidence of and crucially a template for legal concepts and theories of mass sexualized violence that presume the gendered category of sex as a primary site of vulnerability and injury. Events in Rwanda confirmed the diagnosis in the former Yugoslavia, together creating the ability to produce (and prosecute) mass rape as crimes against humanity or genocide in the ICTY, the ICTR, and other international legal forums. Setting the war-raped as the subject of law—in this case one who can also be made mass, whose injury is more than one's own—alters (but does not displace) the individual as the premier subject of international law.[164] However, it does recalibrate group identity formation through the inner workings and structures of law and the analogic functions of making mass rape through undifferentiated comparison to far-flung, troubled locales, to other states in monumental collapse. This process reforms the foundations of international law, amending its utmost respect for state sovereignty, which must now be qualified or even suspended in the defense of all humanity. The categorical possibility of mass rape—as a mass crime befalling a population—joins territories, peoples, and motivations for conflict across the time and space of legally recognizable warfare and the jurisdictions of international criminal law.

The racialization of mass rape is a heuristic that lets us see how structures of law—in particular international criminal law—create populations to be managed and governed and on whose account state sovereignties may be abrogated by international peacekeeping missions, international courts, supranational governance bodies, and other strategies. It points as well to the generation of concepts and structures that may or may not immediately support clear designations of racialization for the peoples that give rise to them. Yet these concepts nonetheless lay the groundwork for future, gendered group racialization and the designation of certain regions or peoples as unstable or violence-prone. Meanwhile, as I discuss in chapter 3, other contemporaneous instances of statistically significant occurrences of rape (think US border violence, prisons, policing) may not be understood as mass rape and otherwise may not easily become conceivable as atrocity crimes.[165] Because the preservation of state sovereignty is the organizational bedrock and buy-in for states, the ICC's reach is mainly limited to those states who accept its authority, placing powerful states mostly beyond its investigatory and prosecutorial reach.

What I am describing as the racialization of rape is related to but not fully coincident with the racialization of Muslims or Islam. As a range of contemporaneous writings and commentary immediately following the Balkan conflict were quick to note, Bosnian Muslims, including Muslim men, were racialized as secular, cosmopolitan, endangered, and even white in international media, law, and policy.[166] Scholars of Islam, critical ethnic studies, and the Yugoslav conflict often emphasize the degree to which Bosnian Muslims "became the bearers of any possible multiethnic and tolerant future in the region" and in this way imply that "they were already properly liberal subjects in contrast to the groups [mainly Serbs] that were vilified during the conflict."[167] These accounts engage particular historical and political frameworks to make sense of the conflict, including the long history of Islam's place in Europe, Bosnian Islam and its relationship to pan-Islamic movements,[168] the political economy of human rights, and the collapse of a world organized by two superpowers. Yet elite legal feminists understood Bosnian Muslim women through their own inheritances, including the turn to geographic diversity as a way of managing internal criticisms and gaining institutional power partly through an initial emphasis on genocidal rape and the championing of Muslim women in particular as a move against the "archly conservative" states, including those who followed some iteration of Islamic law, that challenged women's rights as human ones. For elite legal feminists agitating against rape in the Balkans, the status of Muslim rapes is ultimately distinguished, I argue, through the creation of the mass raped as a population, which was made possible by another misreading of "ethnic" conflict—this time in Africa with the tragedy in Rwanda.

Although the ICTY took pains to distance itself from the designation of "a victor's court,"[169] publicly prosecuting sexualized violence in the conflict from all sides, the Office of the Prosecutor "at the same time concentrated its efforts on a case [Kunarac] that viewed the rapes as systematically aimed at Bosnian Muslims" by Serbian soldiers, police, and other paramilitary forces.[170] Understanding this provides a fuller portrait of how multiple and overlapping processes of theorizing the significance of Bosnian and Croat Muslim women's rapes generated different and sometimes contradictory kinds and sites of racializing tendencies. These rapes helped generate legal concepts and structures that may or may not immediately support clear designations of racialization for the peoples who give rise to them, but that nonetheless clear paths for future and gendered group racialization. The installation of rape within international human rights, humanitarian, and criminal law should be understood as part of broader global operations and hierarchies of race. This includes, as I discuss in chapter 3, the connections between the theories of sexual consent and coercion developed as a result of conflict in the Balkans and the subsequent sexualized exclusion of Muslim detainees from the protections of international law by the US government.

The advent of genocidal rape and the subsequent racialization of rape also fed designations of and resolutions of ethnic conflict. For instance, the creation and maintenance of new nations in the Balkans were not merely abstract exercises in statecraft and international governance but instead altered the literal and metaphorical terrain on which their citizens live, requiring newly nationally segregated, racialized citizens, whose proper state practices of citizenship depend upon the nominal reinscription of ethnic identity categories that had been much more fluid before the 1990s. The Dayton Accords, which set the terms for "peace" in the region, while nominally against ethnonationalism, nonetheless anchored ethnic identities through the terms of its peace. The Bosnian and Federation constitutions that flowed from the Dayton Accords contained provisions that "require that a certain percentage of government offices be reserved not only for representatives of the different ethnic groups, but also for individuals who themselves are of a certain ethnicity."[171] The Bosnian constitution, which required Bosnia to become a party to specific international human rights instruments, also establishes that "regional human rights law as embodied in the European Convention for the Protection of Human Rights and Fundamental Freedoms shall be preeminent over all other law."[172] These sorts of solutions to ethnic conflict—the primacy of regional law for the governance and management of individual states or the creation of new multicultural nation-states—reform subjects' experience of belonging through transformations in gender, race, and sex that produce state, regional, and international governance methods and practices. These methods and practices overlap, converge, and diverge as they individuate and aggregate individuals and groups across local, state, regional, and international scales. In the process, these remedies risked and still risk affording a stable coherence to ethnoreligious categories that subsequently must be managed under liberal state and international legal projects that mark peaceful multiculturalism as emblematic of successful state function. Such state-making projects traffic in the flourishing of human difference through the creation, maintenance, and strenuous preservation and naturalization of ethnoreligious and racialized separations and the configurations of sex and gender required for their support. Genocide, tethered to an understanding of the Yugoslav conflict as "ethnic war," as the name to which it answers, quickly becomes an onto-epistemological project that eviscerates that regions' varied pasts and what might otherwise have been carried forward.

These developments recalibrate international and local understandings of the sociocultural meanings of rape and sexual violence, modifying what states owe to groups who dwell in their borders—and when the international community of states might be moved to act. Designating mass wartime sexual violence as a racialized failing of sovereign states can, for example, isolate such violence from analyses of global capitalism, further justifying international criminal solutions and militarized interventions for global sexual problems that seem to spring primarily from ethnic antagonism and "backward" gender politics. The focus on sexualized violence during and after conflict reflects a panic over collapsed states and disordered economics, wherein moves by neocolonial capitalism to stabilize unstable states resolves a post–Cold War and postcolonial crisis of "ownership" by incorporating those states into a liberal economic order. Legal scholar Anne Orford describes how, in the aftermath of Yugoslavia's breakdown, UN officials imposed political and economic reforms that had been previously rejected by democratically elected Bosnian legislators in the name of righting a region fallen to ethnosexual warfare.[173] Years later, these patterns bear out in other locales. In 2009, Secretary of State Hillary Clinton's response to mass rape in the Congo,[174] which privileged US-led antirape military trainings and funneling millions to the Congolese military, operated in lieu of decisive action to address a prime motivator of violent conflict and political instability in the region: the geopolitical and postcolonial landscape that fosters criminally controlled trade of rare earth minerals—the columbite-tantalite harvested and sold to corporations like Nokia, Motorola, Dell, and Sony that keep the affluent flush in computer chips, cell phones, and game consoles.[175]

One legacy of the sex wars is the racialization of mass rape and its many irreconcilable effects. "Differences" among women and feminist efforts to theorize or otherwise address them are the engines through which radical and dominance legal feminisms take the sex wars abroad, where they feed and are fed by frameworks of war, state sovereignty, and global order at the end of the Cold War.[176] Summoning a subject of international law that is mass, sexualized, and gendered is thus a racializing process that emerges in part through the workings of law—the creation of mass rape as a crime against humanity or genocide fixes its subjects within the circuits of international law and governance that are themselves imperial and colonial projects,[177] although how, when, and where these foundational logics become germane to how and when people and states avail that law requires careful, situated attention.[178]

Submerged histories and representations of conflicts, sexual violation, and the feminist treatments of racial, sexual, and other forms of social and historical difference can resurface if we read simultaneously across and within institutional, legal, and cultural accounts of wartime rape and sexual violence. The genealogy of genocidal rape is formed through international legal feminist fights among themselves and other international law and policy movers and shakers; through local feminist organizing for and against "nationalist" feminisms; through transnational feminists and organizations that operate across international, national, and local scales; and through academic feminisms' attempts to address gendered and sexualized violence in the global house of difference. It includes those who might seek recognition of rape and other sexualized violence as an atrocity that must be addressed while refusing militarized humanitarian responses or privileging shallow ethnonationalist representations of crisis. Understanding law and feminist activisms as transnational amalgams of negotiated, unstable sites of material and theoretical difference provides crucial insight into the ethnosexual logics of international governance and legal advocacy. Thinking about mass rape as something that is made prompts a critical excavation of legal and expert knowledge as contested processes, negotiated by a fractured international legal elite with varying signal commitments and interests, and marked (however imperfectly) by encounters with the multivariate class and national politics of the fracturing Yugoslavia and Rwanda. This approach helps show how the "new wars" inaugurate new forms and subjects of feminist engagement. The racialization of mass rape in this way marks a distinct shift in the place of sexuality in modernity. The apprehension of mass sexualized violence in international law generates new subjects of law, new law, and new links between gendered, racialized, and sexual violence in new world orders that remake but do not shake the imperial and colonial trappings of the old ones.

TWO

States of War, Men as State /
The Tortured Americas,
Genocidal Balkans,
and the Sexual State Form

D URING THE 1980S AND 1990S, Guatemala and Peru endured long, brutal civil wars, marked by the targeting of civilians and indigenous women.[1] The military dictatorship in Argentina in the years known as the Dirty War used sexualized violence against leftist opposition. Yet the presence of rampant and documented sexualized targeting of women, including indigenous women, did not spark popular or legal outrage of the intensity and caliber that occurred in relation to the former Yugoslavia.[2] While the gendering and sexualization of ethnic warfare in the former Yugoslavia and Rwanda rendered sexualized violence visible within international law, naming it "mass" and naming it "genocide," preceding and contemporaneous occurrences of rape and other forms of genocidal sexualized violence against the indigenous in the Americas were approached differently. As feminist human rights attorney Rhonda Copelon wrote in 1994, "Mass rape in Bosnia has captured world attention largely because of its association with 'ethnic cleansing' or 'genocide'" even as "the rape of fifty percent of the women of the indigenous Yuracruz people in Ecuador by mercenaries of an international company seeking to 'cleanse' the land went largely unreported. Similarly, the routine rape of women in the civil wars in Peru, Liberia, and Burma, for example, has drawn only occasional attention. Few in the West remember that the rape of Bengali women also had the distinct genocidal purpose of destroying their racial distinctiveness."[3] Copelon's observation gestures toward a legal and cultural representational complex that merits further attention: the comparative valences of ethnicity and indigeneity in the legal and popular recognition of mass sexual violence.

When sexualized violence in Latin America, indigenous or otherwise, appears in elite legal feminist scholarship at this time, it is not often narrated in ways that take fully into account the varied and numerous histories of imperialism, colonial conquest, anti-left Cold War legacies, and indigenous counterorganizing. These absences exist despite the fact that elite legal feminists like Copelon were enmeshed in regional and global liberation efforts, attending left feminist gatherings, and sometimes even working alongside activists on the ground. Instead, these legal feminists generally portrayed sexualized violence in Latin America either (1) as proof of the general pervasiveness of wartime sexualized violence, or (2) as "domestic violence" or "intimate terror," which they subsequently named torture.[4] In an era when ruling regimes in Latin and South America were under intense scrutiny for human rights abuses, elite legal feminists found torture to provide a recognizable legal architecture within which sexualized violence might materialize in international law, breaking the silence, in this view, of the global suffering of women.

The conceptual triptych of women, silence, and violence—actuated by the framing of sexual matters as private or intimate—claims a certain explanatory power that carries a particular solution: end the silence and stop the violence.[5] Law and the state are positioned in this account as both sites of redress for past violation and as new horizons for justice. But an emphasis on silence does little to illuminate how ideas about rape and sexualized violence in the Americas travel unevenly and across borders, from grassroots activists to international governance elite. That emphasis cannot account for how feminists and other activists in various institutional and informal locations shape the message and the meaning of terms relationally, in and against overarching frameworks of conflict and violation. This "silence" does not show how sexualized violence takes shape in the definitional and procedural orbits of other legally proscribed acts, like genocide or torture and, as is the case with much of Latin America, within constitutionally recognized legal pluralism—or the diverse norms, institutions, and practices that typify postcolonial nation-states, which can include indigenous customary law, national law, and international law.[6] While, as chapter 1 suggests, some elite legal feminists in the 1990s became attuned to "genocide" as a way to short-circuit criticisms of the racial insensitivities of radical feminist universalism, racialized depictions of regional difference were nonetheless already threaded throughout their understandings of what sexualized violence could mean. In other words, elite legal feminists aren't only participating in debates about race, ethnicity, or indigeneity when they struggle with whether to apply, for example, the term *genocidal rape* to discrete situations. Racial and geographic imaginaries—as I argue below with a heuristic that I call the sexual state form—are from the beginning implicated in the social and legal meanings of rape as it becomes an affront to international human rights, humanitarian, and criminal law. These imaginaries affect who is positioned as "silent" and when and how a breaking of their "silence" might be heard. This chapter asks how silences and omissions are discursively produced through legal feminist knowledge of racial and colonial sexualized violence when they are rendered as state-sponsored or -enabled. I argue that contemporary US understandings of and frameworks for naming and addressing societal rape come not only from the successes of US–based second- and third-wave feminist movements in the public sphere but also from how US radical feminist ideologies about sexualized violence continue to underlie the neocolonial and globalizing drives of capital and US empire since the fall of communism.

By the mid-1980s, torture was deemed to be among the most serious affronts to humanity.[7] In the 1980s and 1990s, elite legal feminisms and the intellectual and legal genealogies of domestic violence as torture at once depended upon, invested in, and obscured local decolonial, feminist, transnational, and other activisms against authoritarianism and empire in the Americas. Elite legal feminists and decolonial, feminist, and other activisms coproduced a gendered subject of human rights and an international legal system responsive to it by placing domestic, intimate, and sexualized violation at the heart of torture—an act that, under prevailing definitions of the time, must be committed by a state official or a person otherwise authorized by the state.[8] Yet in doing so, elite legal feminists transformed heterogeneous gender and sexualized violence—due to settler or franchise colonialisms, authoritarian dictatorship, US (and other) empire, and US funding of right-wing militia and military states of which they are fully cognizant—into a binary (and binarily gendered) story of the male state and women's "domestic" torture within it.

In the process, indigenous presence and silence were discursively produced by elite legal feminist efforts to situate sexualized violence in national and international circuits of legal redress. By marshaling eclectic organizing histories and understandings of sexualized harm into a binary story of male state violence, feminist human rights claims have masked continued and continual neocolonial expropriations of land and sideline other ways of being and knowing—overwriting, for example, the plurality of justice mechanisms and debates around them in favor of a progress narrative in which international law redeems the wayward state. "Silences" created the opportunity for elite feminists to retheorize the parameters of state sovereignty through recourse to a global notion of humanity at the moment when the deferred promise of egalitarian justice gained renewed traction within international law and governance. This creation of silence illuminates what Ann Stoler calls "the nature of empire as a moving target" as it operates along "scaled genres of rule that produce and count on different degrees of sovereignty and gradations of rights."[9]

Building on work in queer, trans, and American studies that puts sexuality at the center of race, militarism, and empire, I analyze two influential pieces of feminist legal scholarship: Rhonda Copelon's 1994 article, "Recognizing the Egregious in the Everyday: Domestic Violence as Torture," and Celina Romany's 1993 article, "Women as Aliens: A Feminist Critique of the Public/Private Distinction in International Human Rights Law." Romany's article, as she writes in her acknowledgments, was part of a joint project with Copelon—both were active participants in a coordinated network of elite legal feminists who were attempting to theorize "women's rights," including freedom from sexualized violence, as international human rights.[10] This chapter uses Copelon's and Romany's writings to look at how transnationally produced feminist and US/international feminist legal knowledge of mass sexualized violence depends on largely unacknowledged and silenced—but not silent—conceptualizations of race, indigeneity, and what I call the *sexual state form*. I use the term the *sexual state form* to direct attention to the imagined sexual character of the state and its peoples whose actions become the subject of legal feminist thought and action through their theorizations of legal harm. In elite feminist legal activism and scholarship, the liberal vision of freedom at risk is tethered to the sexual state form: dictators torture, multicultural states in distress commit genocide, and rogue and stateless ethnoreligious actors sow terror. Racialized states, regions, and peoples thus describe, define, and prescribe the contours of sexualized violence as well as its potential modes of redress; they shape the narrative of what sexualized violence is in and beyond calls other activisms might make. Because liberal law does not or cannot fully acknowledge its indebtedness to strains of decolonial, women of color, or other organizing that undermines its authority, it conceptualizes only certain people (or certain "women"—paradigmatically cis-hetero women who are "intimate" with dominant men) as worthy of protection through the narrative that all women are at risk. Before legal action and its complications are even considered or repurposed, the sorts of indigenous and Global South feminist perspectives and activisms that made the conceptualization of domestic violence possible are not always legible in the frame, although their suffering may be evidence of the necessity for it.

To more fully reckon with these interplays, mass sexual or "intimate" violence must be understood not only from within multiple sites and histories of transnational feminist organizing, but also in the diffuse workings of law itself. Recognizing the heterogenous imprint of women of color, indigenous, and left thought and organizing within genealogies of international law and following its continuation through ongoing efforts to address sexualized violence in robust, collective ways is, this chapter suggests, a way to ask different questions and demand different approaches to what is now a global mandate to end rape and sexualized violence. It is a way to counter how the ongoing nonconsensual basis of empire or settler/colonial states—and the sexualized violence inherent to those projects—is overwritten by a liberal notion of sexual consent positioned as a problem between "men" and "women" that must be made public and addressed through international governance, including the militarized and carceral approaches that so often follow it.[11] It is a way to push back against the racial entanglements of regional struggle and sexualized violence exemplified by the sexual state form. The framework and histories of activism in Latin America and the United States that I offer are not meant to be prescriptive or complete.[12] The histories I recount are attempts to flag how a particularized conception of the state, one that denies alternative arrangements of authority or power, is tied to the legal recognition, theorization, and creation of particular forms of sexualized violence. In turn, the state and the violence at issue may then be rearticulated in law as abstract universals and detached from the workings of empire or other mechanisms that distribute and arrange global power.

Encuentros and Desencuentros

While Balkan and African ethnic wars, genocides, and mass sexualized violence would come to dominate 1990s human rights consciousness, the 1980s saw torture and opposition to US-backed warfare in Central and South

America as a locus of activism and activity. With Central America staged as the Ronald Reagan administration's early grandstand against Soviet expansionism in the "Third World," Nicaragua, El Salvador, Honduras, and Guatemala were at the forefront of Cold War political and military contests.[13] US engagement in the region was typified by covert and clandestine operations against counterinsurgency, carried out primarily by local forces and civilians to ensure minimal loss of US lives. "Counterterror" maneuvers counted murder and disappearances as privileged, emblematic, and vociferously disavowed tactics.[14] This vision of warfare, as historian Greg Grandin describes it, was vicious and novel; it included "psychological operations, civic action, and grass roots, human intelligence work, all of which run counter to the conventional U.S. concept of war."[15] The goal: "total war at the grass-roots level."[16]

Historian Michael McClintock credits early 1980s US encounters with Lebanon and other Middle Eastern locales as legitimating the concept of "counterterrorism"; thus "counterinsurgency operations and unconventional wars were similarly sanitized as part of the campaign against international terrorism."[17] In 1981, the Reagan administration dubbed such heretofore unconventional warfare "low-intensity conflict"—a moniker designed to soothe and forestall US public and congressional reluctance to confront Soviet advances and, later, international terrorism.[18] The effects of Central American "low-intensity" conflicts were anything but. As Grandin observes, "After all, it was in Latin America that an earlier generation of US and US-backed counterinsurgents put into place a prototype of Washington's twenty-first century Global War on Terror."[19]

These so-called low-intensity conflicts would also help shape the discursive potential of the ethnic wars, even as 1990s war and statecraft were in many respects a break (a renewed emphasis on ethnicity as martial motivation, the rise of new systems of international law, etc.) from the Cold War Latin American theater. Both locations were embroiled in conflicts that involved more than the formal acquisition of new territory or even, as so routinely charged in the Balkans, with the establishment of ethnic homogeneity. The conflicts were motivated by what V. P. Gagnon describes in the Yugoslav context as "the construction of homogeneous *political* space" as a requisite for imperial economic expansion.[20] As elite US military units trained and deployed local Latin American police, military, and paramilitary counterterror outfits, they sought to unmake social realities that could support oppositional thought and action. As elite Yugoslav politicos manufactured ethnic conflict from within a cosmopolitan society through the imposed reconceptualization of ethnicity as bounded and fixed, they sundered ways of knowing, living, and relating with others, effectively demobilizing the people to whom they were theoretically accountable. That the leveling of political opposition occurs in the service of a voracious global capitalism is an only slightly submerged objective of the homogeneous political imperative. War is indeed, as Foucault succinctly dubbed it, politics by other means.

The Americas, as concentrated sites of US empire and war making, proved particularly salient for US-based or -educated elite legal feminists whose various left-leaning politics found common ground in "improving the lives of women." To reform all scales of law, from the international and regional to the domestic and local, they sought out the "worst" or most harrowing conditions that women experienced as evidence of the bleakness and unjustifiable neglect of "gender perspectives" in law and governance, including the laws of war (as chapter 1 elaborates). Janet Halley traces the formal feminist entrance into law and governance in the 1990s, what she calls "governance feminism," in part to the scaffolding provided by the rise of transnational activist and professional international feminist organizations that had proliferated since the UN Decade for Women (1975–85). The intervening years saw feminist ideas and organizations gain traction during periods of neoliberal state retraction of public services and the concurrent assumption of erstwhile state public duties by NGOs. The proliferation of UN-hosted conferences also raised the profile and traction of "women's" issues.[21]

Alongside Halley's detailed and illuminating contributions, it is worth emphasizing how this rich organizing history did not begin, culminate, or end with the ascent of professional feminism. Otherwise, we risk ensconcing a history of international legal feminisms that isolates "feminism" from other radical left tendencies and platforms. As queer theorist Emily Hobson demonstrates, the "long 1960s," typically understood to range from 1955 to 1975, birthed a "Third World Left": "a wide assortment of radicals—ideologically diverse, working in conversation, and often aspiring to be a common 'Movement,'" who "came to reject the idea that the US nation-state"—and in some cases the abstraction of any nation-state or organization of them—as a unit of legitimate political authority and organization. In other words, the state did not "set the horizon of equality and freedom."[22] Inspired "by anticolonial struggle and Chinese, Cuban, and diasporic black revolutions," these radicals pursued sexual and gender liberation in concert with "Chicano, Asian American, Native American, and Black liberation, forged an antiwar movement and radical underground, and organized women of color, socialist, and other radical feminisms."[23] This trajectory of left organizing frames elite legal feminist interventions in the Americas through divergent transnational social histories that are not about "women." Instead, these histories follow the kinds of sexual and gender liberation and identifications that draw strength from unfolding assemblages of action and thought. Left histories span decades and geographies, from "the height of the late 1960s and early 1970s through Black Power and opposition to the Vietnam War; in the 1970s through socialist and women of color feminism and a growing attention to US intervention in Latin America; and across the 1980s through the Central American solidarity movement."[24] These transnational exchanges brought "anti-imperialism into new areas of struggle and expanded what anti-imperialism meant, including by naming the centrality of heterosexual norms and violence to colonial power"—emphasizing "the multi-gender power of feminisms."[25]

Again, such left organizing was hardly separate from elite feminist legal attempts to create a gendered subject of human rights. Copelon and US gender studies scholar Charlotte Bunch, for instance, attended transnational Latin American feminist gatherings together in the early 1990s, where they strategized about how best to secure women's rights and human rights under international law. Bunch and Copelon also advanced women's reproductive rights as human rights at the 1994 International Conference on Population and Development in Cairo, a view that was ultimately adopted at the 1995 Beijing World Conference on Women.[26] From 1983 until her death in 2010, Copelon, a veteran of the Center for Constitutional Rights, was a member of the founding faculty at CUNY Law School, where she directed the International Women's Human Rights Clinic, which she cofounded with Celina Romany in 1992. The clinic proved instrumental in coordinating feminist responses to the disintegration of the former Yugoslavia and Rwanda.[27] Copelon was active with the NGO MADRE, a US-based transnational grassroots feminist human rights organization dedicated to opposing US imperialism. Founded in 1983, MADRE initially concentrated its efforts in Latin America but quickly expanded to the Middle East and later the former Yugoslavia, sponsoring a Mother Courage II tour that brought local feminists in the Balkans to the United States to raise awareness about the effects of war on women. That tour proved controversial, as nationalist feminists insisted that MADRE recognize the rape of Bosnian and Croat women as genocidal and therefore distinct from the rape of Serbian ones.[28]

The geographic scope of organizing undertaken by MADRE and likeminded feminists speaks to the breadth of US empire and the interconnectedness of the feminist freedom struggles against empire. Yet the enmeshment of anti-imperialist and anti-authoritarian organizing in Latin America with gender and sexuality has its own trajectories and engagements with state violence and promises of freedom. As Ángela Ixkic Bastian Duarte writes, contemporary feminism in Latin America emerged during the 1970s in the shadow of military dictatorships, where women "used the cultural respect for women's traditional gender roles, and the image of mothers and grandmothers, to carve spaces for political agency" and "denounce torture, 'disappearances,' and other human rights violations" at a moment when governments viciously silenced "trade unions, opposition parties, and other traditional political subjects."[29] While, as Duarte notes, these movements were not always expressly portrayed as feminist and might separate themselves from feminism entirely, they nonetheless represent "important watersheds for the creation of a regional feminism during this period."[30] Fights to end repression and denounce the authoritarianism of the Dirty Wars in Nicaragua, El Salvador, and Chile initially spurred feminist efforts in Mexico and Argentina. Yet this feminism never managed, as Duarte and Gisela Espinosa note, "to breach the social and political distance that separated it from grassroots women's groups," including indigenous ones.[31] These rifts were exacerbated during the 1980s and 1990s as feminist professionals began to privilege law and policy over grassroots work—as gender was claimed, as Halley details, as a site of domestic and international law and governance.[32] NGOs and institutionalized feminisms required standardized language in "accordance with the universalizing criteria of the United Nations," which led such feminist organizations to "follow the agendas set by donors."[33] As a result, "institutionalized feminists" distanced themselves from local priorities, lauded individual frameworks of leadership and injury over collective or competing ones, and "established pacts and alliances with governments" and multilateral agencies that "prioritized change in public policy and failed to question economic and political neoliberalism."[34]

Throughout the 1990s, as institutionalized feminisms took root, indigenous women were also constituted as political subjects in Latin America.[35] This emergence occurred through "a discourse in relation to indigeneity that has linked local struggles across the continent with a transnational movement that places racism and political and cultural rights at the center of its demands."[36] The recognition of indigenous political subjecthood culminated in "a series of constitutional reforms [that] recognize[d] the multicultural character of Latin American countries . . . [and] led to a de jure recognition of legal pluralism."[37] While this neoliberal multiculturalism has been championed in some quarters, others have noted that "at the judicial level, the limited recognition of indigenous law and the spaces of community justice in the majority of Latin American states have not included political rights or territorial autonomy, resulting in an additive justice that contributes to decentralization as demanded by international financial organizations."[38] Internationalist feminist organizing in Latin America, with its emphasis on individual rights, including human rights and a focus on sexual and reproductive rights, further split liberal feminists from the main of indigenous organizing. As indigenous organizer Blanca Chancoso puts it, "We talk about land, although our women companions do not need to talk about land. But we [indigenous women] do, because land is not only the farm where we work, it is also the Pachamama, our territory. . . . Violence doesn't come only from the husband or the father, it is also generated by those who have taken over the land."[39]

Copelon first considered theorizing intimate violence against women as torture after attending the 1990 Latin American and Caribbean Feminist Meeting Encuentro Feminista in San Bernardo del Tuyú, Argentina, with US feminist scholar and former Furies member Charlotte Bunch.[40] Initially convened in 1981 in Bogotá, Colombia, Encuentros have annually gathered thousands of feminist activists from almost every country in Latin America and the Caribbean. Encuentros participants hail from "a broad and potentially antagonistic range of public spaces—from lesbian-feminist collectives, to trade unions, landless movements, research and service non-governmental organizations (NGOs), university women's studies programs, revolutionary organizations, mainstream political parties, and State institutions."[41] The sheer breadth of organizing issues and models that converge at the Encuentros has helped nurture a transnational and transborder activist movement in the Americas, one that negotiates "class differences, rural-urban divisions, diverse racial and ethnic formations, age and generational divides, as well as differences in sexual identities and orientations, [and] Latin American and Caribbean feminisms' heterogeneity" in ways that thwart "uniform understandings of key feminist concerns such as reproductive health, education, violence against women, labor rights, sexuality, and (neoliberal) globalization."[42] "While grounded in political solidarity among women, then, the Encuentros and 'desencuentros' [misencounters] within them have fostered productive debates and re-configured alliances and coalitions among the region's feminists."[43]

While indigenous women had participated in previous Encuentros, the 1990 gathering in San Bernardo del Tuyú proved pivotal in organizing indigenous women's regional networks. These indigenous networks developed a structure independent of the feminist and women's movement at a moment when the regional presence of UN and affiliated NGOs and feminists sparked heated debates over the degree of autonomy the feminist movement should have from state and international institutions.[44] "Violence against women" nonetheless performs its mediating work. In the 1990 issue of the Latin American feminist magazine *Aquelarre* (Coven), Carmen Rodríguez describes *des/encuentros* at San Bernardo del Tuyú as diverse in topic but organized roughly under an overarching theme: "All areas of work were covered: sexuality, labour, health, culture, indigenous women, peasant women, daily life, education, power, political and social participation, science, media, law, the economy.... Violence against women in all its forms was, however, one of the areas that got the most attention; the theme of the march that put an end to the conference on Saturday, November 24, in Buenos Aires, was: 'No More Violence against Women.'"[45]

It is in the midst of this dynamic, complex, contradictory, and fraught space of feminist and left organizing that Copelon first links domestic violence to torture.

The Public Home and the Bad Man in It

In the early and mid-1990s, after years of feminist and feminist legal activism against US imperialism in the Americas and gender/sexualized violence in general, Copelon and Romany published a series of articles that framed what they called "intimate violence" (violence between sexual/domestic partners) as torture and therefore a gendered violation of human rights.[46] Unlike popular usages of the word, legal definitions of *torture* generally require four elements: (1) the infliction of severe mental or physical suffering, which (2) must be intentional, with (3) some degree of official or quasi-official involvement present, and (4) the infliction of suffering must happen for a specified purpose.[47] In the mid-1990s, rape and other sexualized violence perpetrated while in the custody of a state official for a specified purpose—which would appear to be very definition of torture—were not automatically recognized as such within international human rights forums.[48] By analogizing domestic violence to torture, Copelon and others not only wanted to correct gendered and sexualized understandings of what torture could be. They also sought to overhaul the relationship between the state and its citizenry. If legally understood as torture, charges of domestic violence would demand state attention, refuting the "persistent trivialization of violence against women," shattering the public/private divide that in theory relegated "intimate" and "private" matters of sex beyond state purview.[49] In the US context, such an understanding of domestic violence could potentially require federal oversight and federal civil rights remedies for such abuses.[50]

In presenting domestic violence as torture, elite legal feminists operating in the international arena furthered an emerging carceral strategy that would bear dividends in US organizing contexts, one that conflated domestic violence with sexism and feeble law enforcement. During the 1970s and 1980s, as feminist legal scholar Aya Gruber writes,

> [US] legal feminists transformed the general claim that patriarchy causes battering to the specific claim that patriarchal criminal *law* is *the* cause of battering. In reconceptualizing [domestic violence] as a matter of men's uncontrolled criminal behavior, many legal activists systematically denied all other antecedents of battering, even marital norms and gendered economic marginalization. They reduced [domestic violence] to the phenomenon of violent sexist men emboldened by weak law enforcement. Strengthening law enforcement soon became the primary goal of the battered women's movement, and radical and antipatriarchy feminists' redistributive, gender norm–upending agenda was discarded as yet another leftist pipe dream.[51]

Knowledgeable of this critical background, Copelon and Romany thus deployed a strategy to bring the gender and sexualized violence within the bounds of international law through the retheorization of certain serious charges, including torture.[52] Copelon and other elite legal feminists argued that recognizing domestic violence as torture would provide a firm grounding for broader social and governance transformation—a place from which to demand that states "correct the systemic discrimination that causes many women, particularly those from poor and minority communities, to fear state intervention."[53] In these ways, recognizing domestic violence as torture was an intended corrective to the "silence" surrounding "violence against women" in international human rights and US federal and state law. It was also an implicit recognition of how "silence" contains differential histories of oppression and exploitation.[54] What Copelon proposed was a relatively straightforward legal device for changing what protections states owe to those who dwell in their borders and a way to "envision human rights in the home."[55]

Despite "the skepticism of some leading mainstream human rights scholars," Copelon ultimately advanced the analogy of domestic violence to torture in a forceful and influential 1994 article, "Recognizing the Egregious in the Everyday: Domestic Violence as Torture." At an Encuentro Feminista workshop on gender violence and human rights, Copelon was, in her own words, "first inspired to think about intimate violence as torture."[56] There, Copelon listened as Las Madres de la Plaza de Mayo, the famous association of Argentine mothers whose children were "disappeared" by the military dictatorship between 1976 and 1983, recounted and theorized abuse in the home under authoritarian conditions: "Several Madres of the Plaza de Mayo in Argentina and women who opposed official torture insisted that what happens to women in violent homes was equivalent to the violence of dictatorial prisons."[57] Copelon came to recognize torture as "a tool of colonial power" through interactions with "women survivors and activists from around the globe—particularly from societies where torture was or is a state practice," who "commonly speak of domestic violence as torture."[58]

Copelon aligned her work against a "feminist essentialism" that "posits a 'women's perspective' without regard to different racial, class, cultural and sexual positions that transform gender and define differences among women."[59] She was adamant that her work not feed divisions between the Global North and the Global South, writing that "gender-based oppression is not a phenomenon that obeys the North/South axis."[60] Although this perspective drove her work, "good faith" has never been incompatible with empire. Yet it is important to try to consider the interventions and innovations that feminists and other activists—elite, legal, or otherwise—sought in law as "a mode of engagement" within a particular "historical juncture."[61] "Why?" and "How?" are the questions, and questions are better than simply cataloging, homogenizing, or dismissing out of hand these feminist interventions as inveterately "backward"—to do this only extols the view from here.[62] What I'm attempting is instead to reposition this past from the vantage of the present. This is an effort to theorize past and current feminist efforts aslant, from a place that accepts that what looks and may be promising now may not be for long or at least will not remain that way.

That said, the operations of law—operations of analogy and the commensurability of harm—coupled with an excess of faith in the liberal state can and do cleave intention from outcome, furthering what Jodi Byrd calls "the syllogistic traps of participatory democracy born out of violent occupations of land."[63] Such "syllogistic traps" are exacerbated by the structure of international law, including human rights, which requires "voluntary" state compliance to its mandates, permitting the exclusion of powerful states from oversight and enforcement.[64] The safeguards of the international order are predicated on geopolitical and historical vulnerability as a mechanism for forwarding political homogeneity—or perhaps more precisely, the "diversities" tolerated by liberalism and capitalism. This includes mandated obedience to human rights instruments in postconflict constitutions crafted by international coalitions, like the post–ethnic war Bosnian constitution (discussed in chapter 1), for example, in the aftermath of war.

Here we might consider how international law and governance function as devices that distribute sentiments—to end violence against women, for example—alongside their other orderings of life, territory, and rights. Like the imperial maps that were a "model for rather than a model of what [they] purported to represent,"[65] legal conceptualizations of domestic violence—and sexualized domestic violence as torture—function as thought maps for a future born of an imagined past and fractured present. Their descriptions are speculative and aspirational—they create legal harm and kick off trajectories of law that cannot describe what they claim to address. Legal feminist motivations are embroiled in a fantasy of silence and relief, of a conceptual framing of sexualized violence that at once responds in some ways and for some people to the quieting imperatives of patriarchal empire, yet somehow is still thought to (or strongly hoped to) escape the racist, imperial, and colonial dimensions of, among other things, international law, which harness and build upon multiple imperial trajectories and histories of powerful nation-states.[66]

If Las Madres de la Plaza de Mayo "insisted" that domestic violence was "equivalent" to torture in dictatorial prisons, the translation of this idea across contexts and into international law—into a legally cognizable harm that is legible within the geopolitics of law's operation—transforms the claim and recasts its motivations. When Las Madres de la Plaza de Mayo link torture to domestic violence, they form this analysis and deliver demands for redress within a history of empire and interference. Later, the administrations of Presidents Raúl Alfonsín and Carlos Menem introduced and adopted legal measures to curb and prevent examples of "domestic authoritarianism," including a 1991 law that allowed men found guilty of "beating women, including wives, partners, mothers, grandmothers, children and other relatives" to be expelled from the home.[67] This, too, is a political framing that is responsive to a particular political history.

Legal feminist attempts to cast domestic violence as torture and dismantle the public/private opposition that structures liberal legal activity—what, in their framing, casts the domestic as the "private" sphere where governments must tread with caution—paradoxically overwrites the fact that it is in "domestic" spaces that Las Madres de la Plaza de Mayo become political subjects. The violence that occurs is already neither "private" nor individual. It is a part of systemic mass, regional violation structured by US interference in the Americas and the state-sponsored disappearance of children. Taking up domestic violence as torture erases the exploitative relationships between states when it casts the damage as a failure of the state to relate properly to the individual. This framing of the public and the private also overprivileges an abstracted racialized (and sexualized) authoritarianism as the structuring rubric for analyzing and defining gendered and sexualized violence, casting authoritarianism as the axis on which the meaning of such sexualized violation turns. Although elite legal feminist critiques of the public/private divide acknowledge its falseness and emphasize state complicity in its maintenance, they also obscure the intensities and mechanisms of that complicity. Those critiques, routed through a small notion of gender, flatten the operations of imperial war making in the name of liberal freedom, sidestep the weaponization of intimate or domestic violence by the US state (largely against poor people of color), and exaggerate the necessity of the state as an organizing unit of political authority.[68]

Structures of law—including the legal elements or components that define violation—matter here. Race, cisgendered heteronormative supremacy, and the geopolitical, economic, and colonial histories that converge to produce "violence against women" are obscured by the metaphorical attempt to link the wretched conditions of women experiencing violence in the home with "political prisoners" abused by "states" through the legal strictures of torture itself. The requirement of state or official involvement in the legal charge of torture provided a crucial frame for how legal feminists understood and analyzed sexualized and domestic violence. The bad man in the home turns the private home into a public one, but torture requires a not only a bad man, but a bad state. In Copelon's and Romany's legal academic work, violence against women is often presented as occurring in a particular perversion of the state: an authoritative, dictatorial one that is matched by a "shadow state" or "parallel" state composed of a male-dominated private domestic sphere. Here, paradigmatic impediments to the realization of women's rights are the masculinist excesses of the exemplary late twentieth-century patriarchal state: ruthlessly violent military dictatorships, particularly in Latin America. In theorizing domestic violence as torture, Copelon finds sufferers of violence against women living under a "system of terror" that constitutes "men as a parallel state in women's lives."[69] Women's captivity in this parallel state prompts her to urge the public recognition of "the heroism of women's efforts to endure and survive, just as we have begun to recognize that of POWs and victims of dictatorships."[70] Privately inflicted abuse, Copelon and Romany suggest, is as damaging as (or perhaps even more damaging than) public or state-sanctioned violence. Privately inflicted domestic abuse "may claim more lives than a brutal dictatorship" and should be a human rights concern.[71]

By analogizing the degree of control abusive men have over their female partners to the sovereign control of states over their citizenry or of armed forces over their prisoners of war—by explicitly contending that "the public/private dichotomy . . . constitutes men as a *de facto* absolutist state in women's lives"—Copelon and others sought to retheorize the internationally accepted legal element of torture that requires active or passive state knowledge, backing, or sanction of the violence endured.[72] These kinds of analysis also call international governance regimes to account by arguing that when international law fails to enact the will of women to be free from sexualized and domestic violence, it fails to fulfill the social contract that authorizes each corresponding state legal order.[73] In this analysis, critiques of dictatorial states or the treatment of captured enemies facilitate the gendered indictment of all states, including erstwhile liberal ones.

The legal arguments advanced by Copelon and Romany envision a global feminist subject in need and neglected by "the state"—there is a war on all women—even as particular states, geopolitics, cultural practices, and "women" (including those actually living on the grounds of war) spur these claims of universality and even as their theorizations of the causes and harms of sexualized violence exceed the traditional rights frameworks they labor within. Romany's "Women as Aliens," for example, begins with a scathing criticism of the state and international law. Specifically, she contends that the abstract structures of state and international law themselves estrange women from liberal guarantees of freedom. Yet Romany ultimately defends the potential of liberalism and the promised justice of the state. Instead of engaging in a strict sort of US gender or sexual exceptionalism that would offer the US treatment of women as the model by which to judge the world, Romany valorizes the ideals of liberal egalitarianism—or what Reddy calls "epistemologies [that] promote an egalitarian principle that figures the liberal state as the ultimate embodiment of the values that enable and guarantee equality."[74] By maneuvering women into the category of the "alien," or those who are bereft of state protection, whose last recourse is the realm of international law and specifically an appeal to human rights, Romany dislocates women from the sovereign authority of any single state. In doing so, she reorders the terms of state authority in the liberal order by subordinating its sovereign authority to the dictates of international human rights law. This changes the relationship of the state to the international order and at the same time forwards liberal egalitarianism—a formation born of a US nationalism that seeks to distinguish itself from European colonialism and empire—as the shared guiding principle of international human rights law.[75]

The crux of Romany's critique, and the source of her belief in a reformed liberal state's liberatory potential, lies in the relationship of the individual to the social, a relationship formed in and against legal, social, and cultural articulations of a public and private sphere. This parsing of the individual from the state "is paradigmatic of a social organization founded on the mythical story of the social contract crystallized by the emergence of the nation-state, via sovereignty theories of the sixteenth and seventeenth century."[76] State responsibility to protect human rights (or women's human rights, represented as largely freedom from sexual and gender violence committed by private actors) follows and augments the liberal state model as it abstracts and expands to generate a working international legal (and legal argumentative) framework. In Romany's view, women as a group are a priori alienated from the state and consequently from the protections of international law—a structural violence that can only be remedied by a reworking of the divisions between public and private that prevent women's rights from achieving true status as human rights: from otherwise "unveil[ing] the hidden accounts, the silenced voices."[77]

The Sexual State Form

Long-standing settler, imperial, and neocolonial histories of violence cannot be explained by thinking only about unilateral relationships between bodies or between the tortured and the torturer, the individual and the state or an international order of states, so I offer the concept of the sexual state form. The sexual state form is the imagined character of the state whose actions become the subject of legal feminist thought and action through their attempts to theorize sexualized legal harm. What constitutes recognizable or evidenced accounts of sexualized violence are, I argue, subtly shaped by imagined sexual state forms and their ability to mirror the most egregious legal forms of violation: dictators torture; multicultural states in distress commit genocide (see chapter 1); and rogue ethnoreligious actors sow terror (see chapter 3). Thinking with and through sexual state forms show them to be driven by desires for state-sponsored sexual remedy that appear already saturated with fantasies of regional and racial difference. The sorting of states and regions through sexual state forms (from the Congo and Rwanda writ large as "rape-prone Africa" or the "ethnic" dilemmas in the former Yugoslavia as a stand-in for the whole of the Balkans) shows how sexualized violence as a concept consolidates law and governance power across areas and geographies. The heuristic of the sexual state form thus "coagulate[s] areas in the service of a queer geopolitics by focusing on the idea of area as a postcolonial form through which epistemologies of empire and market can be critiqued."[78] In this way, it complicates designations of state sexuality as masculine/feminine or penetrated/penetrable through attention to the historical relationships between international governance and sexual protection.[79] The heuristic of the sexual state form is also in analytic solidarity with queer indigenous work. That tradition understands the political not as a struggle between social minorities and majorities but as a "sovereign alignment with and within Indigenous communities" that moves beyond "dominant logics and narratives of nation."[80]

Recognizing sexual state forms in action is recognizing how they are deployed to test and proliferate expanses of international law and governance in a dream that motivates much activist lawyering: the hope that a name for each perceived facet of abuse might someday supply the full portrait of its own redress. For Copelon and Romany, at least in their legal scholarship, this necessitates finding and fulfilling the destiny of the liberal state form, which occurs by theorizing injury tied to particular states, regions, and peoples, and then abstracting and recasting that injury as a problem of all states with "women." Although liberalism is the rationale and the ideological basis for Romany's proposal, the concept of liberalism is actuated through recourse to specific racialized and gendered examples that shape the meaning and scope of what can or cannot be recognized as a liberal state project. Romany's abstract theorizations of state and international legal process are, for example, illustrated through rubrics of torture and terror, fleshed out by accounts of wife murders in Brazil and Inter-American Court of Human Rights challenges, namely, *Velaquez Rodriguez v. Honduras*,[81] that find state complicity for human rights violations in the absence of direct state involvement.[82] Whereas Copelon's vignettes on domestic violence offer more wide-ranging narration of such global incidents, including harrowing US-based examples that depict men's nearly absolute control over women, Copelon and Romany portray women as essentially enduring extreme dictatorial conditions largely devoid of historical and political context. In their academic work, torture sets a template for understanding how and why sexualized violence hurts women. Torture and sexualized and other forms of domestic violence are positioned to share a logical structure, an idea of unyielding, improper, and impermissible force operating on one who is utterly without defense. Each suggests women's relationship to a dictatorial state, shadowed by a parallel state of men, as the appropriate and productive axis for reckoning with gender and domestic violence. Through this parallelism, each severs the disparate historical and material connections between state and "private" violence and empire and the violence of the individual state.[83] As legal feminists analogize the authoritarian abuse of state force and power that defines torture to the inner workings of domestic and familial space—particularly to the presence of abusive men in the home—they mobilize racialized ideas of violent Latin American masculinity to bear on theories of sex and state power.

The sexual state form builds on what Timothy Mitchell calls the *state effect*, or the ideological production of the state through cultural imaginaries and lived encounters with its fragmented and at times incoherent power.[84] The sexual state form, however, emphasizes the theorization of legal harm by actors who cannot be concerned with the historical or political context of any state or group of states, except as an upholder of liberal human rights and an enforcer of the social contract—itself an explanatory device that excuses state violence with the liberal fiction that people consent to be governed. The social contract imagines the individual contract as the essential dispensary unit of freedom. Legal scholar Leti Volpp, drawing on the work of feminist political theorist Carole Pateman, suggests that the social contract is in fact better named "the settler sexual contract."[85] The term *settler sexual contract* is an explicit recognition of the original dispossession of indigenous peoples—"in a terra nullius the original contract takes the form of a settler contract. The settlers alone (can be said to) conclude the original pact."[86] Through this pact, the state also "assumes reproductive futurity, solely on the part of those who are considered fit to be citizens of the settler state."[87] What I describe as the sexual state form is in part another chronicle in the governing fiction of the social contract—one that describes how racialized sexualized violence comes to bear on state sovereignty through the human rights guarantees of international law. In the aftermath, those who engage in recognized, prohibited forms of sexualized violence are not "fit" to be a part of the settler state or humanity.

Attention to legal academic and feminist engagement with the sexual state form shows how legal process and the sociopolitical coordinates that shape legal "strategy"—not only legal outcomes or the administrative enforcement of those outcomes—are forms of state-making, race-making, and dispossession that affect whose violence will or will not be named and addressed. Legal feminist organizing across borders produces relationships and knowledge that must be translated into law, conceptualized and promoted as not simply a harm but a legal one. This line of reasoning allows sexualized settler colonial violence and imperial violence in the Americas to appear within international law as an unmarked problem of state authority in the sense that the state is understood as refusing or otherwise failing to protect those who dwell within its borders. The concept of the sexual state form helps show how existing legal pluralities that shape the meaning of sexualized violence on the ground are simplified or omitted from dominant understandings of "violence against women."[88] The interplay, for example, between the Guatemalan state and indigenous justice forums falls from this narrative.

Liberal responses to indigenous sexualized violation in the Quiché department in Guatemala have led to condemnations of the "rough justice" of the Maya-K'iche'. Anthropologist Rachel Sieder details the case of three men accused of kidnapping a woman and her four-year-old child as well as raping the woman. The men were subjected to community interrogation with "sticks and stones" and subsequently set on fire. They all died. Sieder argues that these actions should be understood not as a state failure to regulate violence but as a form of indigenous self-help in the aftermath of a history of military and paramilitary violence against civilians, "including abduction, displacement, torture, dismemberment, murder and systematic rape [which] . . . together with obligatory participation in paramilitary civilian defense patrols, many of which carried out atrocities against civilians, have left a powerful legacy in many of the local practices and imaginaries of justice and politics."[89] Sieder asks that "rough justice"—which is contested as a practice in the community—nonetheless be understood as articulations of sovereignty and not framed through liberal rubrics that simply position Guatemala as a "weak" or "failed state" because such a view "occlude[s] relations of power, domination and exclusion, and the specific practices which determine the lack of access to justice of most citizens."[90]

Consideration of the sexual state form, then, is an exercise that first asks what "counts" as part of legal discourses about rape and other forms of sexualized violence. This directed attention might help foster ways of refusing what Byrd calls "colonial agnosia,"[91] or how colonialism endures but is not recognized by those who continue to benefit from colonial occupation. As a concept, the sexual state form attempts to bind legal feminist theorizations of gendered and sexualized violence to criticisms of "ethnographic entrapment" that shrink the settler colonial relation to fit the uncompromising measures of multicultural difference.[92] It highlights the "composite genres of rule on which modern empires" are built,[93] from state forums to transnational feminist ones. It entails thinking about the development of sexualized violence as a sociolegal category within the complex of laws and legal doctrine that facilitates and shapes its emergence. The sexual state form ties that sociolegal category to revolutions in the meaning and prosecution of torture and genocide and the consolidation of international law. Locating how sexual state forms operate means tracking elite legal feminists like Copelon to San Bernardo del Tuyú, where interactions with local and regional activists like Las Madres de la Plaza de Mayo and their historicized critiques of sexualized and domestic violence transmute through the universalizing language of state remedy as Copelon famously theorizes the "intimate terror" of domestic violence as a form of torture necessitating state intervention.

These leaps in location are required by law—by its actual networks and operations—if we are to follow the effects of its endless push toward the commensurability of legal subjects and legal harms. The law produces a queer geopolitics and a queer temporal politics that come into relief when we follow the exchange of this person for "woman" and this woman for "women" and this violation for a portable and decontextualized violation called "violence against women" or "sexual violence" or simply "rape" across and within international human rights, humanitarian, and criminal law and governance. Following law and sexualized injury in this way shows that while rape and sexualized violence are key sites of reproductive justice work and organizing, concepts of rape and sexualized violence—permeated by the structure of other crimes, like torture and genocide—can perform the epistemological reproductive work of liberalism as viable or desirable political theory. Reinterpretations of gendered and sexualized freedom align with and help trace the contours of concepts like "'voluntary empire,' 'humanitarian imperialism,' or 'empire by invitation'" or formations that otherwise "hail the advent of a beneficent macropolity endowed with consensual rather than coercive qualities."[94]

Thinking about rape and sexualized violence in this way shows why liberal feminist and other additive attempts to "break the silence" with accounts and exposures of new peoples experiencing these familiar forms of sexualized violation not only fail to acknowledge the full implications of prior and ongoing work of decolonial and other activists (feminist-identified or not) on the issue. They actively submerge the knowledge created by that work. Indigenous organizers in Guatemala, Honduras, and Mexico, for example, have emphasized the inseparability of domestic violence with militarisms, policing, the war on drugs, and resource exploitation.[95] They emphasize how the notion of the social contract naturalizes gendered, racialized, and colonial violence as a state function; here, the state doesn't fail to protect everyone, it succeeds in its foundational mission—its necro-biopolitical and geontological imperative—to protect not only some but the (onto-)epistemologies of some. Recourse to the social contract obscures how alternate formulations might register explicit challenges to consent, state sovereignty, and other liberal political foundations—even as they engage with international law and governance forums.[96] Contestations and appropriations by indigenous or nondominant feminisms or other social actors of terms like *gender*, *sex*, and *human rights* are conceptually papered over by teleologies of torture and sexualized violence that position international law as a perhaps technically complicated but mostly unified site of gendered redress—one that finds authority in its promise to protect against the violence of the wayward state but not against the settler state or the devastations of empire.

To mention these competing formulations of domestic violence is not to reveal the illusory nature of freedom or finally decide what state or sovereign power "really is" or should or should not be. This is not a politics of purity that requires a refusal of law as a tactic or tool or an understanding of rights as either salvation or dupe. This is a story of incoherence, of how politics, injury, and political subjects form and rise and shift. It is one way to think through those shifts in the hope of recognizing and creating solidarities and keeping them in view. This is an account of how the political subject of "woman" or "sexualized violence survivor" is created partly through legal ideas of harm that arise from settler colonial and racial contexts and the corresponding assumptions about the states and regions in which they occur, which shape the sorts of harms they are thought to inflict. What emerges from this method of accounting for legal and activist connections across geographies, bodies of law, and legal systems is a more complicated notion of silence—one where narratives of sexualized violence, its recognition, and its meanings are formed in transnational legal architectures and state-building initiatives that draw on grassroots mobilizations and institutions (including indigenous, feminist, or other formations that can offer other ways of thinking). Feminist theorizations of sexualized violence's legal harm—which rely on racialized sexual state forms to achieve a commensurability of injury across borders, place, and time—won't have it otherwise. The task, then, is to think about how to emphasize activist organizing and knowledge that is essential to the conceptualization of sexualized violence but that falls out of typical legal narratives and theories of sexualized violence. The task is to fracture the ways of thinking that lead to warfare in the name of "women's" rights, binary cis-heterogendered harms, and colonial agnosia by reframing what sexualized violence and "violence against women" can mean.

THREE

My Own Private Genocide /
From Ethnic War
to the War on Terror

IN SEPTEMBER 2006, US president George W. Bush signed the Military Commissions Act (MCA) into law.[1] The MCA established procedures by which to try "alien unlawful enemy combatants" in special military courts called military commissions—not regular US courts—for violations of the laws of war.[2] For many, the MCA departed from domestic and international law in several disturbing ways. Notably, it gave the president the executive authority to detain foreign persons and even US citizens suspected to be members of Al Qaeda or the Taliban by designating them "unlawful enemy combatants"—a term that prior to its passing did not precisely exist in domestic or international law.[3] The term describes a liminal category that the Bush administration set beyond the scope of the Geneva Conventions, which established how combatants and civilians should be treated during armed conflict; it was a designation that the US president and secretary of defense had almost unlimited discretion to apply. As many human rights advocates argued at the time, classifying detainees outside the recognized language of the Geneva Conventions effectively stripped them of constitutional and international humanitarian legal protections, casting them outside of those legal recognitions.[4]

To the consternation of legal feminists, the MCA's repurposing and reinterpretation of established international law also extended to its codified definitions of torture, rape, and sexual violence. Feminist ire was particularly acute given feminist efforts in the 1990s to pull sexualized violence into the orbit of international law by establishing women's rights as human rights and by naming rape and other forms of sexualized violence as actionable war crimes, crimes against humanity, and even genocide. The MCA actively countered that work. While transnational networks of feminist activists, legal scholars, and practitioners had persuaded courts and lawmakers to understand, for example, coerced oral sex as rape, the MCA constricted the definition of rape to include only forced or coerced genital or anal penetration.[5] Although feminist efforts garnered legal recognition of forced nakedness and other forms of sexualized mental abuse as sexual abuse,[6] the MCA's definition of sexual violence required physical contact.[7] Perhaps most disturbingly, the definition of torture put forth by the MCA required specific intent.[8]

Legal feminist Rhonda Copelon was quite vocal about this provision of the MCA. An intent requirement that puts definitional power in the hands (or more accurately, the mind) of the perpetrator—if they had other reasons to do it, then it potentially isn't *that*—would render charges of rape and other forms of sexualized violence almost "impossible to prosecute . . . as torture."[9] Copelon and other experts voiced fears that the bill, retroactively applied, would "absolve American soldiers and their commanders from prosecution for deeds that have occurred since Sept. 11," including the sexualized torture of prisoners at Guantánamo Bay and Abu Ghraib.[10] While perhaps seemingly slight, these shifts in law nonetheless altered the social vernacular of sexualized violence. Requiring specific intent can suspend the question entirely of what counts as actionable force or coercion by eliminating the importance of consent: a particularly dangerous move in contexts of military incarceration. Requiring physical contact for charges of sexual abuse further limits the meaning of violation. Collectively, these redefinitions of law delimit the scope of what rape and other forms of sexualized violence can be. In these ways, the MCA registered among legal feminists as an authoritative challenge that not only contested the legal meaning of rape and sexualized violence in the specific instance but also implicitly raised the broader issue of who may claim to define that violation.

Collectively, these actions threatened, as the editorial board of the *New York Times* wrote, to "turn back the clock alarmingly" on rape and sexual assault and to thwart the "huge progress" that "women's advocates and human rights activists" had made "in the United States and globally."[11]

This situation provokes the central query of this chapter: How, in the wake of 9/11, has the US government been able to understand its treatment of Muslim detainees at Guantánamo Bay and the passage of the MCA to be something other than what it has routinely, publicly, and since the 1990s, aggressively helped prosecute—namely, ethnoreligiously motivated sexualized violence and torture? Why has the US government instead sought to indemnify those in its employ who commit these sorts of acts? What arrangements and concepts of law, states, liability, gender, sex, race, and violence are in play?

From a legal vantage, the claim that the MCA is an affront to feminist anti–sexualized violence work is strictly and perhaps even unassailably true. Changes in law that enervate established definitions of rape and sexual violence undoubtedly turn the clock back on the largely but not exclusively feminist efforts to foreground sexual violence as a criminal, human rights, and at times humanitarian issue that individual sovereign states and the international order have an affirmative, enforceable duty to address. But there is another way to view the sexualized exclusion of Muslim detainees from the protections of international law. This way requires moving beyond single-issue legal precedent within a national body of law. It instead places US legal treatments of erstwhile sexualized violence within transnational feminist and other anti–sexualized violence organizing and then considers the whole of it within the narrative arc of international humanitarian law's understanding of war and the treatment of its prisoners. In this view, legal debates over the parameters of rape and sexualized violence are sites that authorize and enable relationships among states, individuals, and collectives across local, national, international, and transnational sites. These shifting relationships implicate far more than formal institutional positions or cultural consensus on the meaning of rape and sexual violence. They index the acquisition, loss, or alteration of the relationships between people and states that designate freedom. In other words, if leftist feminist and anti-imperial activists in the Middle East understood the critique of sexualized violence at Abu Ghraib and beyond as part of an embedded critique of US imperialism, it is immensely significant that these critiques do not immediately surface in—and in fact are not required in or demanded by—broad legal or social debates about the meaning and significance of sexualized violence.

To this end, a critical historicization of the MCA is necessary to understand how habeas corpus and other legal rights—including protections from sexualized violence—were denied to detainees in the war on terror and used to justify militarized interventions that further wealth extraction (oil) and creation (military expenditures and arms trading) in the Middle East. This chapter searches for those places where law meets what it would seem to deny. I follow the *law beyond Law* method, outlined in the introduction, which considers legal decisions that concern social difference or identity in conjunction with the broader doctrinal, theoretical, and procedural production of law. The method emphasizes the historical, geopolitical, and activist genealogies that shape law's inception, meaning, and impact to disorder law's temporal logics of progress and modernity. This approach breaks from legal feminist efforts to frame the MCA's rollbacks on sexualized violence protections as primarily gendered ones. Such efforts understand sexualized violence as sex discrimination or "women's" human rights in ways that can split gender from the workings of empire, race, citizenship, or national belonging. I break with this approach because concepts of rape and sexualized violence are forged in larger legal systems, histories, and contexts that implicate legal processes, systems, and issues that may seem far removed from sexualized violence.

Building on queer critiques of the war on terror, this chapter looks at how feminists' groundbreaking efforts to prosecute 1990s mass sexualized violence as war crimes, crimes against humanity, torture, and genocide have unexpectedly contributed to the legal reasoning used to deny Muslim detainees the protections typically afforded by domestic and international law. Here, I place a controversial component of the legal infrastructure of the war on terror, the MCA, within two historical narratives that are not often brought together. I not only consider the MCA within the lineage of US legal responses to the attacks on September 11, 2001, but also within activist and elite legal feminist efforts to juridicalize rape and other forms of sexualized violence by moving the "private" problems of rape and sexual violence into the public arena of international human rights, humanitarian, and criminal law. These efforts culminated, as previous chapters detail, at the end of the Cold War and through the 1990s' so-called ethnic wars in the former Yugoslavia and Rwanda. On the shifting terrain of the "new wars," I examine how various legal precedents across bodies of law—from definitions of rape in international criminal law to the protections of the Geneva Conventions regarding appropriate wartime conduct to efforts to require the United States to enforce human rights through civil litigation in domestic courts—enable and are to some extent nullified by the US state's juridical construction of the "unlawful enemy combatant."

Attention to the new wars, I suggest, shows how transnational theorizations of gendered and sexualized violence contribute to legal and governance paradigms of criminalization and armed humanitarian intervention. Contestations over the meanings of race, warfare, rape, and sexualized violence thread through both feminist theorizations of the private as public and war theory's demarcations between civilian and combatant. Attention to these double movements shows how individual legal liability in international law—or the ability for individuals to be held accountable for violations of laws traditionally thought to govern behavior between states—develops synchronically as the meanings of war and mass atrocity also transform. This framing shows, too, how differential orders of law are mobilized to support and address these understandings of violence and the relations that produce them. Ultimately, these maneuvers encourage and further the rise of terrorism (defined in part as unlawful acts intended to intimidate civilian populations for political purposes) as a way to explain the horrors of the world.[12] In this way, I contextualize the US government's recourse to the phrase "unlawful enemy combatants" as part of a sea change in how Global North nation-states conceptualized warfare and security in the wake of the ethnic wars.

As the preceding chapters detail, international law has stretched and transformed over several decades to accommodate changes to the perceived nature of conflict in the post-Soviet era, namely, the rise of parastatal ethnoreligious warfare as a primary mode of conflict and justification for US engagement in the ongoing war on terror. Central to these formulations is who deserves the protections of international law and when it may be summoned on their account. Are women's rights human rights? Are unlawful enemy combatants beyond the reach of the Geneva Conventions? Just as crucially, who is exempt from or subject to international legal protection is shadowed by the question of who may be held responsible for violations of that law. This is a question adumbrated by empire and the geopolitics of knowledge-making that refigure the relationships of states to their publics and other states through gender and racialized framings of sexualized violence as atrocity crimes: war crimes, genocide, and crimes against humanity.

As this chapter details, these notions of racial and sexualized violence circulated and were first tested in US civil and human rights frameworks, but they found ultimate articulation within international criminal law. The 1998 Rome Statute, building on the work of the ad hoc tribunals in the former Yugoslavia and Rwanda, consolidated the previously somewhat inchoate field of contemporary international criminal law, establishing the International Criminal Court (ICC) with jurisdiction over atrocity crimes. As the chapter further explains, the establishment of the ICC and its elaboration of the meanings of atrocity crimes drew upon and formally inscribed binary accounts of gender within international criminal law. The authority of the ICC, as elaborated by the Rome Statute, also formally excluded corporations from the category of juridical individuals liable for atrocity crimes.

The deployment of binary gender and the exclusion of corporations from juridical personhood for the purposes of the ICC were world-ordering maneuvers that cannot be separated from each other or from the broader contexts of war and liability that frame the ascent of capitalism, neoliberal democracy, and (sexual) contract as key rubrics of freedom in the wake of the Cold War and the ethnic wars. Like the broader tangle of jurisprudence from which they emerged, these maneuvers are complex and noncausal but nonetheless constitutive. They have produced the conditions for exempting the United States from respecting the sovereignty of the regions it invades (humanitarian law). They have also furthered a conception of threat and its redress that constructs a particular version of "the individual" unbound from the state as its focus. Through this complex of questions and developments, I understand the MCA's weakening of rape law less as an attack on women's rights than as a window into the refashioning of Islam as racial difference by reordering the relationships between states and individuals. These processes necessarily implicate sexual legal protections because sexuality is integral to the creation and maintenance of racial difference that partitions states, peoples, and regions into zones of freedom and zones of terror.

Queer Times / International Liability and the Remaking of War

Queer feminist critiques from scholars like Chandan Reddy, Judith Butler, and Jasbir Puar have theorized the imperial dimensions and sexualized portrayal of the Middle East and the war on terror. This scholarship vividly and forcefully insists on the centrality of sexuality to nation-building projects and the production of the kind of family and culture that births and rears those worthy of citizenship or other forms of recognition and protection. Much of this work circles notions of "cultural difference" that portray the secular as modern and liberating, while religious orders and associations are deemed backward and dangerously out of time—temporally dislocated from progress. In such accounts, torture becomes a means of policing and establishing "the 'outside'" of "the cultural conditions" necessary "for the emergence of the human."[13] This occurs in such a way, as Judith Butler writes, that "the destruction of populations, their infrastructures, their housing, and their religious and community institutions, constitutes the destruction of what threatens the human, but is not of the human itself."[14] In these discussions of torture, sexualized violence is mostly bounded by incident, place, or peoples—sexualized torture in Abu Ghraib or Guantánamo, for example—and summoned as examples of US empire.[15] In other words, rape and sexualized violence, although understood as conduits of power and not simply as discrete acts, are nonetheless analyzed as dimensions of torture. Torture is the focus, itself a colonizing technology of empire that weaponizes ideas of cultural and national sexual difference to justify the abuse of Muslims caught up in the war on terror.[16]

I build on queer thinking about the war on terror by engaging the US legal infrastructure of that war and its enmeshment with feminist influence in human rights law and other areas of international law. I build on that queer work by considering how the meanings and recognitions of what "counts" as sexualized violence are fundamentally organized and continually reorganized through international law and the geopolitical, historical, and economic contexts that calibrate the conceptual uptake, refusal, or redeployment of its precepts. Organizations of gender, race, and culture that demarcate recognitions and refusal of humanity emerge in part from and through international legal treatments of sexualized violence and the legal scaffolding that supports them. These include international criminal law's establishment of individual legal liability for humanitarian crimes, the preclusion of corporations from prosecution as juridical individuals per the Rome Statute, and the constriction of the meaning of sex/gender[17] to the male/female binary. Together, they shape the social and legal terms of recognition for rape and sexualized violence across various peoples and sites as they alter the relationships between individual liability (who may be liable for what legally recognized acts of sexualized violation) and state responsibility (when consent to be governed entails freedom from sexualized violence).

In this way, feminist innovations in the meaning and scope of sexualized violence are a piece of the new world order that took place at the end of the Cold War. At that time, frameworks of ethnic conflict and mass rape challenged traditional models of warfare that formed the basis of the international humanitarian law. If individual liability for some violations of international law seems a fairly cut-and-dried issue, in the 1990s this was a live legal question and was deeply embedded in the kind of armed conflict the international legal order was authorized to address. To start, some experts at that time understood international criminal law and the related field of international human rights to impose obligations on states, not individuals. International humanitarian and criminal law were largely thought to govern only international conflicts between states and not noninternational conflict.[18] That distinction, as international law expert William Schabas explains, has to do with the relationship between state sovereignty and the meaning of war. The distinction between international and noninternational conflict "exists because states have historically been more willing to accept obligations about the conduct of war and the treatment of victims, especially non-combatants, when the conflict is international in nature. International humanitarian law was originally concerned with reciprocal commitments between sovereign states."[19] By definition, there were no international crimes in noninternational armed conflict.[20] In other words, states didn't and don't want other states interfering with their private business of internal population management, including riot control and civil insurrection, but also their prison systems and policing, their foreign policy and continued settler colonization of land, and their public health (or lack thereof) initiatives—their sovereign authority to govern.

The view that international law applied primarily to state-to-state relations held well into the 1990s. At that time, war came to mean *intrastate ethnic wars*, potentially understood as noninternational conflict, as opposed to warfare that more closely resembled traditional state-on-state or "international" conflict waged by soldiers, other agents of the state, or highly organized "statelike" nonstate actors.[21] As armed and arguably loosely organized groups engaged in large-scale "ethnic" warfare, they antagonized the rationales that animated international humanitarian and human rights law—mainly the preservation of the freedom and lives of civilians, the treatment of captured soldiers, and the rules of conduct during warfare—that preserved the fiction of just wars or justified state violence.

In the first international war crimes trial since Nuremberg and Tokyo, *Prosecutor v. Tadić*, the Appeals Chamber of the ICTY settled the question of the applicability of humanitarian law to some forms of internal conflict: "As early as the Spanish Civil War (1936–39), State practice revealed a tendency to disregard the distinction between international and internal wars and to apply certain general principles of humanitarian law, at least to those internal conflicts that constituted large-scale civil wars."[22] This view was later codified in the 1998 Rome Statute. Yet at the time of the Spanish Civil War in the late 1930s, international humanitarian law did not elaborate on the relationship between international law and internal conflict. In addition, the subsequent development of humanitarian law, as Schabas notes, followed the model international human rights law, which largely reserved its address to states. He writes: "International humanitarian law has developed more or less in parallel with the related field of international human rights law, which, from its very beginning, has addressed individuals' rights vis-a-vis the states that have jurisdiction over them."[23] The founding of a permanent international criminal court and the work of the first ad hoc tribunals since Nuremberg were thus not simply moments of legal consolidation but moments of innovation and choices made that shaped and were shaped by the political and historical contexts of the time.

With states and their agents no longer perceived as the sole or necessarily dominant authors of armed conflict, international legal structures of accountability transformed to accommodate shifting relationships of states, civilians, and nonstate actors to armed violence. If statelessness had largely been the domain of refugees or other migrants, it became an especially threatening space of lawlessness and war that blurred distinctions between the state, armed actors, and civilians in need of protection. Through this spatial reconfiguring, individuals could now be held responsible for violations of human rights or international crime, which had once been intended to govern the behavior of states and state actors.[24] Sexualized violence was integral to these changing notions of the relationships among states, individuals, and armed conflict: *Tadić* did not simply assert the authority of the tribunal to address the conflict at hand. It was also the first international war crimes trial involving charges of sexual violence, and it was the first involving sexualized violence against men.[25] In other words, sexualized violation entered this legal terrain as international humanitarian law staked its authoritative claim in the aftermath of the Cold War. These changing relationships among states, individuals, and armed conflict were in turn integral to changing notions of sexualized violence.

In chapter 1, I discuss how the mass war-raped at this time became a racialized population—a mobile target of international law and governance for states, regions, and peoples vulnerable enough to be caught up in the mandates and procedures of redress enabled by international law. Here, I suggest that the twinned subject of the mass raped (numerous and not always nationally bound) is the rogue, stateless fighter (individualized in an improper relationship to the state and the international order of them). In this way, distinctions between international and noninternational conflict crumble as new understandings of victims and aggressors emerge: the innocents who deserve international assistance and oversight due them by their failed (racialized

and sexualized) states and the one who refuses or is in a prohibited alignment with that state, who has claimed war as his own. The border between
them is newly generative. As the scope of crimes against humanity and war
crimes are broadened to include acts (including sexualized ones) committed
in noninternational conflict,[26] the meaning of gender constricts and corporations are shunted from the juridical category of the individual who may be
liable for international crimes.

Two Sexes, No Corporations / The Rome Statute Story

Unlike the final version of the Rome Statute (1998), which refers to *gender*
nine times, the 1994 draft Statute for an International Criminal Court initially did not contain the word *gender*.[27] Legal feminist Valerie Oosterveld,
describing the controversies that attended the inclusion of the word in the
Rome Statute, frames the struggle to insert *gender* into the document as a
long-standing one that pits conservative and "religious" states and groups
against legal feminist progress. As she writes, "The Holy See, certain Arab
states, and conservative organizations had earlier made their strong views
on the term 'gender' known in other international fora, for example in the
negotiations on the 1995 Beijing Declaration and Platform for Action."[28]
Strong lobbying ultimately carried the day, particularly from groups like the
Women's Caucus for Gender Justice, "which grew out of an organizing effort of a small group of women human rights activists from the Cameroon,
Congo-Brazzaville, Costa Rica, Georgia, Germany, India, Japan, the Phil-
ippines, South Africa, Sri Lanka, and the United States who attended the
February 1997 Preparatory Committee (Prepcom) for the Establishment of
an International Criminal Court at the United Nations."[29] In its advocacy
"for the codification of sexual, reproductive and gender violence crimes of, as
well as for the inclusion of gender sensitive processes and criteria for personnel, the Caucus tried to ensure that the Court would have the capacity to
implement justice for women."[30] Many feminist legal insiders and organizers
would recognize this account. It understands gender's debut in the establishment of the ICC as a progressive, monumental step forward, even if it is ultimately a qualified one: the definition of *gender* advanced by the Rome Statute
has proven controversial. Not only does the Rome Statute hone the meaning of
gender to "two sexes, male and female, within the context of society," it also attempts to foreclose other interpretations of its meaning—"the term 'gender'
does not indicate any meaning different from the above."[31] That final clause,
as Oosterveld notes, "could be interpreted to exclude sexual orientation from

falling within the definition of 'gender,'" and in this way "eliminate persecution conducted on the basis of sexual orientation as a crime against humanity, permitting discrimination on the basis of sexual orientation in the ICC's interpretation and application of law, and excluding the ICC from considering sexual orientation when addressing the needs of victims and witnesses."[32] The formalized constriction of *gender*, its reduction to a seemingly fixed idea of sex, the interpretative ambiguity surrounding not only sexual orientation but also gender identity occur in this moment of triumphant advocacy.

As queer theorist Judith Butler writes, if "hegemonic conceptions of progress define themselves over and against a pre-modern temporality that they produce for the purposes of their own self-legitimation,"[33] then the feminist entrance into international criminal law certainly defined itself against the wayward, backward position of states that follow some iteration of Islamic law and conservative groups. But it also locates progress in a situation in which gender persecution thought to be based on sexual orientation and nonbinary gender identity are potentially excluded, as Oosterveld observes, from crimes against humanity, from the definitional heart of atrocity. That is, gender/sex "progresses" along well-worn binary hetero grooves.[34] Those grooves set the initial conditions for what types of gendered and sexualized violation will be protected through this new articulation of the relationship of the state to sex (this new articulation of the sexual contract) or prosecuted under international criminal law (see chapter 2). The binary shapes the injury, which in turn helps define the perpetrator and the offense. As I discuss in the final section of this chapter, good sex and gender arrangements are protected, and bad ones, stateless and lawless, are the province of the rogue: the individual in violation of the laws of nations who needs less correction than utter elimination. Meanwhile, the corporation becomes the individual who is not one—exempt from prosecution by the ICC. The corporation may be mono- or multinational, but its allegiance to the state and the international order lifts it beyond responsibility for atrocity per the logics of the Rome Statute.

But before the permutations and consolidations of international criminal law inaugurated by the Rome Statute, questions of individual liability were prefigured in a US civil lawsuit that was the first case to adjudicate rape as genocide: the 1995 US Second Circuit Court of Appeals civil tort law case *Kadic v. Karadzic*. The pertinent legal questions—whether the Serbian rapes of Bosnian and Croatian Muslim women would be deemed genocidal, and whether individuals acting in the absence of recognized state authority during internal or noninternational conflict might be liable for violations of the laws of nations—might be considered separate legal issues in traditional legal analysis and have not been addressed as queer or trans ones. The method I have developed posits the recognition of genocide and the extension of liability as conceptually interdependent. The method's attention to how legal issues and concepts are embedded in multiple chains of law makes a queer geography of race, bringing torture in the Americas close to rape in the Balkans. As I will shortly discuss, attempts to use US courts to address torture in Latin America curiously made the civil human rights violations of non-US citizens on non-US soil actionable in a US court of law, setting the conditions by which the charges in *Kadic* could be heard. Situating the *Kadic* decision within its contemporary cultural and legal history across bodies of law shows how legal feminist efforts to explode the public/private divide and debates about who or what might be held accountable for atrocities in and out of war functioned synergistically. Together, they changed the course of discrete branches of law and the world in which those laws operate by establishing the centrality of gendered sexualized violation to international law and governance. I turn to an analysis of the MCA and its understanding of warfare only after offering *Kadic*, US civil case law, as context. What this close reading of rather dry law demonstrates is just how deeply the mechanisms and logics of law affect what rape and other forms of sexualized violence can mean in the new world order. It also shows how deeply radical or dominance feminist ideologies that set gender oppression as a binary operation, the sexual dominance of women by men, are understood to set the terms for what progress and resistance might mean—and where racial, ethnoreligious, and other forms difference can and cannot enter fights for gendered freedom.

Alien Torts Statute / US Civil Law and Its International Effects

Before the dissolution of Yugoslavia, rape and other forms of sexualized violence during armed conflict were rarely presented as integral to a coordinated military campaign and never resulted in anything approximating the levels of attention the subject currently receives. The collapse of Yugoslavia and the fighting in it, distilled to ethnoreligious motivations by most of the outside world, also became a flashpoint for mass sexual atrocity during war due to the upsurge of global feminist organizing in the years following World War II. As preceding chapters attest, feminist theorizations of state accountability for violence against women (later "gender violence") helped instill a logic of violence—as mass and identity-motivated—in international legal jurisprudence and policy discussions that presaged and enabled the rise of identity-based conflict as the paradigmatic new face of warfare at the end of the twentieth century. These motifs are visible in the US Second Circuit Court of Appeals opinion for *Kadic v. Karadzic*. They occur, too, in a broader universe of legal relations that position the fight against torture as an issue that enables the US state to absolve itself of its complicity with tortuous regimes in the Americas by becoming a global enforcer of human rights. The meanings of sexualized violence are entangled, then, in multiple histories of settler colonialism and empire.

The legal mechanics of *Kadic* are not particularly straightforward but are important to detail so that relationships between definitions of rape and other sexualized violence, law, and statecraft can emerge. Plaintiffs in *Kadic v. Karadzic*, represented by legal teams that included Rhonda Copelon and Catharine MacKinnon, alleged that Radovan Karadžić in his capacity as part of a three-man presidency of Srpska, the self-proclaimed Bosnia-Serb republic in Bosnia and Herzegovina, had injured them through planned and systematic human rights abuses carried out by the military forces under his command. The plaintiffs sought relief under the Alien Torts Statute (ATS), which human rights attorneys have used since the late 1970s to allow foreign citizens to bring civil actions in US courts for human rights violations committed on foreign soil. The ATS states, "The district courts shall have original jurisdiction of any civil action by an alien for a tort only, committed in violation of the law of nations or a treaty of the United States."[35] The law of nations includes international custom, general principles of law recognized by nations, and the "judicial decisions and teachings of the most highly qualified publicists of the various nations."[36] Customary international law designates the accepted practices or norms by which most states abide.[37]

Copelon and her colleagues at the Center for Constitutional Rights (CCR)—many of whom were also instrumental in the feminist push to influence the development of the ad hoc tribunals—were well versed in the ATS case law, having innovated its use to champion human rights abuses (including torture claims) on behalf of resident aliens for international rights and customary law violations committed off US soil. Prior to those interventions, the ATS had been left mostly dormant for nearly two hundred years. For such a long-neglected sliver of law, the ATS has august origins. It was promulgated on September 24, 1789, when the Senate and the House of Representatives assembled to debate and ultimately pass the Judiciary Act of 1789. The act established the organizational structure of the federal court system as a three-tiered federal court system, consisting of the US Supreme Court, the circuit courts, and district courts. Congress then set the bounds of each court's jurisdictional reach, determining the content and geographic scope of the cases that would be germane to each. Although the legislative record leaves little indication of the original purpose or intent of the ATS, scholars believe the statute was initially conceived as a bulwark against interference with the safe conduct, rights, and travels of ambassadors, and against acts of piracy.[38] The ATS signaled early US interest in maintaining and abiding by the basic international diplomatic protocols necessary to secure favorable trade relations and uphold customary international law. Roughly two hundred years later, however, the ATS emerged as a centerpiece of legal activists' strategies to enforce international human rights through US federal courts—in effect, giving international human rights law "teeth."[39]

In the original ATS human rights case *Filártiga v. Peña-Irala*,[40] attorneys at the CCR sought civil redress in New York federal court on behalf of the Filártigas, a Paraguayan family. The Filártigas accused Americo Norberto Peña-Irala, former inspector general of police in Asunción, Paraguay, of wrongfully causing the death of Joelito Filártiga by torture. On March 30, 1976, twenty-three-year-old Dolly Filártiga answered a knock on the door of the family home in Asunción. Two uniformed officers then escorted her to the home of Peña-Irala and her brother's battered corpse. Dr. Joel Filártiga—a vocal critic of Paraguayan dictator Alfredo Stroessner—believed that his seventeen-year-old son, Joelito Filártiga, had been tortured and murdered in retaliation by the repressive government. All efforts to seek redress for Joelito's death in Paraguayan legal venues failed, stalled, or were openly crushed by agents of the Stroessner regime.[41]

In the late 1970s, Dolly Filártiga, residing in Washington, DC, learned that Peña-Irala was living in Brooklyn. Dr. Filártiga contacted the US Immigration and Naturalization Service, which detained Peña-Irala and began deportation procedures against him for overstaying his visa. The Filártigas immediately assessed the feasibility of pursuing legal action in US courts against Joelito's murderer. Uncertain of whether such a case could be sustained in the United States, Filártiga's contacts at Amnesty International directed her to the CCR—an organization with robust commitments to international human rights and well known for its innovative legal strategies. There, attorneys, including Peter Weiss, John Corwin, Jose Antonio Lugo, and Rhonda Copelon, suggested a novel, untested approach: apply the ATS to assert US federal court jurisdiction over violations of the law of nations.[42]

Through the ATS, the CCR contended that US federal courts have jurisdiction beyond the sovereign borders of the United States over violations of customary international law—even when both victims and perpetrators are non-US citizens. By interpreting the ATS to incorporate customary international law within the founding statute of the US federal legal system, the CCR suggested that US federal courts were not merely permitted but perhaps even mandated to enforce it.[43] The CCR legal team marshaled an impressive number of international legal instruments, documents, declarations, and treaties in support of their contention that state-sponsored torture and murder are anathema (at least rhetorically) to most nations under customary international law. Peña's actions in his capacity as inspector general of the police in Asunción, they argued, violated the UN Charter, the Universal Declaration on Human Rights, and the American Declaration of the Rights and Duties of Man, among other foundational agreements.

The district court dismissed the original complaint, but on June 30, 1980, the US Second Circuit Court of Appeals reversed the lower court's decision, largely adopting the CCR's expansive construal of US federal court jurisdiction under the ATS. The second circuit court held "that deliberate torture perpetrated under color of official authority violates universally accepted norms of the international law of human rights, regardless of the nationality of the parties. Thus, whenever an alleged torturer is found and served with process by an alien within our borders, [the ATS] provides federal jurisdiction."[44] The *Filártiga* decision set and continues to define the basic scope of contemporary ATS litigation. A key innovation of the decision is its "dynamic" vision of international law, where that law is not simply "a set of rules etched in stone" but a collective pursuit of "'the general assent of civilized nations.'"[45] Although aspects of the applicability of the ATS to human rights abuses remain at issue,[46] the CCR's original contention that federal courts have jurisdiction over some civil wrongs committed beyond US territory if they violate the laws of nations has nonetheless spawned over four decades' worth of litigation.[47] This is "freedom" built through empire. But neither *Filártiga* nor subsequent ATS human rights litigation anticipated a central question—and enduring legacy—of *Kadic*: should individuals, operating outside the sanction of recognized state authority, be liable for violations of customary or other forms of international law? The notion of genocidal rape would help settle this question.

Kadic, Individuals, and the Laws of Nations

"Most Americans would probably be surprised to learn that victims of atrocities committed in Bosnia are suing the leader of the insurgent Bosnian-Serb forces in a US District Court in Manhattan."[48] These inaugural lines of the second circuit appellate court case *Kadic v. Karadzic* were not just a nod to popular conceptions of the purpose of US federal courts. They also signaled a legal controversy at the very heart of the case. At issue in part was whether US federal courts had subject matter jurisdiction or the requisite authority to address the specific kind of legal claim at hand. Writing for the majority, Judge Jon O. Newman's opinion in *Kadic* reversed the lower court decision. The second circuit ruled that Radovan Karadžić—whom the last US ambassador to Yugoslavia dubbed the "Heinrich Himmler of the Balkans"[49]—could be found liable for genocide, crimes against humanity, and war crimes in his private or official capacity because these crimes are universally proscribed regardless of whether or not they are committed by a state or nonstate actor.[50]

Karadžić claimed that the plaintiff-appellants "have not alleged violations of the norms of international law because such norms bind only states and persons acting under color of a state's law, not private individuals," even as he simultaneously styled himself as president of the Republic of Srpska, a Bosnia-Serb military faction with territorial ambitions situated in Bosnia and Herzegovina proper.[51] Looking primarily to prior ATS case law and jurisprudence, district judge Peter K. Leisure dismissed the plaintiffs' cases for lack of subject matter jurisdiction. Leisure grounded his decision in a prior second circuit case that defined states as "entities that have a defined [territory] and a permanent population, that are under the control of their own government, and that engage in, or have the capacity to engage in, formal relations with other such entities."[52] Leisure concluded, "The current Bosnia-Serb entity fails to meet this definition."[53] The second circuit did not mince words in its rejoinder: "We do not agree that the law of nations, as understood in the modern era, confines its reach to state action. Instead, we hold that certain forms of conduct violate the law of nations whether undertaken by those acting under the auspices of a state or only as private individuals."[54] Leisure appeared, the second circuit further noted, "to have deemed state action required primarily on the basis of cases determining the need for state action as to claims of official torture . . . without consideration of the substantial body of law . . . that renders private individuals liable for some international law violations."[55]

In *Kadic*, the inner workings of law, the popular view that ethnic antagonisms drove Yugoslavia's collapse, and legal feminist organizing converged to reframe the relationships among individuals, mass violence, and the state. The appellate court rendered its decision after it accepted the trial court's factual record, in which rape, forced prostitution, forced pregnancy, and other abuses were taken to be part of "a genocidal campaign conducted [by Bosnian-Serb military forces] in the course of the Bosnian civil war."[56] Legal issues played out against a backdrop of factual claims that, because of the structural difference between a trial and appellate court, the appellate court presumed "true for the purposes of the appeal."[57]

The appellate court began with the understanding that the plaintiff-appellants, "Croat and Muslim citizens of the internationally recognized nation of Bosnia-Herzegovina," were the victims (or representatives of victims) of "brutal acts of rape, forced prostitution, forced impregnation, torture, and summary execution, carried out by Bosnian-Serb military forces as part of a genocidal campaign conducted in the course of the Bosnian civil war."[58] In this way, the appellate court followed a mandate of legal practice and reasoning that parsed the question of whether state action is always required from an assessment of the type of violations that might not require state action. This logical fissuring was productive. In *Kadic*, rape and sexualized violence were viewed from the start as part of a genocidal campaign—a designation that helped set the stage for the analysis of the applicability of the ATS and the terms of its expanded reach beyond the actions of the state, its representatives, or the "state-like."

Once it was established that private individuals may be liable for some violations of international law, then the import of the present allegations could assume center stage, and it became more difficult to maintain that well-settled, serious abrogation of international customary law—such as allegations of war crimes, genocide, and crimes against humanity—exceeded the scope of ATS intended jurisdiction. Structuring the argument in such a way naturalized the second circuit's unequivocal, path-breaking legal pronouncement that "appellants' allegations that Karadzic personally planned and ordered a campaign of murder, rape, forced impregnation, and other forms of torture designed to destroy the religious and ethnic groups of Bosnian Muslims and Bosnian Croats clearly state a violation of the international law norm proscribing genocide, regardless of whether Karadzic acted under color of law or as a private individual."[59]

The ruling marked a shift the course of US legal history: it was the first instance where a federal court explicitly established valid federal jurisdiction for suits alleging torts committed anywhere in the world by states, state actors, or nonstate actors against non-US citizens in violation of the laws of nations.[60] In the words of Jennifer Green, who represented plaintiffs in *Doe v. Karadzic*, "The [1995 US circuit court] decision continues to be a milestone decision cited by US courts."[61] But it was also a case, as Catharine MacKinnon attests, that "changed the face of the international legal order."[62] The case "helped to spur an international movement against gender-based violence, especially in conflict situations," and influenced the development of international law.[63] According to Green, *Kadic* "was discussed in international advocacy efforts relating to the then fledgling ICTY—which only came into existence in 1993— and 'contributed to the campaign to recognise rape as a human rights violation and as a form of torture and genocide.'"[64]

The *Kadic* court reached this conclusion given the material facts of the case (extensive allegations of mass rape and murder) in the context of how it understood the conflict in the former Yugoslavia as ethnoreligious warfare (warfare premised on identity group aggressions) that by definition predisposed these conflicts to charges of genocide. By framing these discrete legal questions, read within a matrix of feminist theorizations of sexual violence summoned to bolster a post-Soviet world defined by identity group aggressions, transformations in the court's understanding of the nature of the modern state itself were written into legal discourse and beyond.

Feminist Splits / *law beyond Law* and Procedural Meaning Making

Allegations of genocidal rape and forced impregnation allowed the second circuit to rule that private individuals were able to author international human rights violations. The decision speaks to the work of feminists by publicizing events in the disintegrating Yugoslavia and the court's understanding of the nature of that warfare—even if, as chapter 1 elaborates, naming rape as genocidal flattened and obscured the contested legacy of sexualized violence and difference in US feminisms and those in the former Yugoslavia. Furthermore, the procedural workings of the case as it wound its way through the federal court system collapsed theoretical and strategic differences between legal and other feminists. In this way, the technical operations of law helped produce and consolidate a body of feminist legal jurisprudence (Law) and "a" feminist legal perspective.

Kadic initially began as two separate civil actions that were consolidated on appeal. *Kadic* became the caption under which they were given their day in appellate court. The first civil action, *Doe v. Karadzic*, was the product of feminist and human rights attorneys and activists working with the CCR. On behalf of two unnamed young girls, *Doe* sought to represent a class comprised of "women and men who suffered rape, summary execution, other torture or other cruel, inhuman or degrading treatment inflicted by Bosnian-Serb military forces . . . between April 1992 and the present."[65] The CCR, the International League for Human Rights, and the International Women's Human Rights Clinic of the CUNY Law School (led by Rhonda Copelon and Celina

Romany) submitted the complaint on behalf of the plaintiffs. The attorneys in the other civil action, *Kadic*, took a different approach. Catharine MacKinnon expressly sought an emphatic understanding of rape as genocide, rape as torture, and rape as war crime when she filed *Kadic v. Karadzic* on behalf of her clients, who were named as individuals and not as a class.[66] Because the two cases were collectively dismissed at the district level for the same reason (lack of subject matter jurisdiction), *Kadic* and *Doe* were collectively heard on appeal as *Kadic v. Karadzic*.[67]

MacKinnon opposed the *Doe* limited fund class claim for several reasons. She argued that a class claim could preclude future relief for uncontacted members of the class and potentially limit the ability for class members to sue subordinate tortfeasors (perpetrators).[68] Inadequacy of representation, or the fact that class members could have little or no real contact with their legal representatives, became a controversial issue. Yet the very real question of whether class action suits could be successful human rights strategies also became racialized for MacKinnon. Explaining her opposition to the limited class fund claim, MacKinnon stresses, "Some of the affiants in the *Kadic* motion supporting the decertification noted [that] the *Doe* class usurps many of the functions of an elected representative, which is undemocratic. It could even be termed colonizing."[69] She continues: "What is stolen from them when they are violated can be partially or potentially returned to them through a process that does not reduce them to the ciphers of group membership the way their perpetrators did. It treats them as more than the sum of the injuries done to them. It gives them back a voice in their fate, and the dignity of a place at the table."[70]

MacKinnon's recourse to the word *colonization* does more than merely nod to the rhetorical supremacy of representative democracy. It mobilizes imperial, racialized power inequities to assert MacKinnon's—and also dominance theory's—sensitivity to the lived and legal meanings of racial and other forms of historical social difference, while simultaneously casting colonization's "end" through just the application of law. The differences in approach between *Kadic* and *Doe* signal radical, unresolved splits in legal feminist theorizations of the relationships among gender, sexuality, race, war, and violence. Attention to those differences reveals how legal mechanisms and strategies can give credibility to certain ideas about how sexualized violence and colonialism, for example, are related through critiques of legal choices and court practices. In this case, the *Doe* attorneys' decision to file a class action lawsuit opened the door for MacKinnon to emphasize dominance feminism's sensitivity to racial and historical social difference, while retaining a disdain for "the ciphers of group membership."[71] In this vision, the individuating impulse of liberal subjectivity became the conduit for the recognition of difference, of voice—a necessary corrective to the charge of rape as genocide, with its emphasis on group vulnerability. The critique of class action thus furthered a remedy for genocide that is individuating—that retains the value of the individual and is suspicious of collectivity. Befitting capitalism's ascendency in that moment, liberal individualisms—autonomous subjectivities—were the correct turn. The reduction to group membership (collectivism: the echo) was the route to genocide.

The related and embedded issue of individual liability performs conceptual mirror-work. It allows the formal extension of genocide, crimes against humanity, torture, and war crimes into realms of sexualized violence by explicitly recognizing the individual as fungible for the state and the kind of crimes once attributed solely to it and its agents. If sexualized violence now authorizes the intervention of international governance and domestic state apparatuses, then the individual ability to be held accountable for violations of the law of nations functions as a counterbalance. As sexualized violence becomes a new frontier for governance, the terms of governance change.

In other words, during the 1990s, individual international legal liability and women's rights as human rights and individual international legal liability for violations of humanitarian law developed in tandem. Both emphasized the duty for states and the international order to police and punish individual actors for conduct that would have once lain outside their jurisdiction. The liberal feminist platform to curb violence against women urged an expansion of state and international jurisdiction into the private realm of sexuality and the family, actuated through the liberal vaunting of the individual as redress against violent forms of collectivism. This is not to say that legal feminists, liberal or radical or otherwise, necessarily believed or believe that sex or intimate matters have ever been truly private. It is instead a recognition that feminist efforts to break the legal fiction of private sex in the 1990s extends the reach of the state and the international order into new domains of governance. As chapter 2 details, these efforts necessarily implicate what I call the sexual state form, or the imagined character of the state whose actions become the subject of legal feminist thought and action through their theorization of legal harm. This chapter extends that observation. The sexual state form ties the imagined nature of the sexualized injury to the character and operations of the racialized state—or in this case its disintegration in the clutch of ethnoreligious terror. The sexual state form also shapes what will be appropriate legal and social responses or remedies as it acts against and within existing legal frameworks across local, national, and international registers and within old and ongoing operations of settler colonialism and empire. Correspondingly, international law embraces the private individual as a public actor (and in the context of terrorism especially) as a manifestation of an improper and dangerous collectivism subject to international legal oversight.

Again, these proliferations of state and international oversight occurred specifically in the midst of ethnoreligious conflicts that provoked a crisis in the meaning of warfare previously organized through the prism of the Cold War. The post-Soviet reorganization of legitimate and illegitimate global violence gave feminists an opportunity to fuse ethnic violence with mass sexual violence, raising sexual violence to global attention by figuring it as a central problem of the "new wars." The changing face of warfare, from state-on-state violence to nonstate aggressors, signaled and facilitated individual accountability for mass atrocities as violent conflicts were increasingly framed as ethnic wars. With states no longer perceived as the sole or primary authors of armed conflict, international legal structures of accountability also transformed.

The Times of Individual Criminal Liability

Through its mandate to adjudicate atrocity crimes, the Rome Statute remapped the global geopolitics of risk and security. The terms of the new security, however, were routed through the codification of the gender/sex binary as a limit on what might be considered crimes against humanity. This brave new world of crime also codified corporate exemption from individual criminal liability at the same moment that the individual criminal liability of natural persons underwent dynamic expansion. These conditions made possible feminist progress and innovations in the meaning of rape, and they were shaped by how the new international legal system was forged in relation to the domestic criminal regimes of its potential member states. New legal and social understandings of rape and other forms of sexualized violence in this way were predicated on a recommitment to state sovereignty even as a new system of international law emerged to delineate risk and deliver justice in the post–Cold War era.

The rise and permanent institutionalization of individual criminal liability accompanied equally noteworthy procedural ambitions in post-1990s international criminal law, including the formalized melding of the common law adversarial system with the civil inquisitorial system in what Allison Marston Danner and Jenny S. Martinez describe as "the clash of the common and civil law traditions."[72] These tensions are nested in the "enduring conflict" of a system that draws from the conflicting motivations of three distinct legal traditions: international human rights law, domestic criminal law, and transitional justice.[73] For Danner and Martinez, the aspirational justice of human rights doctrine and the principles of individual culpability that characterize domestic criminal legal regimes are particular sources of tension.[74]

Individual culpability, or the idea that punishment should only attach to conduct for which an individual is personally responsible, is the bedrock of most modern criminal legal doctrine and its domestic execution. Correspondingly, most domestic criminal systems hew to a rule of lenity, which shields defendants from unexpected expansions of the law and the criminalization of new acts or practices.[75] The formation of the ad hoc tribunals and the ICC risked running roughshod over the specific, absolute protections domestically afforded to criminal defendants in favor of the aspirational, contingent, and abstract norms promoted by the human rights legal tradition by establishing individual responsibility over collective assignations of guilt.[76] The fallout, the authors warn, could reverberate at the domestic and international levels. New regimes that avail transitional justice forums might find their credibility undermined where large swaths of the population (not solely individuals) supported, participated in, or actively condoned the prior government's atrocities; such charges dogged Nuremburg. Relatedly, expansive versions of joint criminal enterprise doctrines (a theory that considers individual members of a group responsible for group actions that flow from a common plan) might also lead to trouble. It might seem laudable when a defendant is held liable for an array of crimes associated with genocide or ethnic cleansing.[77] However, when the same doctrine is applied by a domestic national government to figure all persons who provide any sort of support to a terrorist organization, however loosely defined, as liable for all the crimes of its members, the tensions between human rights and domestic criminal traditions are set on full display.[78]

If the rule of lenity did not shield individual actors from international criminal liability, then the principle of complementarity—a principle that privileges adherence to past practice as a form of legitimacy and fairness—did protect corporations from being directly prosecuted by the ICC. The principle of complementarity is simply that the ICC "will complement, but not supersede, national jurisdiction . . . the International Criminal Court will act when national courts are 'unable or unwilling' to perform their tasks."[79] In other words, for "fairness" and legitimacy purposes, the ICC is beholden to (and its founding statute drafted to reflect) the extant criminal law of its member states. David Scheffer, the US ambassador-at-large for war crimes issues from 1997 to 2001, describes the tenor of the UN talks leading to the

Rome Statute in July 1998 as follows: "The court was originally designed to hold natural persons accountable for atrocity crimes.... Also, at that time, there were an insufficient number of national jurisdictions that held corporations liable under criminal law.... The principle of complementarity under the Rome Statute, a principle dependent on compatible criminal law in state party jurisdictions, would have been crippled as a consequence. Finally, the proposal would have imperiled the ratification of the treaty by many governments given the novelty of corporate exposure to criminal liability before the ICC."[80] These collusions of international criminal and domestic criminal legal regimes make visible the entanglements of state projects of discipline, normalization, governance, and control as they relate to capital and international legal frames. These relations are instrumental in establishing the relation between the governed and the governor that we call "freedom" or "oppression." They operate at multiple sites and across multiple times, as the "originary" and exportable freedoms of the good liberal state (e.g., principles of individual culpability) are reframed and redistributed through interactions with the international human rights and international criminal legal regimes they were marshaled to inspire. Elizabeth Freeman's "deviant chronopolitics"—or the notion of embodied, pleasurable "relations across and between times"—acquires other dimensions when lifted and applied to the circulation of legal doctrines between domestic criminal legal regimes and their international legal counterparts that enable the terms of recognition and prosecution of mass atrocities.[81] Principles or rules that underlie and enable legal censure or protections applied to achieve "gender justice" please the attorneys, scholars, and activists who strive to ensconce rape as an international crime; the legal protections they achieve are cast as historic triumphs of feminist advocacy stretching back years. Yet those principles undergird multiple strands and theories of law that endure beyond the life span of the justiciable issue. In this way the operations of law sustain uneven geopolitical terrain that can exacerbate the conditions that prompt recourse to international law in the first place. For example, when theories of responsibility, like joint criminal enterprise, are extended and entrenched within international criminal law, they give legitimate ground for future domestic restrictions and interpretations that further and will be furthered by the close and coming recognition of Muslims as global terror incarnate.

The ideas and effects of legal justice, then, exist in multiple historical present moments and project into multiple futures. What I offer here in this brief reading of international criminal law is a framework for evaluating the fuller dimensions of what counts as feminist progress. That progress depends on the melding of systems of civil and criminal traditions within international criminal law. Attention to the inner workings of law show how feminist legal advocacy helps supply the conditions of culpability (the scope of juridical personhood, appropriate arrangements of gender/sex) that stabilize the geopolitical ascent of the United States and capitalism. Corporate exclusion is the perfected logic of the conjoined ascent of individual human rights as freedom and the imagined decline and active rejection of collective forms of property and life. The accompanying codification of the gender/sex binary is a supporting move—one that circumscribes what kinds of lives are allowed to suffer gender persecution in international criminal law, delineating what arrangements of gender and sexuality will be proper to the state and the international order. The gender/sex binary and its attendant forms of sociality—which intimacies or private lives will be protected—as the next section elaborates, help stabilize, homogenize, and clear the political space necessary for the extension of rights as handmaiden to global capitalism backed by military might.

Foregrounding the nonlinearity of the exchanges between the subject of law and the mechanics of law forces renewed appraisals of law's conceptual and historically embedded relations to freedom. These relations are best approached not just through the rights they bestow or crimes they name but also by analyzing how the governor and the governed are changed and how their relationships to each other (and to others in and across the assemblages of international law and governance) are transformed. How racialization works globally—how racialized groups are perceived locally through the domestic implementation of internationally inflected doctrines—is thus partially accomplished through such instances of legal texts and concepts caught touching (or torturing) across histories and times.

These meetings and melding of law provide a noncausal coherence that buttresses the ascendance of individual criminal liability for atrocity crimes when civilians are increasingly understood to be targets of state-backed or otherwise organized warfare. If targets of war or parastate violence, why not perpetrators of its crime? If rogue, stateless, and perhaps not quite civilian, why should they be protected by the Geneva Conventions? These recalibrations of risk and blame, premised on the sanctity of state sovereignty and enacted through human rights principles, extend the reach of war and liability into the erstwhile civilian realm. This extension initiates securitization strategies through all sectors of society, furthering and furthered by the process in which mass sexualized violence engenders massed and geographically mobile populations in need of supranational oversight.[82] As such, this chapter elaborates and extends what I have called the *racialization of mass rape*, or how feminism and efforts to address state-sanctioned sexual violence through bodies of international law, humanitarian policy making, global securitization strategies, and militarisms interact to effectuate and maintain pathologized nationalities, geographic regions, and peoples subject to predatory capitalist accumulation.

The uptake of individual liability within international criminal law does not ultimately let states off the hook. Instead it conceptually fuses sexual risk with the operations of the state, shifting the locus of blame to include not only individual actors but the collective entities that produce them: sexual threat emanates from failed states and failed individuals identified in part through multisited feminist organizing. These framings extend the reach of states' legal obligations from the domestic public into the domestic private sphere and, under certain circumstances of state failure, allow the international order of states to enter into the sovereign reaches of individual state prerogative in the name of gender and racial democracy. This logic and atmosphere helped form and facilitate President George W. Bush's ability to propose, support, and ultimately usher the MCA into law. The rise, reinvigorations, and refinements of individual legal personality in international law set the stage for the valorization and indemnification of US-employed torturers engaged in ethnoreligious sexualized abuse.

The MCA and Muslims

In the words of President Bush himself, the MCA "provides legal protections that ensure our military and intelligence personnel will not have to fear lawsuits filed by terrorists simply for doing their jobs."[83] As Bush's remark suggests, the MCA was prompted by CIA interrogators' concerns that the Detainee Treatment Act of 2005, which prohibited torture and coercive interrogations, implied potential liability for interrogators and could result in disbanding the interrogation program in secret CIA prisons. The MCA response was to depart from established international and domestic law. The MCA eliminated habeas, stripping detainees of their right to challenge their detentions in US courts. It also curtailed suspects' ability to examine all evidence presented against them and failed to unequivocally bar testimony acquired through witness coercion, sexualized or otherwise.[84] Once again, recall that the MCA also "reinterpreted" the legal parameters of torture, rape, and other sexualized violence.[85]

The debates, people, and law surrounding the MCA are not only a chapter in the legal and cultural trajectory of post-1990s global treatments of sexualized violence. They also demonstrate how specific constructions of terrorism helped curtail or cultivate the recognition of certain instances of rape and other sexualized violence as mass or systemic violence. Judith Butler, Jasbir Puar, and Amit Rai have analyzed terrorism studies experts like Jerrold Post, who during the 1980s hypothesized that terrorists have "pathological personalities that emerge from negative childhood experiences and a damaged sense of self."[86] Puar and Rai continue to detail the more invidious dimensions of this psychology of terror, premised on the Western, heterosexual presumption of the desirability and viability of the nuclear family and patriarchal models of masculine authority. Here, terrorists emerge as racialized and sexually disordered emblems of not only failed heterosexuality but failed cisgendered heterosexuality—ciphers for the frustrated gendered labor arrangements and racialized intimacies of the nuclear family. The superficial result is a portrait of terrorists as "anarchic ideologues" (who rebel against the society of their parents) and "nationalist-secessionists" (whose loyalty to parents manifests in rejection of external enemies).[87] These terms describe terrorists' orientation to family and state power as extrainstitutional and unpredictable; they are improperly autonomous subjects (see introduction), bound neither by traditional familial obligations nor state-based restraints. They are an affront to the social and subjective arrangements that enable contractual freedom or the ability to make contracts (including sexual ones) without coercion or duress—what became, at the end of the Cold War, the evidence of freedom and proof of the well-run state.

The term *unlawful enemy combatant* reflects the conditions in which it was newly forged: where US terrorism studies meets the new wars that feminisms helped define. These were the times of ethnoreligious and sexual massacres that rampaged beyond state control, killing civilians indiscriminately *and* with targeted animus. These were the times of ranging menace that toppled divisions between public and private realms, disquieting the sovereign prerogatives of the state and revising what may be pitched as the human demands of international law.

The rise of stateless combatants in international law and security policy correlated with the entrenchment of individual criminal liability within international law,[88] setting the stage for future interpretations that would accept that liability as a basic tenet. The ambiguity of nation-state affiliation that describes terrorists today echoes descriptions of ethnic wars and low-intensity conflicts of the past, which were in turn enmeshed in contemporaneous Western political descriptions of jihad. As Oliver Roy writes in 1994, "Jihad ignores the ABC of war according to Clausewitz. . . . Jihad knows no borders;

it has an instrumental vision of the state, which ends up being devalued.... The ethical model that is at the heart of the notion of jihad prohibits political structures."[89] In this view, as anthropologist and legal scholar Darryl Li notes—and despite local contexts and connections to sovereign states and competing iterations of political universality—the notion of a "global jihad" lacks what Carl Schmitt dubs a "telluric orientation," a "tie to the soil, to the autochthonous population, and to the geographic particularity of the land."[90] As Li writes, "Transnational jihad thus appears as a form of warfare that is rootless, ruthless, and boundless."[91]

The notion of a "rootless, ruthless, and boundless" transnational jihad might itself be considered part of a conceptual apparatus that Junaid Rana names "racial infrastructure," or "a spatial formation in which the social, political, and economic relationships of racial systems operate through dominance and discursive power."[92] Racial infrastructure facilitates and feeds a particular incarnation of what others have called the security industrial complex and what Rana calls the "terror-industrial complex." In Rana's view, "The impact of the terror-industrial complex is far more extreme than a representational mistake based in the fear mongering of Islam and Muslims. Rather, it is the larger systems of structural violence that are normalized through the workings of concepts such as race and permanent war that create an unprecedented flexibility in the workings of social domination and capital accumulation."[93]

This flexibility adheres in the term *unlawful enemy combatants*, which also and crucially describes a racialized, gendered, and sexualized threat that after the 1990s was irreparably tied to boundless, violent unrest and war. As such, efforts to contain an already geographically, governmentally, and sexually devious opponent demanded (so the thinking goes) a further recasting of the potential boundaries of what had largely or arguably been state-based international legal proscriptions: torture, crimes against humanity, war crimes, and other legal violations that had been refashioned alongside the entrance of rape and other sexualized violence into international criminal, humanitarian, and human rights law.

On its face, the MCA offers a straightforward differentiation between Muslims/"unlawful enemy combatants" and the United States as a means of spatially and geographically differentiating between the sexually free and the sexually oppressed. The MCA racializes Muslims as bad, the United States as good, US women as free, and Muslim women as cowed and utterly dominated. As many scholars have recognized, the perceived threat that Muslim women face from Muslim men (read: free-range, war-waging, terrorist) leaves them categorically susceptible to assignations of sexual vulnerability.[94]

What has remained out of frame is how the notion of the vulnerable Muslim woman feeds off legal theorizations and prohibitions of rape and gender violence that transnational scholars, activists, and attorneys produced in the midst of the wars in the former Yugoslavia and Rwanda and how these produced structures of liability that produce broader reorganizations of race and power. The MCA serves at once as another pathway to US sexual exceptionalism, while also reinforcing the sanctity of the nation-state as a space of political cohesion in a time of roving threat. Because US citizens could be deemed "unlawful enemy combatants" per the MCA, US soil could be further militarized and policed to prevent "excessive globalization" or political space that is impermissibly heterogeneous. What Puar famously recognizes as the failed heterosexuality of the terrorist in the post-9/11 moment is an echo of the struggle at Rome to recognize the targets of atrocity crimes—what version of the human must be protected—as anything but cisgendered and heterosexual, much less to recognize forms or arrangements of embodiment that invoke other systems or worldviews entirely. In this way, "unlawful enemy combatants" are the exemplary, historical heirs of the violent substate combatants that post-1990s international criminal humanitarian law guards against, for which terrorist studies sounds a psychofamilial warning.

For these reasons, I suggest that the US government–proffered term *unlawful enemy combatants* should be understood as more than a transparent effort to work around the Geneva Conventions and simply maximize US power. Instead, it might function as a categorical alternative that uses the racialized language of the new wars and the new recognition in international law of civilians as true targets and, if nonstate actors, perpetrators of war, to describe an allegedly new breed of terror and threat—one that lurks within and beyond any state boundary or proscriptions and in this way places himself (it is almost always a "him") beyond the boundaries of the human subject of human rights. This is an enemy to which the state—or organization of states—owes little or nothing because it not just antistate, it is anti–all states—a logical and anxious end to the cracking of the public/private fiction that is the foundation of liberal law.

Sexual Barbarism and the Entrenchment of Militarized Humanitarianism

As the war-raped and sexually violated entered the international juridical sphere as an at-risk population, armed intervention, in retroactive fits and starts, became an appropriate and morally just reproach to humanitarian crises.

At the dawn of the 1990s, the question for international humanitarian law was, to put it crassly, how "bad" was wartime rape? Was it, in fact, a war crime and consequently a trespass of acceptable military behavior? Was it a crime against humanity or genocide—violations that strike against the core of juridical notions of humanity? Or was it a more routine misfortune—regrettable, but understood as an affront to dignity, not a crime of violence that stains the idea of the human? Over the course of that decade, wartime rape and other sexualized violence were statutorily embedded in international criminal law as war crimes and crimes against humanity and were prosecuted as constitutive acts of genocide, transforming the literal letter and dominant interpretations of international law and governance instruments and protocol. As war rape and other sexualized violence were defined and prosecuted as systematic mass crimes instigated by military, state, or parastate command, the character and components of rape and sexual violence were recast. The concept of sexual consent was scripted in response to mass sexual violence and ethnic war. That wartime (and shortly thereafter, postconflict) rape and sexual violence could emerge as a large-scale global problem subject to international governance and international legal criminal scrutiny hinged on its ability to be perceived in international humanitarian law as befalling vulnerable civilians en masse. Those populations of the sexually violated are now a feature of governance that entrenches "sexual barbarisms" as a barometer of civilization.

If the breakout of violence in the Balkans inaugurated a new worldview where threats emanate not solely from individual states but also from indiscriminate zones of ethnoreligious violence, then it signaled as well a devolution in states' ability to fully represent the enemy and contain sexual risk. This diffusion of sexual risk in and across state boundaries is in turn a comment on its own transmutation from a largely individual discrete or encapsulated threat to a diffuse, seemingly boundless collective menace. To consider specifically the sort of risk produced by mass wartime sexual violence, the UN Population Fund's (UNFPA) 2010 "State of World Population" report is instructive. The report, titled "From Conflict and Crisis to Renewal: Generations of Change," chronicles "how conflict and protracted humanitarian emergencies affect women and girls and men and boys" and focuses primarily on the long-term effects of wartime rape and other sexualized violence.[95] The report frames wartime and postconflict sexualized violence as problems that exceed the temporal constraints of the event, necessitating extended oversight.

The opening lines of the report, penned by UNFPA executive director Thoraya Ahmed Obaid, set the tone: "Gender-based violence, including rape, is a repugnant and increasingly familiar weapon of war. The immediate toll it takes extends far beyond its direct victims, insidiously tearing apart families and shattering societies for generations to come."[96] In two sentences, Obaid positions gender violence (including rape, almost disproportionately so) as a progressive threat that spreads from individuals to their families to the whole of society. "Experience over the past decade," Obaid continues, "underscores the need to tear down false barriers between crisis, recovery and development.... War and disaster do not cause gender-based violence, but they often exacerbate it or allow it to strike with greater frequency."[97]

The UNFPA report follows on the heels of UN Security Council Resolution 1820, adopted on June 9, 2008. While Resolution 1325 from 2000 was the first to address the effects of armed conflict on women, Resolution 1820 was the first to explicitly hold "that rape and other forms of sexual violence can constitute a war crime, a crime against humanity, or a constitutive act with respect to genocide."[98] It was also the first to call on member states "to comply with their obligations for prosecuting persons responsible for such acts."[99] Resolution 1820 claims gendered (and generational) sexualized violence (if not sexuality more broadly) as the purview of international law and governance in explicit terms that also trace changes in warfare. War exceeds its temporal limits and its spatial presence. Armed conflict degrades into conflict zones, where the probability of and proximity to armed violence define geographical regions and the people within them. At the same time, the bleed of sexualized violence in and out of war brings international humanitarian law and the laws of war to bear on governance protocol beyond war. In 2009, UN Resolutions 1888 and 1889 cemented the UN's position that addressing sexualized violence was an essential component of achieving global security during and after conflict, particularly when undertaking pre-cease-fire humanitarian access and human rights agreements, demobilization, reintegration, and security sector reform. Feminist calls to end violence against women in this way helped force the reappraisal of designations of international and internal conflict and the role of nonstate actors (erstwhile civilians) in war. What flowed from this positioning was a familiar array of remedies for those who work in the vein of gender securitization and militarisms, among them UNFPA task forces in Colombia and Rwanda to "sensitize" the armed forces and local police to gender issues and, in the case of Rwanda, actively recruit and promote women with the ranks of the Rwanda National Police.[100]

I do not extract these sentences or those of the UNFPA report to condemn *en tout* the intentions behind them. Rather, I highlight UN Resolution 1820 and Obaid's introduction to the UNFPA report to mark the entrenchment of rape and other sexualized violence in international law and governance, where literalization of the "gender war" metaphor popularly used to describe social and civil attacks against women's interests has manifested at the heart of the violent disintegration of the nation-state. This confluence underscores the racial infrastructures that allow gendered sexualized violence to set off the political and economic arrangements of an expanding military humanitarian industrial complex. What begins in conflict does not end when the conflict subsides but mutates from the targeted risk of rape or other sexualized violence into a generalized threat that has become increasingly indicative of total social collapse. Gender violence, rape, and other forms of sexualized violence are now international concerns during and after conflict because they are able to be theorized, experienced, and represented as a foreclosure of the liberal promise of the state and of a piece with the new wars—a threat that emanates from within and beyond the official confines of certain individual state governments, peoples, and regions.

Such theorizations of rape and other sexualized violence position sexuality as a pivot between the individual, the population, and the state—as "the precise point where the disciplinary and the regulatory, the body and the population, are articulated."[101] This pivot illuminates some of the stakes of rape and sexual violence gaining prominence within international law in the context of ethnic conflict. Because international criminal law encompasses crimes against humanity and genocide, rape and other sexualized violence gain entry to international law and jurisprudence not just as severe acts befalling individuals but as mass crimes. In the initial, formative conflicts in the former Yugoslavia and Rwanda, the creation of populations of war-raped and sexually violated were themselves subdivisions of overarching and suffering ethnic and ethnoreligious populations—conditions framed to echo the inception of human rights regimes after World War II. For these reasons, it is impossible to parse the occurrence of mass sexual violence and the new wars—complete with ethnic rivalry "origin stories"—nor is it possible to extract the advent of militarized humanitarianism from the tales we tell about the nature and rationales of modern warfare or who will or will not be responsible for its "excesses."

From this vantage point, the MCA and its ilk do not simply "turn the clock back on rape and sexual violence" as much as they mobilize gender and sexual norms in the service of statecraft, war, capital, and ultimately cisheteropatriarchal and neocolonial visions of gender freedom. In this regard, the now-infamous calls to wage literal war in the name of women's human rights are not entirely at ideological loggerheads with the MCA and related provisions and practices that constrict international legal and normative meanings of rape and other sexualized violence. Instead, a broad view of law and its contents—as a complex of doctrinal precepts and cultural forces— helps reveal the MCA as a shadow of that already shadowy call to "save women" in the name of "global gender equality." No matter how the clock turns on rape law, such antigender violence mandates are for now hostage to a militarized humanitarianism that will wage war for peace and torture and violate in the name of freedom.

FOUR

Two Title IXs /
Empire and the Transnational
Production of "Welcomeness"
on Campus

SCENE 1 / A FEMINIST SCIENCE STUDIES GRADUATE SEMINAR AT A
STATE UNIVERSITY (2017). The first-year assistant professor is transmas-
culine. They ask their students to bring an object to class that shows some
entanglement of animality and sexuality. A student offers a photograph of a
dragon-headed dildo. A white cisgender student dubs this a "sexual assault"
and on other occasions describes the experience as "like a sexual assault." The
assistant professor must report to their department chair and the Title IX
office, where they are ultimately compelled to lead a Trans 101 educational
session for all faculty on campus. The university is concerned that the assistant professor is engaged in behavior that would be impermissible for "any
other man on campus."

SCENE 2 / A PERFORMANCE ART EVENT AT A LARGE RESEARCH UNIVERSITY (2019). The performer is transfeminine and from the Global South. The performance they deliver is a comment on how violence is globally distributed through Global North rubrics of "rights." A white cisgender female graduate student later christens the whole performance a "sexual assault." Speaking on behalf of all in attendance, the student alleges that the performer assaulted the whole audience (more than a dozen audience members). Included in this number is the assistant professor—nonbinary, not white—to whom she addresses her complaint. As a mandatory reporter, the assistant professor must now contend with the institutional response to the complaint and report the (and their) "assault" to the university's Title IX office. Repetitive and opaque bureaucratic operations are set in motion.[1]

SCENE 3 / THE US DISTRICT COURT IN KANSAS (2017). Jane H., a woman enrolled at Haskell Indian Nations University, an institution under the control and management of the US Bureau of Indian Affairs, accuses two fellow students of rape and seeks relief under Title IX. Judge Thomas Marten dismisses the lawsuit, writing that the federal government and the university were immune from damages under the doctrine of sovereign immunity, which holds that the federal government cannot be sued without the express consent of Congress. The decision further holds that the plaintiff's Title IX rights are inapplicable because Haskell Indian Nations University is not an institution receiving federal assistance within the meaning of those statutes. In other words, the allegations are not found to be "properly before the court." Other civil forms of redress, including torts claims or allegations of due process, and criminal proceedings are not barred in this pronouncement, but Title IX is foreclosed.

WELCOME IS A FEELING. Derived from the Old English *wilcuma*, the word first described a feeling about someone—*the person who is coming is pleasing*. Later, it became a form of greeting (*you will receive a warm welcome*), a reaction of pleasure or approval (*the decision to proceed was a welcome one*), an invitation to do a certain something (*you are welcome to join us*), or a term used to indicate relief in relinquishing control or possession (*you are welcome to it*).[2]

That feeling of welcome has long been essential to feminist understandings of "good sex"—an act and aspiration that is not solely defined by the presence or absence of consent. As legal feminist theorist Robin West writes, "Consensual sex, when it is unwanted and unwelcome, often carries harms to the personhood, autonomy, integrity and identity of the person who consents to it—and that these harms are unreckoned by law and more or less unnoticed by the rest of us. The possibility that the liberal valorization of consensual sex that is so central to liberal de-regulatory projects legitimates these harms ought to concern us far more than it has, at least to date."[3] Since West wrote those words, however, campus and feminist legal activisms have renewed their interest in Title IX, the federal law prohibiting sexual discrimination in federally funded education, as a vehicle for combatting sexual harassment, including sexual assault. Debates have raged over what counts as prohibited speech or conduct.[4] Despite the primacy of consent to liberal law, these debates have turned not only on what constitutes as consent but also on the appropriateness of consent as a marker of "good sex"—as the appropriate gauge of whether sexualized speech or conduct is wanted or welcome and not simply assented to. As an attempt to militate against the limits of consent and adjust for the perceived lack of sexual bargaining power between male and female students, some college code of conduct policies, for example, prohibit "unwelcome" sex—regardless of whether consent was obtained.[5] A rightful apprehension motivates these discussions and protocols, although it equates, analogizes, and glosses: on the battlefield and in the classroom, in the boardroom and on the assembly line, beneath the objective marker of consent lies a world of coercion that is structurally produced but bears down and manifests in the individual sexual encounter—the pressure to comply. This is the fear of the "unwelcome yes."

Most feminist, queer, and allied scholarship has viewed the embrace of sexual welcomeness to be a mostly "welcome" one. Suspicious of contractual configurations of consent, these fields have taken up alternate rubrics for assessing "good" sex—for example, suggesting various ways to center expansive theories of autonomy, agency, vulnerability, or self-possession as the structuring conceit of the inquiry.[6] In this way, they rail against viewing sex and desire as transactional, contractual, or even necessarily individual.[7] Such work has critiqued law's presumption of a rational subject whose coherence and validity depend on the ability to make wholly informed and emphatic decisions about their sexual lives and encounters, particularly in the moment.[8] But even work that is suspicious of determining sexualized violence through the framework of sexual welcomeness has not properly theorized possession— *you are welcome to it.* More pointedly, while Black and other women of color, trans, and indigenous activists and scholars have long criticized a consent-based model of sexual freedom,[9] the move from consent to welcomeness as a sociolegal concept has not been accounted for by contemporary scholars as part of transnational projects of empire—even though the mechanism of their advancement has, I argue, occurred through the geopolitics of global sexual violence and their attending, vicious distributions of labor and property. In other words, the gendered, sexualized, and racialized historical formations of property and possession that make contemporary notions of bodily welcomeness thinkable and feelable are largely absent from scholarly and other conversations about sexualized violence on and off campus. Who gets to talk about what signals welcomeness in sex—whose denials of welcomeness will activate the dim juggernaut of institutional bureaucracy? Who remains undifferentiated by desire, merely a population at risk?

Social identity or individual relationships alone (professor, tenured or untenured; staff or student; queer or trans or cisgender) do not control for the scenes above and others like it. These are also stories of settler empire and law, of how bodies of law, civil and criminal, are triggered (or not) by different bodies in different spaces. Ultimately, these are stories about how underlying lines of force animate different bodies in different places—different people in different places—positioning them to make different subjective "sexual" claims. In the above scenes, each perceived violation—named *sexual*, named *assault*—is made possible by competing understandings of consent, coercion, force, and welcomeness: the legal terms of art and social lexicon that recognize sexualized violation. These contestations of meaning play out in what questions drive the inquiry and allow the violation to be named and seen. In the first two scenes, did the students agree to experience or feel OK or even good about what happened in the classroom—was the experience welcome? And in the third, did the US government, regardless of what Jane Doe did or felt, agree to be potentially liable (was the rape charge "welcome" to the government)?

In what follows, I look at how campus bodies become living archives of uneven histories of violence that lie beneath the charge of sexual violation by reading for divergent, transnational genealogies of consent, coercion, and welcomeness in law and policy instruments that would govern sexualized intimacies on college campuses. In particular, I'm concerned with how the idea of the "unwelcome yes"—or how consent can be copresent with coercion—has been taken up in informal and institutional conversations about campus sex. Who gets to talk about what signals welcomeness in sex on campus? What counts as "sex" on campus? What follows is an account of how property and sovereignty as concepts and claims are staked through the sexualized body, in and through the shifting parameters of what counts as consensual or coercive sex and what creates something that is called sexual welcomeness and recognized as such. What follows is also a call to consider how far we might follow a narrow notion of sexual injury—of what justice we pursue and deny in its name.

With this in mind, I look at not one but two Titles IXs. Each concerns the 2013 reauthorization of the Violence against Women Act (VAWA). This legislation contains provisions that impact how Title IX of the Civil Rights Act, the federal law prohibiting sex discrimination in federally funded education, is administered—including how campus crime data would be defined for the purposes of mandatory public reporting requirements.[10] The 2013 VAWA also contains its own Title IX, subtitled Safety for Indian Women. This Title IX builds on the 2005 VAWA's inclusion of tribal title, when the federal government recognized the "unique legal relationship between the United States and Indian tribes creates a federal trust responsibility to assist tribal governments in safeguarding the lives of Indian women."[11] Title IX of VAWA recognizes tribal criminal jurisdiction over some cases of domestic or intimate violence regardless of their Indian status, provided that tribes ensure certain enumerated due process protections. I use the coincidental titling of the 2013 VAWA's provisions regarding tribal authority and the Civil Rights Act's prohibitions on sex discrimination in education as an invitation to probe the versions of consent, sovereignty, and authority that circulate beneath the banner of "violence against women." This framing animates the workings of both criminal and civil rights law in relation to tribal nations' continual negotiations of sovereign authority. It also realigns ongoing debates about sexualized violence on campus—and the meanings of sexual consent and coercion—by considering the United States as a transnational space and bringing a feminist analysis that is cognizant of settler colonialism into the frame. From this perspective, I consider the relationships between campus sexual securitization initiatives and tribal nations' jurisdictional struggles with the federal government. Specifically, I examine how these relationships are actuated through antigender and antisexual violence legislation. Such activisms summon multiple genealogies of violence and transnational interplays of activisms that must be interpreted and harnessed within law. In turn, that process shapes the content, meaning, and scope of human rights, civil rights, and criminal wrongdoing and the enabling language of them—in this case ideas of force, consent, coercion, and that welcome feeling.

At the heart of this exploration lies the tension between ambiguous definitions of sexual consent and coercion and the legal frameworks that would counter or clarify them—including versions of affirmative consent (which require some indication that the acts are more than merely assented to) or the potentially consent-defying notion of welcomeness. The problem of sex on campus is not only, as the thinking goes, because consent and its individualized rubrics of transaction underlie liberal visions of sexual freedom or even because the history of the contract in its many iterations has been differentially and unevenly applied to children, the enslaved, women, and the disabled (to name a few).[12] It matters how theories of consent, coercion, and now welcomeness have been conceived of, interpreted, and actuated through systems and bodies of law that span national borders and subject areas.

Consent, coercion, or welcomeness as sociolegal concepts are formed *and felt* through the disavowal of imperial, cis-hetero settler colonialism, racial suffering, and dispossession that is at once articulated through the interplay of civil (Title IX of the Civil Rights Act) and criminal (Title IX of the VAWA) law and the rationales for penalizing (or failing to penalize) sexual violation that accompany those systems and bodies of law. This process triggers questions of epistemic authority: Who or what can recognize the presence or absence of "sex" or "good sex"? Who might determine the contexts in which sex or good sex can occur? In other words, who effectively determines what sex and sexualized violence are or can be? What does this mean in settler or other colonial spaces, where feelings of "welcomeness"—sexual or otherwise—are made possible by what Jodi A. Byrd, Alyosha Goldstein, Jodi Melamed, and Chandan Reddy call the logics of propriation, or "a conception and practice of the proper, propriety, proprietorship, and proprietary claims that instantiates property as a relation to private and public"?[13] How are the logics of propriation activated not simply through the pronouncements of law (what it says it does) but through interactions between bodies and processes of law? How might women of color, decolonial, and queer theorizations of bodily pleasure and sexuality offer other ways of understanding—of making—sex and sexual violation on and off campus?

Through this framing, the inclusions, omissions, and interpretations of the Title IX stories that begin this chapter come into fitful relief. On college campuses and tribal land, authority still speaks in the antiquated language of family, of the parent and the ward: the lingering effects of in loco parentis for the students and the "special relationship" the US federal government historically claims with tribal nations.[14] The inaugurating scenes cohere if the adjudication of each claim of sexual violation is understood to labor in the service of establishing permissible sexual arrangements as proxies for permissible property arrangements, realized through gendered, racialized, and colonial intimacies of governance. In writing this, I do not mean to offer the state or any law as the primary site of meaning-making. What I suggest is that ideas about the character of the state or nation, submerged beneath liberal, individuating frameworks of consent and coercion and activated through various types and bodies of law, have shaped ideas about what sexualized violence and even sex is—what it feels like, and what it can be. Attention to the transnational production of sexualized violence must concern activist and legal debates about sex on campus and be centered in discussions of the meanings of sex, good sex, and welcomeness that shape and are shaped by our understanding of the bodies, institutions, and lands that hold our lives.

The Transnational History of the VAWA and Its Civil Remedy

If an unwelcome yes for a college student can be heard in some specific (if limited) terms and an active no at Haskell Indian Nations University cannot, the difference between them is partly one of law and its internal negotiations—negotiations that are transnational at the root. Before I explore questions of law and settler nationhood in the two Title IXs, I want to revisit the circumstances in which the original 1994 VAWA came to be and the controversy over its inclusion of a federal civil remedy for rape—the ability to sue for civil money damages in a federal court when district attorneys failed to prosecute. What thinking prompted the recourse to civil law in the midst of an omnibus crime bill? The controversy surrounding the first iteration of VAWA helps show how the kind of violation rape may be—not only what the act entails but how its harm might be conceived, described, and recognized—depends on disparate theories of the state, rape (specifically), and other forms of sexualized violence (generally), and their corresponding bodies of law. The fate of certain provisions contained in the 1994 VAWA show how international crises of the place and meaning of nation-states at the so-called end of history were mediated through rubrics of diversity in the post–civil rights era. In the case of rape and other forms of sexualized violence, these mediations depended on theorizations of rape as both criminal and civil issues.

Hailed as the fruit of feminist coalitional organizing throughout the 1980s and 1990s and spearheaded by Senator Joe Biden, the 1994 VAWA established the Office on Violence against Women in the Department of Justice, allotting $1.6 billion toward the investigation and prosecution of violent crimes against women.[15] The 1994 VAWA also imposed automatic and mandatory restitution on those convicted. The 1994 VAWA, originally passed as part of the Violent Crime Control and Law Enforcement Act, on its face expunges the histories of anticarceral feminist activisms that preceded it.[16] In what later sparked a major constitutional controversy, the 1994 VAWA afforded those who experienced "private" gender-motivated violence a federal civil remedy: the ability to sue the perpetrators for money damages in federal court.[17] The 1994 VAWA's federal civil remedy developed from the work of legal feminists like Catharine MacKinnon and Robin West and, according to Biden and supporters, was "the single most important part of VAWA."[18] Modeled after nineteenth-century law to protect Black people in the wake of the Civil War, the civil remedy was meant to counter gender bias and discrimination in state courts by asserting that violence against women was a civil rights violation. In this way, the civil remedy depended on a certain understanding of what the experience of rape was like (that a "women's" no or other resistance was not readily believed) and a certain understanding of the state (that the federal government and its courts, not the corrupted justice system of individual states, could best guarantee the civil rights of women).

Importantly, legal feminists advocating for the civil remedy, like MacKinnon, presented it as a means of avoiding the perils of criminal law. If the harms of rape are exacerbated by—or perhaps can be said to include—the failure of local courts to "listen to women, " this failure to listen was also specifically understood as a failure of criminal law and its venues, which require a higher evidentiary standard of proof of criminal behavior.[19] In the context of the legislation—and despite VAWA's carceral commitments, which "protect" women with mandatory arrest provisions for domestic violence and simultaneously authorize the construction of women's prisons—positioning rape as a civil rights violation was simultaneously understood by its proponents to signal a lack of faith in the criminal justice system. In this way, the civil remedy suggests, however fitfully, that justice for sexualized violence could be made possible beyond the reach of the criminal justice system, even as it harnesses civil rights firmly to punishing carceral logics.

The federal civil remedy was famously struck down by the Supreme Court's 2000 decision in *United States v. Morrison*—the same year the VAWA was reauthorized and expanded. The effectiveness and desirability of these measures notwithstanding,[20] how did this happen in the era of women's rights as human rights? Feminist law professor Reva B. Siegel and law professor Robert Post characterized the Supreme Court's decision in *Morrison* as "enormously consequential."[21] For Siegel and Post, *Morrison* and another case decided during the same term, *Kimel v. Florida Board of Regents*, represent "the first time since Reconstruction that the Court has declared that Congress lacked power to enact legislation prohibiting discrimination."[22] These cases, both restrictions on congressional power, tell how the fissures and inchoateness of state power affect the meaning and significance of sexual violence. In *Morrison* the Court held that the extension of a federal civil remedy was an impermissible exercise of congressional power—an act in excess of the authority granted Congress by the Commerce Clause and the Fourteenth Amendment's Equal Protections and Enforcement Clauses. Roughly speaking, the federal government had to justify its right to regulate places of public accommodation or places that offer some service to the general public, including privately owned businesses and facilities. In the 1964 case *Heart of Atlanta Motel v. United States*,[23] the US Supreme Court located the congressional power to uphold the public accommodations provisions of the Civil Rights Act on Commerce Clause grounds. The idea here—the bread and butter of every constitutional law classroom, if not every cultural studies one—is that because discrimination can substantially affect interstate commerce, Congress has the ability to enforce antidiscrimination provisions under its broad power to regulate interstate commerce. In this way, the justification for the federal government's interest in antidiscrimination provisions is ineluctably tied to bodies tossing in hotel beds and cans of soup loaded and hauled along the freeways—to the easy exchange of money, hand to hand and across state borders.

Restoring (and expanding or curtailing) civil rights, as Lisa Marie Cacho writes, has "always been tied to expanding US sovereignty and racial capitalism."[24] Yet how civil and criminal strategies are actuated through law, how they fall differently on the many groups or populations to whom they apply, matters. If the origins of contemporary civil rights protections lie in *Heart of Atlanta Motel*, subsequent legal decisions have changed the meaning of civil rights guarantees, their scope and application, in ways that change the relationship of civil rights to the economic health of the state and, in turn, what exactly a "healthy" state looks like. The majority in *United States v. Morrison*, for example, required that only economic activities that directly and not indirectly influence interstate commerce were subject to public accommodations.[25] Chief Justice William Rehnquist, writing for the majority, justified the distinction due to "the concern that . . . Congress might use the Commerce Clause to completely obliterate the Constitution's distinction between national and local authority."[26]

This abbreviated account of VAWA's short-lived federal civil remedy shows not only how civil rights guarantees are bound to the economic life of the nation-state—to the trade flows of people and property—but also how civil and criminal codes, carceral and civil rights logics, are linked and mediated through multiple, complex, and potentially contradictory ideologies of the sexual state form. (The *sexual state form*, a term I describe at length in chapter 3, describes feminist imaginaries of sexual harm and how such harms are tied to the bad behavior imagined to result from particular kinds of states and state failure.) Matters of trade as well as the boundaries between federal and state jurisdiction shape the meaning and recognition of actionable sexualized violence and contour the relationships between states and their publics. By regulating (or refusing to regulate) sexualized violence at the federal level through civil remedy, the US Supreme Court creates a particular account of what sexualized violence is. The notion that rape is a federal civil rights issue that should be governed and remedied by the state through the logic, laws, and remedies afforded federal civil rights affronts is undercut after *Morrison*. This notion of what sexualized violence is then mediates federal and local concentrations of power and the meaning of rights in a carceral state built on dispossessed native lands. Judicial wrangling around civil rights and sexualized violence affect how sexualized violence, civil rights, and tribal sovereignty are relationally imagined.

In the case of the federal civil remedy, legal feminists cast the US federal government as a guarantor of rights—one whose credibility as a capitalist liberal democracy depends on its inclusion of women's issues made possible by the continued, mediated denial of its status as a settler state. They cast civil rights, premised on achieving equality, as the proper analytic for understanding sexualized violence—understood as complementing and pushing against a patriarchal criminal framework.[27] Although these feminist approaches to law may think in terms of which legal paradigms to employ—equality or criminal ones, for example—as Rehnquist's words attest, an overarching and contrasting view about the nature of the state ultimately carries the day. In *Morrison*, democracy depends on curtailing the federal government and preserving local authority—federal civil rights remedies can intrude on more localized codes of civil and criminal law.

In the text of and debates surrounding the 1994 VAWA alone, carceral logics of punishment (of which the federal civil remedy is and arguably is not a part) are checked by federalist concerns over the balance of power among the federal, state, and local governments. The state demand to uphold women's rights shapes and is shaped by these issues of governance and statecraft that arise from long-standing US constitutional debates about what balance of power is necessary to secure liberal freedoms. These debates are themselves predicated on and rationalized by economic calculations, including the economic health of a state made possible by the dispossession of indigenous lands.

At the heart of this, once again, lies the question: Who is capable of recognizing sexual consent, coercion, or welcomeness—of explaining what sort of violation sexual ones are? Even as the possible legal venues for addressing sexualized violence constrict with the denial of the federal civil remedy, the gesture toward civil rights reinvigorates the work captured by the term and disavowed. Here are the echoes of the radical social transformations of 1968 and global decolonization movements distilled into an extension of rights, whether civil or human ones. VAWA submerges this scaffolding and these questions even as it enlivens them, as the above account details, in queer legal kinship. In other words, this controversy in US governance that pitted the federal government against state and local authority was embedded in a broader debate about the character of the democratic nation-state and the meaning of freedom and diversity in a post-Soviet but pre-9/11—or at least the US 9/11—moment. As the following section details, ideas about what rape and sexualized violence are and are "like" drew from transnational feminist conversations and legal organizing efforts. Those conversations and efforts were shaped by their historical moment: the Cold War's end and the rise of multiculturalism and diversity models for interpreting racial injustice and dispensing "equality." These ideas about the character of the US state—multicultural, democratic—justified global war making, expropriation, and exploitation in its name, even as the possible avenues of state redress for rape that occurred in its territorial boundaries (for example, the federal civil remedy) needed to shrink to support it. The very notion of a federal civil remedy for rape—one that tacitly admits the failure of the US state to manage its diversity—ran at odds with the global role the United States took up the in the 1990s: the defender of "women," the bane of ethnonationalism and of mass rape.

VAWA's Civil Remedy and the Ethnic Wars

As VAWA was being discussed and implemented in the early 1990, the Balkans erupted. Rwanda shortly followed. The United States would look to Europe and Africa to soothe its own racial troubles. In the process, it cast racial and gendered antagonisms through the prism of ethnoreligious conflict, subsequently valorizing secular multicultural and diversity projects of "inclusion" as the essence of racial, gendered, and sexual freedom. The ensuing conflicts in the Balkans and Rwanda and the ascension of mass ethnic rape to international attention kindled particular understandings of the relationships among consent, coercion, and the possibility of a welcome yes.

Platforms of diversity and multiculturalism that rose to prominence throughout the 1990s were some of the latest iterations of the US state's postwar embrace of a liberal race paradigm. The liberal race paradigm, as Jodi Melamed writes, "recognizes racial inequality as a problem, and . . . secures a liberal symbolic framework for race reform centered in abstract equality, market individualism, and inclusive civic nationalism."[28] That concept of racial equality harnessed official state-backed antiracism efforts to individual rights in a familiar refrain that deemed alternative or systemic analyses of racial injustice or economic exploitation as biased, non-neutral, and therefore racist approaches to the problem of historical difference.

The US management of race through diversity and multicultural logics, however, also occurred within what Neda Atanasoski calls an era of "post-socialist imperialism" that was "based in humanitarian ethics."[29] Self-heralded as a diverse and tolerant state, the United States marshaled this idea of civil rights to justify its role as "protector and enforcers of rights, now on a global scale" against other knowledge systems, especially socialist ones.[30] This nationalist multiculturalism positioned the United States as "a model for multicultural democracy that Eastern Europe might look to during its [post-Soviet] transitional period."[31] In this analysis, diversity and secularism came to signify liberal democratic freedom. Ethnoreligious difference writ large substituted for the opposite: oppression, unfreedom, and barbarism. In this imaginary, human rights—"secular" to the core and parsed from decolonizing accounts of freedom and justice through the notion of multicultural inclusion—became the only viable "ethical politics."[32] Notions of sexual freedom further modulated the politics of inclusion. In the United States, ideas about race have been amended (to use Chandan Reddy's term) by debates around the meaning of gendered sexual freedom. This state interest in defending sexual freedom can justify past global violence by the state and authorize new violence in its name: "It is sexual freedom—as the evidence of civilization and progress—that at this moment most powerfully disallows a reckoning with its own conditions of possibility, redeeming . . . the very state that . . . global sexual and racial violences have built."[33]

From this vantage, the reasons for the civil remedy's failure take on new resonance. Multiculturalism as a state project could not be vented through a civil rights remedy without echoing the strong centralized state of socialism and suggesting that women's rights could not be trusted to local US institutions—that modernity was in fact a horizon event, distant and perhaps unachievable. Despite the call of "women's rights as human rights," the federal civil remedy sat ill at ease with a liberal vision of US multiculturalism. Yet the definitions, theorizations, and conceptualization of rape that were formed through transnational antisexualized violence organizing and newly consolidating instruments and institutions of international law nonetheless would affect US antisexualized violence organizing and lawmaking. While state "identity politics,"[34] so to speak, can help create the meaning of sexualized violence in US legislation like VAWA, contemporary transnational feminist organizing to affect international law has also shaped the boundaries between concepts of consent and coercion that would impact theorizations of consent, coercion, and force in US domestic law.

Legal feminists' framings of war rape and human trafficking helped deprivilege consent as the premier marker of good sex. War—and not the metaphorical kind—allowed legal feminists to emphasize how endemic coercive conditions undermine meaningful consent. This invigoration of coercion frameworks has surfaced as something akin to welcomeness in contemporary Title IX debates. Attention to legal feminist writings and activisms shows how theories of sexualized violence travel transnationally, affecting both international and domestic law by transforming what counts as evidence of sexualized violence and who is authorized to see it—what can "properly appear before the court."

International Law and the Fight for the Criminal Universality of Rape

Discussion and debates about VAWA's civil remedy were contemporaneous with the establishment of the ICTY and ICTR—whose founding statutes were promulgated in 1993 and 1994, respectively. Their statutes and supplementary materials, which collectively define the jurisdiction, operating procedures, and institutional roles and rules, mark a distinct turn in the history of international law, as international criminal law and international humanitarian law underwent a process of consolidation. Genocide, crimes against humanity, war crimes, and other violations of the laws of war were selected as violations meriting tribunal inquiry during deliberations leading to the promulgation of the statutes. The enumerated crimes falling under tribunal jurisdiction were culled "from the immense body of [international humanitarian law] then suspended across a wide range of treaties, trials, and other authorities"—in other words, from existing sources and forms of international criminal liability.[35]

The tribunal statutes mark the first explicit codification of rape and certain forms of sexualized violence as violations of international criminal law. Under these statutes, however, rape is "not a free-standing crime but must be charged as an act of war, genocide, or crime against humanity."[36] The explicit inclusion of rape and other forms of sexualized violence in the tribunal statutes was part of a sea change in feminist influence in international law and inched toward the establishment of the universal criminality of rape through the reputational heft of (and prior work accomplished in) the intersecting triad of international law invoked by the conflict: international criminal law, international humanitarian law, and international human rights law. Because the new international criminal tribunals promulgated discrete rules of procedure and evidence, legal feminists had ample opportunity to propose, debate, and craft definitions of sexual violence crimes and ancillary technics, including the scope of applicable defenses and allocations of burdens of persuasion, among themselves before the Rome Statute negotiations.[37] These negotiations were attended by state delegates and NGOs, including those representing the umbrella organization, the Women's Caucus for Gender Justice.[38]

For elite legal feminists, the international criminalization of rape hinged on eliminating or minimizing consent to charges of war crimes, genocide, crimes against humanity, or other violations of the laws of war. Those enmeshed in the consent debates were split in their approach. In international legal negotiations, lectures, and law journals, MacKinnon pressed for an absolute deprivileging of consent in the construction of the crime of rape. A proposal compiled by Center for Constitutional Rights–affiliated attorneys Rhonda Copelon, Jennifer Green, Patrick Cotter, and Beth Stephens in an effort to "influenc[e] the rules adopted by the Tribunal for the prosecution of rape and other sex crimes" initially advocated a presumption of women's nonconsent in all rape cases due to the inherently coercive circumstances of war.[39]

In their respective Rules of Procedure and Evidence, the tribunals ultimately fell short of disallowing consent as a defense to allegations of rape and sexual violence and thus construing rape solely through the lens of coercion.[40] The tension between consent and coercion, however, played out in tribunal and ICC litigation, where abstract debates involving individual self-actualization and the structural inequality of the war zone encountered the ideological and juridical burdens of naming rape a mass crime, as genocide or as a crime against humanity during conflict marked as ethnoreligious or ethnic.[41]

Two early cases, *Prosecutor v. Akayesu* and *Prosecutor v. Kunarac,* for example, resurfaced a strong theory of coercion that militated against consent as a defense, transforming the legal notion of rape.[42] In 1998, the Trial Chamber I of the ICTR in *Prosecutor v. Akayesu,* in conjunction with a charge of rape as a crime against humanity, defined rape under international law for the first time. To be classified as a crime against humanity, rape must be committed:

(a) as part of a widespread or systematic attack;
(b) on a civilian population; and
(c) with knowledge of the attack.[43]

In other words, to be actionable as a crime against humanity, rape must be part of the large-scale or geographically widespread rape of civilians.[44] The mass or widespread (and, in the case of the genocide charge, aimed at group destruction)[45] aspects of the crime mitigate definitions of rape premised on individual consent. The *Akayesu* court went further, fortifying feminist theorizations of rape as a crime of coercion by naming rape as "a physical invasion of a sexual nature, committed on a person under circumstances which are coercive" and defining sexual violence, which includes rape, "as any act of a sexual nature [not limited to physical invasion of the body, penetration or physical contact] which is committed on a person under circumstances which are coercive."[46] The *Akayesu* court expressly articulated a theory of coercion as independent of "a show of physical force," finding that coercion instead might consist of "threats, intimidation, extortion and other forms of duress which prey on fear or desperation" and crucially that coercion "may be inherent in certain circumstances," such as armed conflict or militarized ethnic intimidation.[47] In praise of *Akayesu*'s definition of rape, MacKinnon writes, "Arguably, for the first time, rape was defined in law as it is in life."[48]

This theorization of inherently coercive circumstances departed from a liberal portrait of autonomous desiring individuals that has underwritten certain conceptualizations of sexual consent. As MacKinnon writes:

Where coercion definitions of rape see power—domination and violence—nonconsent definitions envision love or passion gone wrong. . . . This crime basically occurs in individual psychic space. . . . Coercion definitions, by distinction, turn on proof of physical acts, surrounding context, or exploitation of relative position. . . . The crime basically takes place on the material plane. Accordingly, while consent definitions tend to frame the same events as individuals engaged in atomistic one at-a-time interactions, coercion definitions are the more expressly social, contextual, and collective in the sense of being group-based.[49]

Rape is a "form of aggression" that is responsive to the atmosphere of aggression and violence within which it occurs. As such, rapes can include not only intercourse but also "acts which involve the insertion of objects and/or the use of bodily orifices not considered to be intrinsically sexual."[50] Rather than list what acts and body parts might constitute rape, the *Akayesu* judgment declared that "the central elements of the crime of rape cannot be captured in a mechanical description of objects and body parts."[51] In doing so, the court took a cue from the nearly twenty-year legal feminist effort to revoke the primacy of consent in rape determinations and classify rape as a form of torture prohibited by various human rights instruments.[52] While ICTY, ICTR, and ICC secondary and tertiary documents narrow consent as a defense to rape and sexual violence during armed conflict, *Akayesu* refused to render nonconsent a matter of proof for the prosecution on the grounds that the circumstances of ethnic conflict are inherently coercive, thus alleviating the need to probe questions of individual sexual consent for acts found to be part of larger campaigns that constitute crimes against humanity, war crimes, or genocide.[53]

Subsequent case law has not always followed the framings of consent and coercion present in *Akayesu*. I do not intend the foregoing analysis to be construed as a definitive account of the state of international law. Instead, I spend time on it to provide a historical point of entry for further inquiry into how state protections, race, and sexual violence are cast in feminist international legal scholarship as criminal violations that occur under coercive circumstances—and how these theorizations return back to the United States within sociolegal theorizations about the meaning, harm, and primacy of rape and sexualized violence. At the sites of definitional wrangling over what constitutes rape and sexual violence—which include the parameters of consent and force but also ancillaries like age or marital status—the contestations around rape become apparent and public. Yet these border disputes are not typically construed as political projects that depend on culturally specific framings of gender, race, sex, and violence—or genealogies of feminism that construe the relationship between the "individual" and the "collective" through those framings. Border disputes around the meanings of rape are instead understood as an opportunity for legal clarification. They are evidence of the need for restorative gestures geared toward positioning the law to reflect what women experience in life. The notion that the legal naming of rape and sexual violence primarily serves to align the law with a universal experience or meaning of those terms obscures the law's role in creating legally and culturally recognizable experiences of rape and sexual violence. The internationalization of legal debates about rape and sexual violence make this clear.

In what follows, I consider how debates about the utility of consent and the meanings of coercion, innovated in the midst of genocidal ethnic conflict and resonant with radical feminist models of sex as dominance, bleed into discussion of what constitutes welcome sex in the United States. Contestations over the meanings of sexual consent and coercion traverse civil and criminal, domestic and international theories of wrong, harm, and violation.[54] Welcomeness as a social, legal, or policy threshold for good sex is a transnationally produced and racialized concept. Here again, the notion of the US state as democratic watchdog and the global feminist antisexualized violence project too often depend upon the exclusion of US settler colonial interiors from any analysis of the global, international, or transnational.

Defining Sexual Assault and Harassment

Back to this essay's inaugural scenes, which require that we hold close two unruly things: trans and queer vulnerability to accusations of sexual assault for presenting educational content (examples that are not facially recognizable as assault but are nonetheless named and investigated through that charge) and legal elisions of indigenous rape, where a charge wears the familiar skin of sexualized violation (rape) but is actively excluded from the purview of Title IX. In the first, "sexual assault" stretches and in the second, it vanishes. In the first, entering the classroom or performance hall sets the stage, so to speak, for an unwelcome yes (a subjective calculus, the individual's avowed offense) that can be heard by civil law and its administrative apparatuses. In the second, the objection to rape proper (the utterance of "no" at the moment of violation and later, the lodging of the complaint—and later still, the paperwork filed in court) ultimately cannot. How does this happen? The confusion is the fruit of US law and feminist activism that largely equates sex discrimination, the formal prohibition of Title IX, with rape or sexual assault.[55] The sensationalism of sexualized "violence" covers the more mundane operations of discrimination that include access to educational programs and other nonsexualized sorts of workplace disparities. That equivalence helps mask how empire generates the concepts and terms of sex discrimination as well as how the mechanisms of their administration—bodies of law, civil and criminal—are triggered (or not) by different bodies in different spaces.[56]

Although the meaning of *sexual assault* is mutable, varying across federal and state law, some general sense of the term nonetheless surfaces through sheer accumulation of legal thought and practice. The criminal offense of rape, for example, is generally understood to be nonconsensual sexual penetration by use or threat of force. The US Department of Justice defines sexual assault as "any nonconsensual sexual act proscribed by Federal, tribal, or State law, including when the victim lacks capacity to consent."[57] The phrase "nonconsensual sexual act" typically denotes rape, attempted rape, or fondling—more precisely, penetration; some contact with genitalia, breasts, buttocks, or other "intimate" body part; or exposure of those body parts, which all involve some kind of physical intrusion and bodily proximity. Under general criminal law principles, the presence of a "yes"—whether affirmatively expressed verbally or through performative action or otherwise reasonably implied—has mostly been conceived of as a total defense to a charge of sexual impropriety.[58] As legal scholar Aya Gruber explains, liability for rape under general criminal law principles cannot occur if the partner is honestly believed to be willing, "regardless of the reasonableness of that view."[59] In supposed contrast, unreasonable actions that do not intentionally cause harm generally result in civil liability.[60]

Clean theories of civil and criminal law are complicated by the sometimes civil and sometimes criminal offense of sexual assault and the legal theories of harm that underlie these respective bodies of law—not to mention the range of standards (negligence or general criminal law principles, for example) that apply to shape the meaning of prohibited sexualized violation. Title IX, for example, addresses sexual assault as part of a more comprehensive project of prohibiting sex discrimination in all federally funded education, including K–12. Under the auspices of Title IX, sexual assault is understood as a form of sexual harassment, and sexual harassment comes in two kinds: the infamous "quid pro quo" variety (and here, suddenly, Dr. Hannibal Lecter of *The Silence of the Lambs* fame appears to tell us something nasty about trans desire) or as part of a creation of an environment hostile to learning. More precisely, the US Supreme Court has defined hostile environment sexual harassment as (1) unwanted or unwelcome but also (2) sufficiently severe or pervasive as to (3) have a detrimental impact on the complainant's work or educational experience, (4) so much so that conditions are evident not just to the complainant but to a reasonable person. In other words, there must be an objective dimension to any determination of sexual harassment under law.[61]

That definition prompts the perennial question: What constitutes an objective or reasonable perspective? What matters in these determinations are the social and cultural coordinates through which legal theories are read which animate what kind of violation rape or other forms of sexualized violence might be—how they are justified and classified within civil and criminal jurisprudence. Should rape be understood as any other criminal violation, where the state of mind of the accused matters to its recognition, or as something else, more akin to the civil law precepts that govern sexual harassment, where the goals of the state purportedly align with equality or antisubordination interests? Robin West makes the case that the presence or absence of consent can be a valid criterion for determining whether certain forms of sex are criminal, whereas MacKinnon is less interested in that distinction. As MacKinnon puts it, "An equality standard, such as the one applied in civil law that recognizes that sexual assault is sex discrimination, requires that sex be welcome. For the criminal law to change to this standard would require that sex be wanted for it not to be assaultive."[62]

Because Title IX of the Civil Rights Act is first and foremost an instrument of antidiscrimination law, these controversies and tensions around the legal rationales for prohibiting rape (and in turn, the kinds of state involvement appropriate to the kind of legal problem it presents) have played out under its auspices. Some Obama-era Title IX investigations have taken hesitant, if significant, steps in MacKinnon's direction, all but eliminating the objective requirement for sexual harassment charges.[63] A 2016 investigation at the University of New Mexico concluded, "Title IX requires defining sexual harassment as 'unwelcome conduct of a sexual nature,' including 'verbal conduct' and 'regardless of whether it causes a hostile environment.'"[64] A 2013 University of Montana compliance investigation also defined sexual harassment expansively and subjectively: "Sexual harassment is *unwelcome conduct* of a sexual nature and can include unwelcome sexual advances, requests for sexual favors, and other *verbal, nonverbal, or physical conduct of a sexual nature,* such as sexual assault or acts of sexual violence."[65] These investigations are matched by what Janet Halley describes as "new campus sexual harassment policies [that have shed] 'severity or pervasiveness,' making unwantedness sufficient to show detrimental impact and dropping the detrimental impact and reasonable person requirements. The trend of these incremental rule changes is to invite complaints based on subjective unwantedness alone."[66]

While at the time of this writing, Betsy DeVos's Department of Education mulled proposed changes to the administration of Title IX and actively suspended some of the interpretations of the Obama years, the shifts Halley points to around the social meaning of sex and sexualized violence are in many ways a fait accompli. The thinking on sex has changed—for better and worse, the category of "bad sex" has expanded. The bad sex avalanche of #MeToo, the heightened profile of Title IX as the premier instrument for addressing bad sex on campus, and the dedicated envelopment of sexual assault beneath the banner of sexual harassment have facilitated the kind of allegations present in the classroom and performance scenes with which this chapter begins. Here, the thinking goes: sexual assault is a form of sexual harassment, and sexual harassment is unwanted. No dragon-headed dildos, no trans professors talking anywhere near sex, no queer ones, no lone brown denunciation of white supremacy from the stage—these are about "sex," and none of this is wanted. These are unwelcome, so these are sexual assault. No question or counterargument—Did the student consent to "uncomfortable" learning? Was the content really bad? Could the professor in the class with the picture of the dragon dildo have engaged the class in a more responsible way?—is broachable, much less persuasive, when the analogic counterpart of sexual harassment (understood here as something "unwanted" and "sexual") is rape.[67] The sight of the dragon dildo and the critique of white supremacy delivered through brown femme performance have been declared unwanted, and questions to the contrary are crude, even cruel, denouncements of what we already feel and know: a yes can be unwelcome and within the coercive architectures of the entrepreneurial university, this is incontrovertible.

Activists, scholars, artists, and professional organizations have nonetheless marked the dangers of such an expansive understanding of sexual harassment,[68] while others have uncritically championed these interpretations[69] or questioned whether they ultimately matter.[70] Yet this shift in cultural—and as many worry, legal—knowing itself depends on a selective genealogies of anti–sexualized violence law and organizing that are caught up in liberal definitions and condemnations of only certain breeds of violence. Such genealogies create an atrophic notion of force or power that delimits the meanings of consent and coercion to the site of sex, even as they destabilize and continually offer new interpretations of what sexualized violation and by proxy "sex" actually are. In other words, in the context of sexualized violence, coercion and force by definition do not consider differences in kinds of force or coercion to be anything other than analogic, proof that sexual violence occurred. These elisions allow the unwelcome yes—an individual, exceptional, and subjective condition whose presence signals the existence of sexualized violence—to emerge.

Making the Unwelcome Yes, Part I / The US Sex Wars

If, as Janet Halley writes, "the real vision of emancipation is a world in which women have sex only when they desire or want it," the legal question becomes how to best establish the norm.[71] Halley understands the rise of the unwelcome yes as part of a turn back toward the dominance feminism of MacKinnon.[72] For over forty years, in international legal negotiations, lectures, and law journals, MacKinnon has pressed for an absolute deprivileging of consent in constructing the crime of rape. In her view, an "emphasis on nonconsent as definitive of rape views the crime fundamentally as a deprivation of sexual freedom, a denial of individual self-acting."[73] Yet in war or peace, MacKinnon argues, "the realities of compulsion and lack of accord in sexual interactions overlap and converge," necessitating an "emphasis on coercion as definitive" in establishing the occurrence of rape—a crime she recognizes as one of power and inequality.[74] She continues: "When a sexual incursion is not equal, no amount of consent makes it equal, hence redeems it from being violative. Call it sexual assault."[75]

This genealogy of legal feminist thought tracks a conceptual merger of sexual harassment with rape/sexual assault (see chapter 1) through the enduring feminist concern with the sort of force or coercion that is typically prerequisite for any charge of rape or sexual assault. In and out of the realm of sex, force or coercion has been theorized as physical (violence visited on one's person or others or threat of such), economic, psychological (manipulation, threats), and circumstantial (involving, for example, drunkenness) or one born of perceived structural inequality (age, disability, and other status categories or situations thought to incapacitate, including war). What force is sufficient to preclude meaningful consent is the question, and it remains a live one. The predominant feminist genealogy of sexual harassment and rape/assault in the United States takes up the relationship among force or coercion (more broadly, "violence"), sex, and gender. This route stages contemporary grapplings with the scope and meaning of sexualized violence as foremost a rehashing of the US sex wars, a rehearsal of the same thirty-year-old fights by some of the same feminists. Emily Bazelon's 2015 *New York Times Magazine* piece "The Return of the Sex Wars," for example, tracks Title IX controversies on campus through this narrative arc. There, Halley cautions against "treating sex exclusively as a danger from which women should seek the authorities' protection," while MacKinnon urges everyone to acknowledge that "women [live] in a state of subordination . . . with pornography, sexual harassment, prostitution, child sexual abuse, domestic violence and rape as core elements in male domination" and mobilize state power to correct it.[76] Then and now, in US domestic and international jurisprudence, Halley and MacKinnon embody ideological positions that support and are supported by particular configurations in law—in matters of sex, what constitutes force, consent, or coercion?[77]

From this vantage, there are only variations on a theme. The critical roots and routes of this thinking locate the fight on particular terrain: changing the definition of consent, force, or coercion changes the relationship of the state to sexualized violence, including sexual harassment. How criminal understandings and civil understandings of rape/sexual assault produce and differentiate who will be in a protective relationship with the state (for all of the many problems that entails) and who will be cast beyond it slips from view. Crucially, Black legal feminist theorists and other women of color interventions (for example, what Angela Harris calls "nuance theory," in which Black women's experience, including legacies of enslavement, are simply construed as variations of white women's experience) fall from the record.[78] What falls away, too, are how Global South (including decolonial antirape) activisms, themselves part of larger liberation projects, are used to create and justify social and legal understandings of sexual consent, coercion, and welcomeness in the Global North. What falls away is how the genealogy of the sex wars eclipses and erases other contemporaneous narratives of force and coercion that depend on global distributions of violence that are not limited to the arena of "sex."[79]

Elsewhere, US feminist legal theorists are quick to note that sexual harassment does not have to be sexualized.[80] The legal definition of sexual harassment, adopted by the Supreme Court in *Oncale v. Sundowner Offshore Services, Inc.* (523 US 75, 1998), provides that legal prohibitions against sexual harassment simply mean that "it is unlawful to harass a person . . . because of that person's sex," noting expressly that "harassment does not have to be of a sexual nature." This repositioning of sexual harassment as a gendered labor issue and not solely a sexual one loosens the chain of conceptual conflations that culminates in the equation of sexual harassment with rape or sexual assault. Yet staying within the bounds of law, treating its self-diagnoses—its self-help—as definitive statements of its practice, intellectual terrain, and operations narrows desire to what is sexualized. Limiting desire to what is already sexualized loses what women of color and indigenous feminisms and queer/trans studies and activisms insist: desire is bigger than "sex." It is rangy, uncontainable, and steeped in the legacies of colonialism, chattel slavery, and cis-heteronormativity. In other words, the question should be how do constrictions and expansions in the theorization of desire map onto and affect theorizations of the force or coercion that results in unwanted or illegal sex (while on the way making an idea of sex)? In the case of Title IX, what vision of the university guides the deployment of those terms?

There are other ways to read law—not to correct it or provide another, totalizing alternative to it but to simply admit (and admit to) something else, something that is obvious even now from the legal record. Following how law shapes gender—who gets to be (or is forced to be) what kind of "woman" per the VAWA, who gets to claim "unwelcomeness" and awaken the machinery of civil rights—makes a small window that lets us glimpse how civil and criminal legal responses to sexualized violence are often only truly distinguishable by *how* they perform mediating work in the service of imperial and settler colonial legacies. In other words, the legal feminist preoccupation in criminal or civil law with broadening force to consider how "psychological, economic, and other hierarchical forms of force—including age, mental and physical disability, and other inequalities, including sex, gender, race, class, and caste [may be] deployed as forms of force or coercion in the sexual setting, that is, when used to compel sex in a specific interaction" is not simply rethinking force to make sexualized violence visible to law.[81] Instead, debates over the scope of what constitutes force are rethinking the meaning of sex and what must be absent from it to make it good. Broadening force can, in other words, fold other violence—settler, capitalist, imperial—into sex and subordinate the whole beneath the state-bolstering strictures of civil rights, human rights, and criminal law. A genealogy of force, consent, and coercion that prioritizes the sex wars alone is (to borrow Frantz Fanon's words) a "history that others have compiled."[82] Recall instead that Blackness, transness, indigeneity, and postcoloniality emerge in part as social historical categories that are produced (and produce whiteness) through a differential, sexualized notion of deviance and danger.[83] What can they teach us about the utility and sociolegal development of words like *welcomeness* as antidotes to the issues affixed to "consent"?

Making the Unwelcome Yes, Part II / Crime, Consent, Civil Rights, and Tribal Sovereignty

Against genealogies of law that culminate in debates about force and sex, or labor and access, we might examine the many namings of what makes up "violence against women" in the eponymous act as a way to surface other epistemological reckonings, ones that agitate against sexualized violence while remaining suspicious of the state, its territorial ambitions and cis-hetero-intimacies. Enter the two Title IXs. The first, part of the 1968 Civil Rights Act, is often reductively couched within the genealogy of the sex wars. The second Title IX, of the 2013 VAWA, is another story entirely, one of settler colonialism and genocide.[84] This is a different genealogy of force and its centrality to sexualized violence. It is in part a story of indigenous feminist organizing to hold the US government accountable for what it has forcibly wrought while enhancing tribal sovereignty.[85] As such, Title IX of the VAWA might be seen as an inheritance of broader struggles for indigenous sovereignty, such as those of the pan-indigenous American Indian movement, that understand "US imperial militarism and US domestic law enforcement as entwined elements of the same power structure."[86] It is also part of contemporary indigenous struggles undertaken by organizations like the Seven Dancers Coalition (Haudenosaunee), the Sacred Circle, and the Cangleska Domestic Violence Program (Oglala) against settler colonialism, carcerality, and sexualized violence. These organizations receive US government funding for programs and also recognize that "under the settler state, government systems are never benign instruments of care."[87] These genealogies and their ongoing effects come into relief when we trace what sexual consent and coercion can mean, and when and for whom they matter.

The Violence against Women Act was originally passed as part of the 1994 Violent Crime Control and Law Enforcement Act—a $30 billion piece of legislation that, as Emily Thuma notes, allocated funds to hire 100,000 new police officers and build 10 billion dollars' worth of prisons across the country. The legislation also applied the "three strikes rule" to a number of federal crimes and terminated funding for prisoners' pursuit of postsecondary education—all while "earmark[ing] unprecedented federal funding for improving the prosecution of sexual and domestic violence as well as providing services for victims."[88] The subsequent changes the 2013 VAWA inaugurated on campuses and tribal lands could be seen simply as illustrative of a carceral feminist creep, a desire to find solutions to sexual problems through paradigms of punishment and criminal logics administered by the state.[89] Yet VAWA's "universal woman" isn't cohesive. It is an amalgam of injuries with different standards of recognition and different remedies all grouped under familiar names: sexual assault, domestic violence, stalking, human trafficking, or campus crime. VAWA's treatment of sexualized violence is a differentiated vision of sexual welcomeness that stems from different theories and genealogies of the relationships among force, sex, and gender.[90] This vision is fitted in the matrix of laws that distinguish campus spaces from tribal ones and actuated by the interplays of civil and criminal articulations of law. These interplays are about whose theorizations of what sexual violence is and whose anti–sexualized violence work speaks for all and whose speaks for some. The focus on sexual welcomeness that some university policies have considered or adopted is undergirded by convolutions in law that trend toward looser and more expansive definitions of what law will recognize as a civil or even criminal "sex offense" on campus, while rape at Indian Nations universities fails to register under the auspices of Title IX, a civil law.

Title IX of the 1964 Civil Rights Act, the Clery Act,
and the 2013 Reauthorization of the VAWA

The 1990 Jeanne Clery Disclosure of Campus Security Policy and Campus Crime Statistics Act (Clery Act) requires institutions of higher education that participate in the federal financial aid program to collect and report crime data to the Department of Education and publicly disclose campus statistics by publishing annual security reports. The 2013 VAWA reauthorization amended the Clery Act to mandate campus reporting for incidents of "dating violence, domestic violence, and stalking."[91] Jacob Gersen and Jeannie Suk understand these additions as a fundamental expansion of the criminal justice system's reach through administrative law and bureaucracy, shifting how the US state interprets its duty to guarantee sexual safety within and beyond its borders.

Because different jurisdictions differ over the definition of crime, the Clery Act has defined what constitutes crime for reporting purposes. The Department of Education's 2014 final rule implementing VAWA's changes to the Clery Act makes no bones about it: "We believe that this makes it clear that all incidents that meet the definitions in [VAWA] must be recorded in an institution's statistics, whether or not they are crimes in the institution's jurisdiction."[92] As Gersen and Suk write, "The bureaucratic reporting regime includes not only crimes but also quasi-criminal or noncriminal incidents that federal regulations define as reportable crimes for Clery Act purposes.... Leveraging crime statistics reporting to require that schools report criminal incidents, even when they are not crimes in that jurisdiction, allows the federal bureaucracy to expand its regulatory reach."[93] Additionally, the Clery Act's definition of "sex offenses" retains lack of consent as an element or essential part of the proscribed violations, but the Department of Education, which administers the law, insists that "all sex offenses that are reported to campus security authority must be included in an institution's Clery Act statistics ... regardless of the issue of consent."[94] In this way, VAWA impacts potential Title IX investigations, opening the door, as Gersen and Suk argue, to "liability for sexual conduct that is called criminal but may not be even a civil wrong."[95]

This expansion, however, is about much more than criminalizing logic per se or ending sexual violence and discrimination. Looking at Title IX of the Civil Rights Act in relation to Title IX of the 2013 VAWA shows how legal constructions—not simply responses—to sexual assault and harassment are mediated by social and institutional relationships that certainly include gender but also federal funding relationships to universities, carceral modes of governance, federal agencies' relationships to Indian Nations universities, and the disavowed but still animating notions of in loco parentis and trust responsibilities that underlie them. Accompanying modulations in the relationships between consent and coercion as they traverse bodies of civil and criminal law function as technologies of racialization and settler nationhood consolidation. For as the 2013 VAWA amends the Clery Act in ways that expand the breadth of what might count as criminal sexual(ized) harassment on campus, the possibility of availing Title IX at Indian Nations universities is nonetheless subject to competing doctrines, theories, and bodies of law. That complex of law not only precludes the recognition of rape or sexual harassment—as if these were temporally fixed and self-evident—but materially changes what those terms mean. Thus laws like the VAWA bring forward not only differential legal treatment of those who experience rape or other forms of sexualized violence but also different understandings of what rape and sexualized violence legally are. Amendments to the Clery Act, which modify how sexualized violation will be understood or recognized, expand what it might mean to be violated on some but—as the opening third scene details—not all campuses and certainly not tribal lands. The takeaway here is not, as a traditional analysis would posit, a failure of law's calibration—the often-recited "discrepancy between female experience and the law's definition of rape."[96] Instead, this analysis evinces how civil and criminal legal precepts operate in settler nationhood through particular and particularly sexualized bodies. These operations of law in turn compromise the utility of legal categories like sex and gender as descriptors of or uncomplicated avenues of redress for that vast and elastic range of abuse.

Title IX of the 2013 Reauthorization of the VAWA

Ruminating on the prevalence of sexualized violence against indigenous women, President Obama deemed it "an assault on our national conscience."[97] Muscogee legal scholar Sarah Deer locates the problem elsewhere: in the dilemmas of federal and tribal sovereignty, where the tolerance for sexualized violence on Indian lands is "a fundamental result of colonialism, a history of violence reaching back centuries," where the dynamic of "intrusion on [indigenous] lands and culture by an external, hostile outsider" is played out "on their bodies and souls rather than on the land."[98] Who gets to talk about what signals (sexual) welcomeness, what fills its shape, and who is merely a population at risk?

Title IX of the 2013 VAWA, subtitled "Safety for Indian Women," recognizes tribal criminal jurisdiction over some instances of domestic/intimate violence regardless of their Indian or non-Indian status, provided that tribes ensure certain enumerated due process protections. The recognition of "special domestic violence criminal jurisdiction" has been framed as a partial *Oliphant* fix because it modifies the US Supreme Court's 1978 decision *Oliphant v. Suquamish Indian Tribe* (435 US 191). Infamously, *Oliphant* held that Indian tribal courts do not have the inherent authority or jurisdiction to prosecute or punish persons who do not have Indian status—in part because of a fear that tribal justice methods would inadequately secure the civil rights of the defendants.[99] However, this extension of the ability to prosecute or punish those of non-Indian status is an uneven extension of criminal jurisdiction to Indian courts. As indigenous activists and scholars have emphasized, Title IX of the VAWA does not allow for the prosecution of nontribal members for crimes beyond domestic violence—crimes like sexual assault, child abuse, human trafficking, or non–intimate partner rape remain beyond its purview.[100] Importantly, the VAWA framework of violence against women describes the harm of domestic or intimate violence as an interpersonal one between "men" and "women."

This is the backdrop against which the events of *Doe v. Haskell Indian Nations University* (266 F. Supp. 3d 1277 [D. Kan. 2017]) unfolded—one of jurisdictional entanglement and sovereign denial. Haskell Indian Nations University is one of thirty-two accredited tribal colleges and universities in the United States. It is federally funded through the Tribally Controlled Colleges and Universities Assistance Act of 1978 and managed by the Bureau of Indian Affairs. In *Doe*, under the theory of the sovereign immunity of the United States, civil redress through formal antidiscrimination legislation (Title IX) is foreclosed: the US government cannot be sued without its consent. Here lies the actual (and not merely feared) failure to extend rights protections, where civil rights are wielded as weapons to deny tribal sovereignty while the erstwhile civil rights of Indian students are outright denied through jurisdictional clashes and gaps, frustrating the promise of full citizenship that civil rights guarantees purportedly provide. If the notion of sexual welcomeness might be construed on campus as the individual negotiation of particular histories of force, the withholding of civil rights denies even that individuated reckoning. Contextualizing Title IX's operations within VAWA lets us catch how competing visions of force, sexual violence, and violation are relationally formed, which in turn contours social understandings of what rape socially and legally is (a civil rights violation? a crime? something else?), what sex is, and who participates in its naming and recognition. What form of government or governance can handle the task of determining proper sexual relations is overlaid and activated by the stories we tell about what we want, what we desire, and what falls in the domain of sexuality proper and what does not.

Remaking the Unwelcome Yes

The stories we tell. The three scenes that inaugurate this chapter map some of the ways that sociolegal ideas about sex and desire create the terms and conditions for sex and sexualized violence to exist and be recognized. They pose a set of deceptively simple questions: What counts as sex or even the sexual—what falls within its orbit? What counts as good sex or good speech or conduct about sex, and how can we tell when it is happening? Rather than dismiss these accounts as sex panics in the first two scenes or failures of law in the second, is there another way to understand these charges of "sexual assault"?

In the case of the trans professor's classroom and the art performance, the objection is not simply that that the actions that occurred were nonconsensual. What students index, however fumblingly, by claiming those incidents in the rubric of sexual assault is a more comprehensive vision of what freedom and safety entail—and they use the idea of sex to advance it. What's invoked is uncertain, but it touches on something beyond consent and coercion frameworks—something about what sex and good sexual and other politics might look like, who may say what and do what to whom and where and when. The impulse is beguiling; it is first and foremost a vision of justice. Yet the language of sexual assault holds sway. The narration is suffused with the language of sexualized violence, sexualized danger. The door shuts on the suffocating room. Meanwhile, at Haskell Indian Nations University, an alleged physical assault cannot be viewed as "properly before" the US District Court. Title IX is no point of entry.

The opening scenes gain social meaning and cohere as individual and collective violation, and are mediated and obscured by settler colonialism and the nation-state through deployments of civil and criminal law. In the first two scenes, consent and welcomeness as diagnostics for sexual assault or sexual harassment consolidate the scene of violence to primarily the individual sexual encounter or series of encounters. The scene of "sex" is the lone agentive site marked by either the presence or absence of "true" consent (whether there was enough or appropriate evidence of consent) or the overt presence of the unwelcome yes—the rupture between act (consent and its fictions) and affect (what one purportedly really felt). But the unwelcome yes in and out of law has depended on more than the proffered vision of gendered sexual vulnerability.

Law matters here. The possibilities it names help secure the social meaning of sexualized violence and, in turn, what availing antisexualized violence law as a site of justice or bare relief can accomplish or foreclose. Here, sexual assault or rape becomes both metaphor and simile for strong feelings of dispossession or exploitation (a single art performance becomes "sexual assault" or viewing the image of a dildo is "like a sexual assault"). It also becomes a catch-all descriptor for a range of sexualized violations (a picture of a dildo isn't interpreted as "sexual harassment" but is named "sexual assault"). What makes these first two scenarios possible is the unwelcome yes—one that places the scope of sexualized violation as an individual encounter or experience that is subjectively either wanted or unwanted, regardless of whether consent was given, enthusiastically or otherwise. What is crucial here is how easily sexual consent as a concept is confined from other forms of consent (the consent to be governed, for example, or consent to the mostly abysmal conditions of graduate student labor and learning), as if what they index had nothing to do with desire, the welcomeness, or unwantedness of the encounter.

Attempting, for a moment, to insert other forms or theories of consent into the discussion is an attempt not to rehabilitate the liberal contractual subject but to fracture it—and to fracture it through the inner workings of the law. Unwelcomeness, unwantedness, consent: what material conditions engender the subjectivities necessary for these affective formations to take hold? Or alternatively, how do racial, imperial, and settler violences unfold in and out of law to shape the possibilities and ideas of welcomeness? Could they be marshaled to shatter a reliance on the individual experience of sex as the language of liberation? Beyond legal technics, what forecloses Title IX at Haskell Indian Nations University is a failure to imagine another kind of unwelcome yes—one that accounts for the brutal histories that led to the management of the university by a federal agency. How might those histories be brought into sharper relief? As legal and social theory and as embodied feeling, the contemporary unwelcome yes, which sets college students in proximity with the war-raped of the Global South, is made possible by the materiality of race, indigeneity, and global capitalism in a postsocialist era. How do we readmit and admit their historical roles—let them in, confess them?

Here is another story. In the 2011 heyday of the Occupy movement, Chancellor Linda Katehi, of the University of California, Davis, infamously permitted campus security to pepper-spray students involved in a campus protest. For Katehi, the university's proximity to Oakland set the stage for a tale of trespass and endangerment. In Katehi's words, "The issues from Oakland were in the news and the use of drugs and sex and other things, and you know here we have very young students."[101] Yet campus innocence, pitched against the racialized threat of always Black and brown Oakland, is not only a matter of protecting an undifferentiated "youth." Katehi justified her actions by stating "We were worried especially about having very young girls and other students [interacting] with older people who come from the outside with knowledge of their record."[102] Katehi feared that unknown "nonaffiliates"—people with no relationship to the university or the town of Davis—would endanger "very young girls" on a campus that apparently knew little of drugs, sex, or "other things." But Katehi also invoked a particular administrative, policy-based fear: "[I]f anything happens to any student while we're in violation of policy, it's a very tough thing to overcome."[103] Here, as Doyle notes, the policy at issue is Title IX,[104] and the conceptual integrity of sex and security blur: "A metonymic chain of associations accumulates (Oakland [Black people], drugs, sex, young girls, older people, outsiders, violation) to bring the Chancellor to her fear: 'older people from outside' interacting with 'very young girls.'"[105] Individual student sexual safety is enacted as violence on the collective student body and the people. For Doyle, this blurring is illustrative of "abuses of power and authority as connected to the shape of sexism on college campuses."[106] I would add is that these abuses of power and authority are subtly and not so subtly assembled through (and assemble) the mutable architectures of desire—who is welcome, when and where—that root and route in and out of law, its bald pronouncements and technical inner workings, in ways that outpace "the shape of sexism" and the rubrics of the security state. The idea of student sex—whether accompanied by a "yes" or "no," whether welcome or unwelcome—rests on an edifice of political decision making and the presumed authority of a land grant university's propertied claims: UC Davis, sits on Patwin lands.

The immediate tableau of police and sex and students and the overwriting of indigenous land claims describe how the specter of sexualized violence might be mobilized in ways that are less than liberatory; this is a comment on how the university wields Title IX to discipline and erase other relationalities. Yet if the language of dangerous sex is how the campus manages protest, it seems worth considering what protest might in turn have to say about "sex." How might we narrate contemporary campus activisms if we keep an eye trained on those whom VAWA separates and places in proximity and how those proximities appear or do not appear in campus organizing work? The social meaning of Title IX depends on the statute's stated imperative to prevent sex discrimination in federally funded education. But it also depends on the matrix of laws, precedent, and legal theories that make Title IX cognizable in a legal system that exists in relation to international law, other bodies of domestic law and jurisprudence, transnational organizing, and its own settler colonial foundations. The social meaning of Title IX depends on the transnational historical contexts that animate its interpretation and enforcement. But importantly, the social meaning of Title IX rests on the conditions that shape the meanings of the terms of law—and how terms like *consent* and *coercion* gain legal meaning through feminist and activist theorizations of such violence.

From this perspective, I turn back to campus protest not to detail a collision with or disciplining of campus protest by "sex" but to imagine campus protest writ large as generating other visions of "sex" and "violence." Another calculus of consent, coercion, and force lies in campus activisms that are coalitional, embedded, embodied, and responsive to the depressingly routine calculations of a university that, as many note, has never been in the service of the "public" in its entirety.[107] This perspective flips the traditional theorization of the unwelcome yes on its head and multiplies it. Keeping with the example of UC Davis, the potential and potentially enthusiastic yes of the students to protest or more with Oakland "outsiders" is unwelcome for the university. This unwelcome yes exists in a space whose racial, settler, and class coordinates render it unpalatable (if not unthinkable) to the university administration. The potential and potentially enthusiastic yes of the students to protest or more with Oakland "outsiders" might make a space where sex and pleasure aren't anathema to serious political work or learning, where decolonial critiques of the word *occupy* might also surface. The challenge of protest is then a proliferation and intensification of what hangs between the image of the university as a site of respite and all that must be overwritten, suppressed, and repressed for the thinnest version of student sexual safety to move front and center to preoccupy the administrative imagination.

Campus protests might then be read alongside the university's production of what Jennifer C. Nash calls the student as "sexual citizen"—steeped in affirmative consent policies, calls for bystander interventions, and fear and liability. This "sexual citizen" is contoured not only by the failures of affirmative consent or welcomeness to secure sexual freedom but by the university's continual amplification and proliferation of sites of vulnerability and risk for those who are expendable (not welcome, not desired).[108] At UC Davis today, the lack of accessible all-gender bathrooms, the persecution of Students for Justice in Palestine, escalating tuition and fees, students' and other campus workers' exploitation, bare-bones "support" for indigenous, gender, and ethnic studies departments and those within them—the list goes on—create structures of value and desirability. These distributions of resources are distributions of desirability and power. They enable a slow, creeping corrosion that consumes what we need to thrive while demanding trust in the benevolence, goodwill, and decision-making capabilities of that which and those who would destroy us. Protest on these and related issues can be authoritative challenges to the state, the family, and the institution as sites of unqualified remedy or haven. They can also be experiments in other forms of relationality, kinships, and solidarities that leave staid versions of the heteronuclear family in the dust. As such, they challenge the organizing logics of "sex" that underpin institutional authority: where those in charge always know what to do and will do the right thing, where the family is the location of love, the university a paterfamilias extraordinaire. The challenge of these protests, then—inchoate and contradictory as they are—might be read productively against the theory of an unwelcome yes that places the scope of sexualized violation as an individualized encounter or even a series of encounters that endlessly circle the failed negotiation or imposition of an act or speech that represents something named "sex."

If we build backward, through the activisms and law that bring us to a critical discussion of welcomeness, the challenge of protest within the political economy of the university may be construed and fostered as an implicit challenge not only to any assumption that sexualized violation could ever be fully cognizable with the adoption of an appropriate legal standard. Protest also challenges (and might further be encouraged to challenge) the idea that "the sexual" itself is not always a concept under construction—that multiple demands springing within and beyond its name don't tell a better truth than the desire for a single meaning. Using campus protest to retheorize the unwelcome yes can be a way to mark the different conditions that produce sexualized violence and its multiple meanings. Retheorizing the unwelcome yes can be a way to intervene on staid interpretations and genealogies of law. Protest can be a challenge to the notion that with enough or the right kind of logic, it will somehow all make sense. Starting there would reemphasize strains of feminist and queer analysis and praxis mostly stricken from the record: ones where sexualized violence and fights against it cannot be cleaved from empire, white cis-heterosupremacy, and a settler state—where pleasure (what is welcome, what is wanted) is staked on those fraught and fought-for grounds.

Epilogue /
Decolonial and Abolitionist
Feminisms and the Work of Rape

I am the history of rape
I am the history of the rejection of who I am ...
I have been raped
be-
cause I have been wrong the wrong sex the wrong age
the wrong skin the wrong nose the wrong hair the
wrong need the wrong dream the wrong geographic
the wrong sartorial I
I have been the meaning of rape.
—JUNE JORDAN, "Poem about My Rights"

First published in the November 1978 edition of *Essence*, June Jordan's "Poem about My Rights" contains no further, explicit mention of rights beyond the initial titular reference. In some ways, this omission might be understood to prefigure and track recent critical work on the subject of rights that looks beyond its language and associations for ways to live together on different terms. That work plumbs the shadows cast by rights regimes to consider how, as Jodi Melamed and Chandan Reddy write, "the very terms and categories that drive and define modern politics—such as rights—constitute the means of racializing human beings in order to differentially (de)value them, as necessary for existent and emergent modes of capitalist accumulation."[1] Rights, in other words, redeem the capitalist order. Their promulgation marks a cut against the violence of the past, a break, a way of saying, "Those ways are behind us." Rights signal the recognition of the individual who can make choices, who can participate. The rights-bearing individual is set against the undeserving: the terrorist and increasingly, again, in Trump's America, the usual subjects/suspects.

Taken globally, the effects intensify. Rights have been vehicles for capitalism's worldwide extension, clearing swaths of land and priming territories and peoples for governance and freedom on its terms. Given this, Melamed and Reddy propose a turn away from "idioms of individual rights to life, capital, or community" and toward the work of social movements that emphasize "collective social existence through the plural form."[2] Doing so, they continue, means respecting other language and others' language, the terms "used by social movements [that] don't sound political-juridical, but more like love, kinship, jubilee, repair, respect, welcome, name, and be free."[3]

Jordan's poem also opens into collective, plural forms of social existence but through historical, temporal, and bodily disorientations that unfold beneath the title's initial, possessive rights claim. In moving as the poem does toward collective livability, Jordan does not relinquish the language of rights—or even individual rights. "My rights" are significant, and they are elaborated as such in a poem whose subject is so often cast as one of the most intimately individuating of all: rape. Jordan's speaker elaborates "the history of rape" as "the history of the rejection of who I am."[4] That rejection itself has another history: "the history of battery assault and limitless / armies against whatever I want to do with my mind / and my body and my soul." These histories nested within histories—histories that span individual experience and collective dispossessions, armies on another's soil—are for Jordan the stuff of rights, and for Jordan, the stuff of rights is ineluctably the stuff of rape. What is—where is—sexualized injury here, and what counts as proof or evidence of it? How do we imagine its contours, probe them without making it all worse? What can rape and Jordan's history of it tell us about rights—what we all have and what is "mine"?

Together, the poem's use of rights and Melamed and Reddy's anticapitalist critique of rights suspend us, put us in a place between the legal language of rights and the work to which it may be put. Both perspectives on rights offer ways and times of knowing—knowing who we are, what hurts, and who or what is responsible for preventing that hurt or alleviating it. Both approaches propose to track the course of injury from beginning to longed-for end. In what remains, I analyze the poem's recourse to the language of rights and consider what to make of it in the present moment, at a time when certain rapes can be understood as violations of international law that contribute and further exploitative world orderings. Here, I bring the work of rape into explicit conversation with decolonial, anti-imperial, and abolitionist feminist frameworks of transformative justice through the poem's supple and transnational meditations on rape and rights. To do this, I take Jordan's poem at its word: the poem about "my rights" requires an account of history that grafts racial violence within the many and geopolitical histories of rape.

Thinking through the Work of Rape

The Work of Rape, as a book and as a concept, is an effort to credit and keep close two things in any discussion of sexualized violence. The first is the legal, geopolitical, and economic contexts that efforts to combat rape and other sexualized violence may enable. The second is how those contexts in turn create the meanings and terms of the recognition of such violation. The racialization of mass rape, for example, describes the ways that international law's uptake of sexualized violence as an affront to humanity justifies and produces certain populations of the violated to be managed and governed through violence. Rearticulations of the relationships between sexual consent and coercion within international law and governance systems instigate the racialization of mass rape by producing states, regions, and peoples who cannot control their sexualized violence. The resulting splits and divisions affect who will receive attention for sexualized violation and the terms by which they will receive it. International law's entanglements with sex, rights, and war produce cartographies of instability and danger in need of external assistance by those states whose integration into global economic and political systems presuppose a degree of sexual stability.

The sexual state form, or the imagined character of the state whose actions become the subject of legal feminist thought and action through their attempts to theorize sexualized legal harm, furthers and helps produce the racialization of mass rape. If, as I discuss in chapter 1, the war in the former Yugoslavia is "ethnic" and genocidal, then so is the rape. The indictment of all states through recourse to international human rights law that elite legal feminists make at this time nonetheless functions, as I discuss in chapter 2, by "silencing" indigenous responses and frameworks of sexualized violation and authority, positioning the liberal state as the site of redress. In addition, as I detail in chapter 3, the racialization of mass rape is supported by changes in international legal liability that figure the rogue individual operating outside of state sanction (essentially the terrorist) as the one who can now be punished and understood as the cause of global violence. The violences of "good" states, empires, and global capitalism take a backseat to the excesses of the "bad" individual and his bad sex.

It is also important to remember that the legal recognition of sexualized violence depends on women of color, decolonial, "queer," Third World feminist, and related if not coincident activisms and justice forums, including those that do not strictly traffic in liberal and capitalist terminologies and endpoints. They have been essential to the advancement and innovations of feminist social and legal knowledge about rape. Turning to them offers less a set of categorical alternatives to standard or statist accounts of sexualized injury and redress and more a window into other genealogies and meanings that include non- and antistatist responses to "male violence." The method of law beyond Law helps bring these conflicted meanings into frame by making the process and production of law (including legal academic writing and activist and other labor) an archive and object of study that is bound to any discussion of what the law does or what rape is. The method pries "law" open beyond its formal declarations to bring these other ways of being and knowing in range of the current controversies that spit from the TV or roil our campuses.

The work of rape and the method of law beyond Law are attempts to follow how racialized conceptualizations of rape in war shape rubrics of sexual autonomy beyond the context of armed struggle. Social and legal knowledge produced from the grounds of war—at times through the erasure of indigenous sexualized violence—travel through feminist theory, legal practice, and organizing. Such activism and advocacy provide a medium through which international and transnational social and legal theorizations of sexual consent and coercion under wartime conditions enter US jurisprudence as disembodied, abstracted debates about the nature of consent and coercion writ large. Often framed by elite feminists as a gendered battle that pits "women" against "men," transnationally produced epistemologies of rape, as I discuss in chapter 4, justify and rationalize expansive understandings of sexual coercion in US civil rights contexts (in particular through the interpretation of Title IX on some college campuses). In the age of women's rights as human rights, the method of law beyond Law is an effort to show some of the ways that empire, colonialisms, and war become the bloodied grounds that grow rape's legal and social meanings.

The concept of the work of rape is an invitation extended with some urgency, which is to say it is a demand (if an unsettled one) open to revision. Whatever forms it provisionally assumes, the work of rape is at its heart a call to imagine sex, pleasure, sexuality, and violation through a framing that does not cede the moral or ethical terrain of sexualized violence to rubrics of individual pleasure and violation or otherwise disappear the political and economic consequences that follow the pursuit and conceptualization of sexualized liberation through international law or its law-like offshoots. Given this context, acknowledging the work of rape is a refusal to "democratize" pleasure through tweaks in the meaning of sexual consent, uncritically promote the wholesale believability of "women," or assume the coherence of the liberal subject in ways that may engage certain theorizations of structural misogyny but not its "darker" entanglements: capitalism, settler colonialism, empire.[5] The disquieting debates and line drawing around the meaning of sexual consent and coercion are partly the consequences of making "sex" a site of liberation through a partial or instrumental engagement with misogyny. Certain debates about the meaning of gender and sexual freedom— including debates about consent and rape by deception, as I discuss in the introduction—can amount to attempts to resolve and absolve empire, militarism, and racial capitalism with the judicious application of more empire, militarism, and racial capitalism.

But there are other ways of doing things, and they (and we) don't have to be perfect to try them.

Abolitionist, Decolonial, Anti-Imperial Feminisms and the Work of Rape

Abolitionist, decolonial, and anti-imperial feminisms and practices have long focused, in the words of Beth E. Ritchie, a founding member of IN-CITE! Women of Color against Violence, on "moving unapologetically to take power back from the mainstream anti-violence movement."[6] Reimagining the antiviolence movement entails recognizing the state as a source of violence and a refusal to accept the state's project of "redistributing pain" through the racist, classist punishment mechanisms of policing and prisons that multiply damage and further the estrangement of the most vulnerable.[7] As trans legal scholar and activist Dean Spade puts it, US prisons are the "serial rapists and murderers."[8] As many have argued, so are the border patrols, black sites, and occupying forces.

In the wake of the ethnic wars and the rearrangement of international law, I propose that reimagining the antiviolence movement also entails engaging with the narratives of progress and civilization that opportunistically justify interventions in the name of women's human rights, relegating certain regions, states, and peoples as "rape prone."[9] The reimagining of the antiviolence movement requires an account of racial capitalism, law, and sex after the ethnic wars of the 1990s. The social and legal concepts of sexual consent and coercion in the United States cannot be separated from the subsequent international systems of law and governance that divvy up the world according to racialized and sexualized danger—where the legacies and continuations of empire and neocolonialism supply the conditions through which feminists on the ground and elite legal feminists coproduce the parameters of sexualized injury and harm. Gendered and sexualized violence, now ensconced in international law as indicia of affronts to the essence of the human, organize global meanings of property and freedom. Those orderings cannot be separated from post-US 9/11 figurations of Muslim women as singularly oppressed that, as Sara Farris has demonstrated, culminate in "saving" Muslim migrant women by funneling them into low-paying, precarious domestic work.[10] They cannot be separated from the complex of US and tribal lawfare that catches indigenous people and sexualized violence in jurisdictional nets that require complex adjudications of tribal sovereignty. They cannot be separated from attempts to justify the now studiedly international carceral and militarized humanitarian regimes that produce migrant populations, stranding queer and trans people of color around the world and in US detention centers at unconscionable risk of psychic, spiritual, and bodily harm. Yet such examples remain staged as paradoxically and mostly resolutely separated from mainstream US antiviolence movements, even as they are still presented as evidence of global "violence against women."

Confronting this epistemological project of sexualized violence leads me to decolonial feminist and queer theorizations of sex itself. Kim TallBear's work on sexuality and kinship describes an approach to sex, kinship, and I think to the recognition of violence that decenters (but does not dismiss) individual experiences of safety and harm. TallBear asks: "Can we resist naming 'sex' between persons and 'sexuality' as nameable objects? Can such disaggregation help us decolonize the ways in which we engage other bodies intimately—whether those are human bodies, bodies of water or land, the bodies of other living beings, and the vitality of our ancestors and other beings no longer or not yet embodied? By focusing on actual states of relation—on being in good relation-with, making kin—and with less monitoring and regulation of categories, might that spur more just interactions?"[11]

TallBear's questions deliver me back to Jordan, her poem, and the idea of rights in the service of gender, sex, and racial freedoms. The poem forges the speaker's rights and body within the living history of bodies like hers: "the wrong people of / the wrong skin on the wrong continent." What they have endured and continue to endure conspires to create the "personal and idio-syncratic / and indisputably single and singular heart" that beats out of time with the many truths that make it.

> I am very familiar with the problems of the C.I.A.
> and the problems of South Africa and the problems
> of Exxon Corporation and the problems of white
> America in general and the problems of the teachers
> and the preachers and the F.B.I. and the social
> workers and my particular Mom and Dad/I am very
> familiar with the problems because the problems
> turn out to be
> me
> I am the history of rape[12]

In the above lines, "I" and its rights are not separated from the problems of the world by something as decisive as a line break but are literally set aslant, slashed from and tethered to the historical narrative Jordan presents and presences in "the meaning of rape": the "I" that the speaker has been.

What Jordan catches and names "I" is enmeshed in histories, dramas, and violences that are not individual slights but collective ones, mass and massive ones sustained and rippling and felt at once as impersonal and interpersonal ones: "who I am / which is exactly like South Africa / penetrating into Na-mibia penetrating into / Angola."[13] Rights here—the speaker's rights—are an entry into feeling histories that are not separate, contained, or otherwise clearly demarcated across temporalities, geographies, or even people. The condensed and singular history claimed by the poem's speaker, the speaker's claim to be *the* "history of rape," is the place of the personal, the intimate, the subjective experience of vast operations of power. Here is an argument about the necessity and the limits of rights. Here is an argument that chafes when we hone our attention to the moment of felt violation and seek to corral it too neatly into the confines of consent or coercion. Thinking only within those constrictions means we have already lost the fight. The right for the speaker to "do what I want to do with my own / body"—what is passionately claimed—meets its limit in the many pasts that conspire to frustrate the ability of the speaker to assert them and yet nonetheless compose the history of what the speaker *is*. How does this brush up against law, consent, and coercion—enflesh the terms and fill them with blood?

If rape is so often pitched as an indelible mark, a not-getting-over, then Jordan's speaker knows there are things that some people are not permitted to *not* get over. "What / in the hell is everybody being reasonable about" the speaker asks as they list the brutal legacies of colonialism and empire in Africa, when "back in 1966 the C.I.A. decided that they had this problem / and the problem was a man named Nkrumah so they / killed him and before that it was Patrice Lumumba / and before that it was my father on the campus / of my Ivy League school." The intimacies and desire work that regimes of empire and gender/sex produce are a part of being "the wrong people of / the wrong skin on the wrong continent." The father says the speaker "should have been a boy," the mother pleads "plastic surgery" for the speaker's nose and braces for their teeth.[14]

We could add to the speaker's list, include indigenous land seizures and eliminations and the millions of queer and trans slights and killings, death in prisons, death at the borders, wars across the Middle East, all of which bring us, again and again, to the streets. We could also emphasize what keeps the fight alive. Protests, including poetic ones, are not only a recognition of injury—and insistence that it be recognized—but part of that old persistent desire to be otherwise.[15] Protests are surely, to follow José Esteban Muñoz in another context, "an invitation to desire differently, desire more, desire better."[16] Protests are also conflicting, conflicted, and difficult because what we want is never singular or stable but conflicting, conflicted, and difficult—no law could name it—because it is steeped in forms of pleasure and exploitation that move and change. What meaning or vision of rights grounds there?

Chandan Reddy and Jodi Melamed acknowledge the tangle of what we want and what we get through the medium of rights in the following way:

> We cannot not want rights, as Gayatri Spivak says. Yet we *can* not want the differential uses of individual rights that structure the asymmetries of advanced neoliberal racial capitalism and give impunity to its violences. Efforts to separate what rights are from how capitalism, nationalism, liberalism, and colonialism define them have always been a robust part of Black, Indigenous, migrant, third world, peoples' and antipoverty movements. For scholarship to untangle these collective and radical uses of

rights from the capitalist uses of liberal rights abstractions, we have to grapple with *the elitism of our politics of political knowledge*.[17]

In the divided world, law and rights matter. They move us, and sometimes that is the best move because it is the only move: to pivot, to change the narrative. To thicken the plot.

What I have tried to suggest with the work of rape is that "the elitism of our politics of political knowledge" is not just about a de facto condemnation of law, certain tactics or "strategies," or the knee-jerk liberal trick of meeting gendered and sexualized injustice with more punishing law (or simply more law), but about two related and more foundational forms of presumption. The first presumption: ontoepistemologies of sexualized violence that follow Western and Anglo-American legal models of violation are the inevitable or only "practical" modes of assessing the meanings and effects of sexualized violence. The second: what those particular traditions name as sexualized violation can be addressed through that delimited language of rights. Even those shallow accounts of sexualized violence that such law purports to address cannot be fully located within its analytic terms. In that view, law's inner operations and wide-ranging connections—its histories, processes, and embeddedness in other legal discourses and global social systems, including the many systems of international law—remain stubbornly out of frame.

Rape and other forms of sexualized violence cannot be transparently, eternally defined because they are not isolated from the variegated and divided world. "A" gendered universal subject of international law is fractured at once in its formation and by its uptake and interpretation in the many sites in which its summoned. The invocation of genocidal rape in the Balkans and its attempted prosecution in the ad hoc tribunal does a different work in its geopolitical and historical moment than, for example, the prosecution of the genocidal rape of the Maya in Guatemalan national courts. The work of rape is after a queer geopolitics that recognizes how the received postcolonial forms of state, nation, and region are engaged by feminists or other activists in ways that accrue different value or possibility through their historical contexts. In their various pursuits, these engagements change their relationship to empire or colonialism and/or resonate beyond them—what law and law-like structures and some versions of feminism would nevertheless present as a part of the same "arc" toward global gender justice.

I follow a queer methodological philosophy to elaborate the epistemologies and processes that enable these divergent accounts of rape. I use the method of law beyond Law because queerness, as Jasbir Puar writes, "challenges a linear mode of construction and transmission: there is no exact recipe for a queer endeavor, no a priori system that taxonomizes the linkages, disruptions, and contradictions into a tidy vessel."[18] My method shows Law as possessed by itself, ventriloquized by precedent, but also cracked by its assembly of facts—the knowledges that come from other times and imagine other pasts, presents, and futures.

If we wreck the idea of sex as an object and distort the genealogies that center the liberal individual alone as the narrator of injury and redress, if we follow TallBear and INCITE! and read Jordan through them—in other words, if we prioritize a collective and relational knowledge of injury and "sex"—then perhaps we might find some of rights' other meanings through the work of rape.

The End and the Work of Rape

Here is how the poem ends.

> I have been the problem everyone seeks to
> eliminate by forced
> penetration with or without the evidence of slime and/
> but let this be unmistakable this poem
> is not consent I do not consent
> to my mother to my father to the teachers to
> the F.B.I. to South Africa to Bedford-Stuy
> to Park Avenue to American Airlines to the hardon
> idlers on the corners to the sneaky creeps in
> cars
> *I am not wrong: Wrong is not my name*
> My name is my own my own my own
> and I can't tell you who the hell set things up like this
> but I can tell you that from now on my resistance
> my simple and daily and nightly self-determination
> may very well cost you your life

As Jordan's speaker knew, something has to give for the bone-bred knowledge "*I am not wrong: Wrong is not my name*" to transmute into the insistence of a name that is "my own my own my own." Something has to end for that "own name," which is "my resistance my simple and daily and nightly self-determination" to also be understood as a response to the sum of the interactions and histories that preceded and formed that name.

In one reading, a fairly straightforward argument about consent takes center stage. The speaker does not consent to the web of relations that conspire to leave her vulnerable to "the hardon / idlers" or the "sneaky creeps in / cars" or what justifies the "protections" and rejections of parents, the FBI, the teachers that make her "wrong"—what otherwise creates the conditions of her unfreedom. The speaker does not consent to these arrangements of bodies, risks, and desires that leave her unable "to do what I want / to do with my own body." The poem could be thought to end in the consolidation of the autonomous I and its will to power.

Yet the injury here is diffuse, prolific, and always proliferating: risk and autonomy are twinned, and each summons each. The "hardon / idlers" and "sneaky creeps" emerge from the thicket of antirelations that at once give the speaker "her own body"—the fiction of the "I" composed in part by the threats external to it—and would nonetheless cost the speaker her life. What becomes of the hardon idlers and sneaky creeps? Are they forever locked in their descriptive cages or are they subject to the violences that put them on corners and in cars, unknowable here but perhaps not so far removed from the "problem of white America," the CIA, and corporations that so plague the speaker?

Mobilizing the work of rape as an analytic is an act of solidarity with the transformative justice aims of many decolonial, abolitionist, and anti-imperial feminisms. At its most basic, transformative justice, as Mia Mingus writes, requires us to "respond to violence without creating more violence."[19] Transformative justice "acknowledges that we must work to end conditions such as capitalism, poverty, trauma, isolation, heterosexism, cis-sexism, white supremacy, misogyny, ableism, mass incarceration, displacement, war, gender oppression and xenophobia if we are truly going to end cycles of intimate and sexual violence."[20] Following Mingus and many others, it must be a "we" that addresses those many pasts and a "we" that subtends the speaker's rights claims. This "we" is provisional, common, and constantly overextending itself in an "excessive reach,"[21] yet attentive to the "unaligned geographies of difference" that "name how actors from different social and structural locations engage in collective political action, and how they account for and negotiate power differentials."[22] The question and challenge that remains is how "to connect incidences of violence to the conditions that create and perpetuate them."[23] For transformative justice initiatives, thinking through the interrelations of violences is essential work.

Such a commitment might move us to read the speaker's refusal to "consent" as a product of the histories summoned in the poem—all of them and then some. Such a commitment might seek out where the poem opens to knowledges that include and extend past the fact of the day-to-day oppression experienced by the speaker as a part of the African diaspora. In this way, the poem might make a path out of liberal rights (a path made out of rights) through a collectivization of consent's many histories and temporalities. Further, locating Jordan's Black feminism within the Black radical tradition,[24] the poem might be read to avow Édouard Glissant's call "to consent not to be a single being." After all, "genesis," as Fred Moten writes, "is dispersion."[25] The speaker might be thought to refuse the received histories and genealogies of vulnerability, the array of injuries, the layers and layers of them, that position the speaker as "the problem" and put everyone and everything in the poem in harm's way. The refusal might make a path by summoning and situating the histories of sexualized violence in genealogies that are not Western liberalism's or "a" feminism's alone. This path, where subjective experience is abstracted into political value claims (into rights), might veer, disperse, even fade away when routed through the histories of labor, property, race, and indigeneity—of the militarized exploitation of so many beneath multiple regimes of dominance and extraction, including settler empire. What is force, what is welcomeness, what is consent? Who is desirable? Who is suspect? Where and when is it all right to be touched? Who gets to touch whom with impunity? What kind of person wants sex on the street, changes their sex, stays out all night? What makes a state "rape-prone?" What turns numerically significant numbers of rape into socially and legally recognized mass rape? When does the international community care about the rape? What kind of sex is okay? Is this even sex? The poem's claim to rights might become a series of doors opening or otherwise a way to imagine unfolding connections in or out of law—actions and relations, not destinations to arrive at or things to have that invariably guarantee an outcome, like an ace up a sleeve. To follow rights in this way is to pursue a horizon of perpetual conflict.

As the Santa Cruz Women against Rape wrote in 1977, "We do not believe that rape can end within the present capitalist, racist, and sexist structure of our society."[26] They knew and they passionately argued that rape was a "tool used against Third World people" and that prisons "are used to keep all Third World people down." More than forty years later, the entanglements of antirape organizing and international law heighten the stakes and elaborate them. Now, gender and sexual justice are routinely imagined through unacknowledged and disavowed conditions of neocolonialism and empire in the heart of war. Appeals to states and the international law and governance for redress have ramified in stunning ways. The work of rape is one way to retheorize the scope, focus, and meaning of the mainstream anti-violence movement in this time of international justice as a means of seizing power from it. To do so might very well, to rephrase Jordan, cost us certain kinds of life, but these are ways of knowing and not-knowing that we might learn, together and again and again, how to no longer desire.

Notes

Introduction

1. The "Dear Boy" column in *Sassy* was a running feature where indie rockers like Thurston Moore, Jay Mascis, Mike D, Dean Ween, Billy Corgan, and Iggy Pop gave life advice in response to readers' questions. Some of it was surprisingly good, and some of it was unsurprisingly awful.

2. See Engle, "Calling in the Troops."

3. Engle, *The Grip of Sexual Violence in Conflict*, 7, 15. See also Engle, Miller, and Davis, *Anti-impunity and the Human Rights Agenda*.

4. Butler, *Bodies That Matter*, 228.

5. Quoted in Ferber, "Judith Butler on the Culture Wars."

6. Here, I draw on C. Riley Snorton's formulation of race as "the history of historicity" to plumb the relationships between self and history. Snorton, *Black on Both Sides*, 8–9. I also write with Kadji Amin's question in mind: "Could *queer* be rendered lively, then, by an engagement with its *multiple* pasts, by a re-animation of its dense affective historicity, rather than only by a future of continual modification

by something else?" (Amin, "Haunted by the 1990s," 180). *The Work of Rape* is a recent, materialist history of the many, forgotten grounds that grow *queer*, its pleasures and pains, its terms—shame, transgression—and what Amin would term its "affective histories." It is a work "haunted by the electric 1990s convergence, under the banner of *queer*, of same-sex sexuality, political urgency, and radical transgression" (185). But it is also *possessed* by "ethnic" warfare, mass rape, and the geopolitical earthquakes that gave us the ascension of US superpower through global racial capitalism and an enlivened international law. These are the material contexts that enable and underlie some of the affective registers of *queer*.

7. Morgan, *"Partus sequitur ventrem"*; Hartman, *Scenes of Subjection*; Feimster, *Southern Horrors*; Rosén, *Terror in the Heart of Freedom*; McGuire, *At the Dark End of the Street*.

8. A standout engagement would be Williams, *The Divided World*. Another would be Falcón, *Power Interrupted*. Falcón examines how by 2001 intersectionality became a key organizing rubric in the UN agenda against racism. Falcón notes that the radical politics and organizing of antiracist feminists occurred in the UN forums dedicated to racism, which she argues "offered a more strategic context for the activists I interviewed than the forums based on women" (5). *The Work of Rape* might help explain why. Feminist legal studies work in the postcolonial tradition also provides productive frameworks for thinking through the relationships between human rights, sexuality, and governance. See Kapur, "Human Rights in the 21st Century"; Kapur, *Erotic Justice*.

9. Melamed and Reddy, "Using Rights to Enforce Racial Capitalism."

10. This included, as Monisha Das Gupta and Lynn Fujiwara note, "sweeping reforms that engineered systemic changes to the way immigrants gained access to public assistance, due process, and established mandatory and expedited removals. . . . The 1996 triad of laws—Personal Responsibility and Work Opportunity Reconciliation Act (PRWORA), the Illegal Immigration Reform and Immigration Responsibility Act (IIRIRA), and the Antiterrorism and Effective Death Penalty Act (AEDPA)—passed within months of each other." Das Gupta and Fujiwara, "Law and Life," 4.

11. United Nations, "Framework of Analysis for Atrocity Crimes," 1.

12. Fredman, *Comparative Human Rights Law*, xxxiii. The *human* of human rights is aptly described by Sylvia Wynter and Katherine McKittrick as "our present referent of the bourgeois mode of the subject and its *conception* of the individual, that of the *concrete individual* human subject" (Wynter and McKittrick, "Unparalleled Catastrophe for Our Species?," 47).

13. This analysis is informed by work that links racial subjectivity to property regimes and formations, particularly the notion that possessive ownership as a legal justification for property manifests in "the materialization of abstractions in the subjectivities of the owner and owned, colonizer and colonized" (Bhandar, "Property, Law, and Race," 205). See also Best, *Fugitive's Properties*; Bhandar,

Colonial Lives of Property; Ferreira da Silva, *Toward a Global Idea of Race*; Harris, "Whiteness as Property"; and Lowe, *The Intimacies of Four Continents*.

14. I refer to the end of the Cold War to mark the advent of particular international legal systems, but am informed by work in Asian American Studies that complicates the periodization and significance of the Cold War. See Baik, *Reencounters*; and Yoneyama, *Cold War Ruins*.

15. Arvin, Tuck, and Morrill, "Decolonizing Feminism."

16. Batha, "Yazidi Girls Sold as Sex Slaves."

17. I use the term *sexualized violence* to emphasize the instability of the category and as a way of yoking together separate legal concepts like sexual assault and sexual harassment. This accomplishes two things. First, it emphasizes the historical blurring between the two concepts and the instability of the "sexual" as category, which I discuss more fully in chapter 4. The term *sexualized violence* also more fundamentally comments on the opacity of the harms—these are not settled or obvious or eternal. I considered using "sexualized violation" instead of violence, but found this to be a version of the problem of expecting changes in language to accomplish the sorts of epistemological heavy lifting that the broader argument makes.

18. Brockes, "#MeToo Founder Tarana Burke."

19. Phipps et al., "Rape Culture, Lad Culture and Everyday Sexism," 1. See also Buchwald, Fletcher, and Roth, *Transforming a Rape Culture*.

20. Brownmiller, *Against Our Will*.

21. Rodríguez, "Keyword 6," 120.

22. MacKinnon, "Where #MeToo Came From."

23. MacKinnon, "#MeToo Has Done What the Law Could Not."

24. MacKinnon, "Where #MeToo Came From."

25. Freedman, *Redefining Rape*, 2.

26. Consider, for example, how MacKinnon harnesses #NiUnaMenos in Argentina to #MeToo alongside Veronica Gago's account of #NiUnaMenos and the "International Feminist Strike." In Gago's account, "feminism becomes more inclusive because it is taken up as a practical anti-capitalist critique" (Gago, *Feminist International*, 45).

27. MacKinnon, "#MeToo Has Done What the Law Could Not."

28. Suk, "'The Look in His Eyes,'" 202.

29. Davis, "Rape, Racism and the Capitalist Setting," 40.

30. Davis, "Rape, Racism and the Capitalist Setting," 42, 45.

31. Deer, *The Beginning and End of Rape*, x.

32. Quoted in Hanssens et al., "A Roadmap for Change."

33. Quoted in Hanssens et al., "A Roadmap for Change."

34. Abu-Odeh, "Holier Than Thou?" See also Al-Ali, "Sexual Violence in Iraq."

35. Abu-Odeh, "Holier Than Thou?"

36. Early US historian Sharon Block notes that the *Oxford English Dictionary* locates the original use of the term *rapist* to the last quarter of the nineteenth

century, "when a United States newspaper referred to a 'nigger' rapist" (Block, *Rape and Sexual Power in Early America*, 244). Rape has long been used, as Block and numerous other scholars have observed, as a signal of social transgression and a project of national and cultural consolidation. But it has changed since the 1990s: changes in the recognition and meaning of sexualized violence reflect and enact global changes in land, changes in capital, changes in fortune.

37. Gupta, "Orientalist Feminism Rears Its Head in India."

38. Reddy, *Freedom with Violence*, 17.

39. Reddy, *Freedom with Violence*, 17.

40. As Wendy Brown writes, "The viability of a radical democratic alternative to various political discourses of domination in the present is not determined only by the organization of institutional forces opposing that alternative but is shaped as well by political subjects' desire for such an alternative" (Brown, "States of Injury," xi).

41. Here I follow Nadje Al-Ali, who cautions against overly simplistic analyses of "root causes" of sexual violence that pit "culture" against "structure": "dichotomous approach—focusing on patriarchal cultural attitudes and practices on the one hand and imperialist policies and neoliberal economics on the other—is unhelpful and more reflective of specific, and often quite divergent, positionalities rather than the complex empirical realities we are facing as activists and academics" (Al-Ali, "Sexual Violence in Iraq," 14).

42. See Angela Harris's "nuance theory," which I discuss in more detail in chapter 1. Harris, "Race and Essentialism in Feminist Legal Theory."

43. See Hong, *Death beyond Disavowal*; and Reddy, *Freedom with Violence*.

44. Hong, *Death beyond Disavowal*, 64. Thinking about incommensurable forms of sexualized violence within women of color and queer/trans of color traditions helps account for what is called "difference" without reifying an idea of the norm or otherwise temporally fixing that "difference" as static, unyielding, locked in an eternal meaning, or uncritically valorized as progressive. See Reddy, *Freedom with Violence*; Amin, *Disturbing Attachments*; and Chu and Drager, "After Trans Studies."

45. The ad hoc tribunals for Yugoslavia and Rwanda were the first of their kind since Tokyo and Nuremberg. They were followed by the 1998 establishment of the world's first permanent international criminal court with the jurisdiction to prosecute atrocity crimes, including crimes against humanity, genocide, and war crimes. See chapter 1.

46. Transnational feminisms consider the circulation of ideas and social practice on a global scale through attention to gender diversity—to inequalities and commonalities produced by late capitalism in specific historical (and not solely national) contexts. I use the term in appreciation of Ranjoo Seodu Herr's insistence that transnational feminisms (or feminist inquiries or activisms that occur at the supra-national level) must be in allegiance with Third World and indigenous feminisms. I discuss the impact of the work of rape on transnational feminisms more fully in in the following chapters. See Herr, "Reclaiming Third

World Feminisms." See also Blackwell, Briggs, and Chiu, "Transnational Feminisms Roundtable"; and Kaplan and Grewal, *Scattered Hegemonies.*

47. Halley, "Where in the Legal Order Have Feminists Gained Inclusion?," 3.

48. Halley et al., preface to *Governance Feminism*, xii.

49. Halley et al., preface to *Governance Feminism*, ix. See also Karen Engle's careful and recent publication, *The Grip of Sexual Violence in Conflict.* That work tracks the creation of "common-sense" understandings of rape that rely on gendered tropes of innocence and demands for carceral redress, cast women as vulnerable and without the capacity to be perpetrators of violence, and essentialize ethnic groups as especially "shamed" or even "torn apart" by the experience of sexualized violence. In contrast, *The Work of Rape* begins, but does not end, with the entrance of rape into the halls of international law. It does not keep the problematic of war rape locked behind those doors or in the spaces of intrafeminist fights. Instead, building on women of color, queer, and trans of color critique, and decolonial critiques of racial capitalism, *The Work of Rape* searches through the connections between rape in conflict and rape on campus and examines how they are enacted and sustained by the ever-shifting abstraction of rape. I do this by tracking the theorizations of sexual consent and coercion—how they are made— that would bind women together in global sisterhood, even as they reorder the relationships between peoples and states through the mechanisms of international law and the charge of atrocity crimes. *The Work of Rape* does not contend that "rape" simply imposes First World feminism onto Third World locales. It does not argue that Western framings of rape otherwise "distract" from economic or developmental critiques advanced by some sectors of the feminist Global South. Instead, it figures the formulations of rape developed in this moment as racial, economic, and geopolitical management. By this I mean that rape as an abstraction holds the space for a renegotiation of the histories of imperialism and settler colonialism. It manages these histories through the grafting of sexualized violence onto mass international violations like genocide, war crimes, and crimes against humanity. The transformations in the meaning of rape wrought there matter here, where I write from within the United States. They matter now.

50. Mackinnon, *Feminism Unmodified*, 50.

51. To approach governance feminism as "dominance feminism" versus "the rest" risks flipping and reenacting the dominance feminist script, leaving Third World feminisms and other activism in a relation of acute victimization. They are cast as either perpetually at the mercy of authoritarian feminist theory from the Global North or accepting of its postulates because they are at best misinformed. For an account of law as a site of subaltern discursive struggle, see Kapur, *Erotic Justice.*

52. The group Las Madres de la Plaza de Mayo is a case in point. These mothers defied the military dictatorship to publicly assemble and protest after their children were "disappeared" by the Argentinian state during the so-called Dirty War (1976–83). As I discuss in chapter 2, the Madres influenced the development

of regional feminisms in Latin America. Yet in the past, the Madres have rejected feminism as a "bourgeoisie" distraction but have nonetheless participated in large-scale regional feminist gatherings (Encuentros Feministas), theorized and agitated on the problem of domestic violence, and even traveled to the International Criminal Court negotiations in Rome only to be thrown out for disruption. The Madres' president, Estela Barnes de Carlotto, attended the ICC negotiations in an effort to have forced disappearances codified in the Rome Statute as a crime against humanity. Once there, the Madres refused financial compensation and exhumation of bodies and called the offer a "betrayal" because it would legally stop the dictatorships' disappearances from being considered ongoing crimes. See Glasius, *The International Criminal Court*, 80. The Madres had "no faith" in proceedings that the assumed the legitimacy of the Argentine state and made their disapproval known when they stole into "the plenary hall, unfolded a banner reminding the delegates of the unresolved plight of Argentina's 30,000 'disappeared' political prisoners and disrupted the speech of the Argentinian justice minister. Eventually, they were forcibly led away by . . . uniformed guards." Howe, "The Madres de la Plaza de Mayo," 43.

53. Scholarship within feminist international relations has largely focused on analyses of rape as a weapon of war with a focus on states and the international governance order. An organizing question for this scholarship is why and how rape becomes a feature of armed conflict. One strand of this literature attempts to discern war rape's place in what Elisabeth Wood calls a "typology of political violence" (Wood, "Rape as a Practice of War"), where social and structural conditions create the opportunity for the practice of sexualized violence and "the fulfillment of base, individual desires or collective 'mythology'" (Meger, *Rape Loot Pillage*, 9). See also Kirby, "How Is Rape a Weapon of War?"; and Wood, "Variation in Sexual Violence during War." Another camp tends to view rape during warfare as a strategy of violence like any other. See Dolan, "War Is Not Yet Over"; and Leatherman, *Sexual Violence and Armed Conflict*. An incipient body of work explores international security and gender violence in feminist analyses of political economy. See True, *The Political Economy of Violence against Women*; and Meger, *Rape Loot Pillage*. Another emergent strand of research calls for inquiry into "how the imaginary demarcation of the 'right' bodies to be protected manifests itself in particular racial, national and gendered lines, both in scholarly work and in policy-making." See Drumond, Mesok, and Zalewski, "Sexual Violence in the Wrong(ed) Bodies," 1147. In contrast, *The Work of Rape* brings the methods and subjects of queer of color critiques, transnational (including decolonial) feminisms, and scholarship in racial capitalism to bear on the notion of sexualized violation and how the idea of sexual injury is formed through the operations of law.

54. Queer of color critique is not often engaged by scholars who describe the import of sexualized violence within international law in terms of how it might activate state obligations to end it. See Eriksson, *Defining Rape*. Queer of color critique and racial capitalism are not brought to bear on historical accounts of

sexualized violence, which often posit rape as transhistorical (meaning the act or violation is evident) and also context dependent (meaning the rationales and causes of it may vary). See Heineman, *Sexual Violence in Conflict Zones*.

55. Queer of color critique, positioned as an inheritance of women of color and indigenous feminisms, springs from a "founding engagement," as Roderick A. Ferguson writes, "with the contradictions inherent in liberalism" (Ferguson, "Queer of Color Critique," 18). See also Tompkins, "Intersections of Race, Gender, and Sexuality," 173. In these historical and materialist tellings, US civil rights and related forms of governance become a key ideological component for the reproduction of US state rule. This embrace of civil rights shored up a state rocked by radical, antinationalist, anticolonial, and antipatriotic organizing across a variety of fronts during the long civil rights movement. Such rights extensions and recalibrations are not simply an imposition or an ending. They transform the terrain and meaning of racial struggle, creating new terms, conditions, and applied meanings that are also sites of subject to seizure, appropriation, or outright rejection.

56. Reddy, *Freedom with Violence*, 29. Again, this is not to say that gender and sexuality reference ahistorical or static particularities but to suggest that as contested sites of social, political, and legal meaning—not simply referents for individual or group "identity"—they can have something to tell about how power and capital operate through "difference."

57. Reddy, *Freedom with Violence*, 17.

58. In this way, *The Work of Rape* draws inspiration from queer work that seeks to globalize race, racism, and racialization in relation to queer bodies and capitalist regimes of value production. See Amar, *The Security Archipelago*; Liu, *Queer Marxism in Two Chinas*; Rao, *Out of Time*; Savcı, *Queer in Translation*; and Shakhsari, *Politics of Rightful Killing*.

59. Nguyen, *The Gift of Freedom*, 4.

60. Foucault, *The Birth of Biopolitics*, 63.

61. Nguyen, *The Gift of Freedom*, 10.

62. Atanasoski, *Humanitarian Violence*, 6.

63. Atanasoski, *Humanitarian Violence*, 6.

64. As Jennifer Suchland notes, academic treatments of transnational feminism often do not consider the second world. That "lack of focus on the second world obscures the fact that it has always been a part of the global" (Suchland, "Is Postsocialism Transnational?," 838).

65. Brown, *States of Injury*, 23.

66. Wynter, "Unsettling the Coloniality of Being/Power/Truth/Freedom," 260.

67. Jakobsen, "Perverse Justice," 25.

68. Jakobsen, "Perverse Justice," 28, 27.

69. Jakobsen, "Perverse Justice," 26.

70. Jakobsen, "Perverse Justice," 26.

71. Williams, *The Divided World*, xv.

72. Williams, *The Divided World*, xxl. In this way, the work of rape supports the advent of what Paul Amar calls the "human-security state," which relies on "humanized security discourse that generate[s] particular sexual, class, and moral subjects . . . to define political sovereignty and to articulate the grammars of dialectically unfolding and internally contradictory forms of power" (Amar, *The Security Archipelago*, 6).

73. Consider efforts by feminists to classify rape and other forms of sexualized violation as decidedly not sex. "Women's rights advocates in the U.S. have made the distinction between sex and rape for a long time. By defining rape and sexual assault as an act of violence and not sex, we are placing the validity in the voice of the assaulted, and accepting their experience as central to the truth of what happened. . . . What we understand by centering the perspective of the assaulted people is that there was no sex happening regardless of the act" (Deb and Mutis, quoted in Puar, *Terrorist Assemblages*, 97).

74. See Reddy, *Freedom with Violence*, 165. Reddy begins this work with the figure of the gay Pakistani immigrant, whose "juridical appearance" must, Reddy argues, be "situated within the context of the neoliberal restructuring of state power" (151). Reddy sees the US legal sphere as "one site where the nation's official records are maintained and reproduced, giving those who seek identity through the law a history of their kin" (165).

75. Williams, *The Divided World*, xvii.

76. Brownmiller, *Against Our Will*.

77. Franke, "Putting Sex to Work," 1161.

78. Puar, *Terrorist Assemblages*, 113.

79. By *internationalist*, I reference individuals and groups operating with allegiance to the umbrella-style governance principles promoted by the UN and affiliated organizations that nonetheless privilege the nation-state as a legitimate and principal locus of political power. Internationalist perspectives provide a stark contrast to transnational feminist approaches to "violence against women."

80. Holland, *The Erotic Life of Racism*, 43.

81. Projects to end sexualized violence can be complicit with a bionecropolitical neoliberalism that Grace Hong recognizes as "an epistemological structure of disavowal" that "*affirm[s]* certain modes of racialized, gendered, and sexualized life, particularly through invitation into reproductive respectability, *so as to* disavow its exacerbated production of premature death" (Hong, *Death beyond Disavowal*, 7).

82. Haraway, *Staying with the Trouble*, 50.

83. Brown, *States of Injury*, 22.

84. Somerville, "Queer Loving," 337.

85. *Loving v. Virginia*, 388 U.S. 1 (1967).

86. Puar, *Terrorist Assemblages*, 118.

87. MacKinnon, "Reflections on Sex Equality under Law," 1288.

88. Spade, *Normal Life*, 5.

89. I develop this method in conversation with legal feminist Martha Fineman's vulnerability theory. Fineman recasts equality-based arguments premised on special group vulnerability in favor of an analytic focused on how institutional and social relationships distribute risk and resilience across different populations and institutions. From this perspective, sexual assault and harassment are not simply problems faced by "vulnerable women" who are failed as a group by patriarchal law and policy. Rather, the laws and jurisprudence of sexual assault and harassment, of discrimination and criminal violation, might instead be approached as aspects of an "institutional system designed to mitigate certain forms of vulnerability." For Fineman, then, vulnerability exceeds the singular subject and is an analytic that travels across individuals, groups, and institutions, asking what ideas, power structures, lives, or institutions are protected and who or what is left at risk. See Fineman, "The Vulnerable Subject," 21; and Marvel, "The Vulnerable Subject of Rape Law," 2042.

90. If race, as Grace Hong writes, calls forth some of "the names for what has been rendered unknown and unknowable through the very claim of totalizing knowledge," what happens if we approach some of the structures that shape "sex"—in this case the legal and social notions of consent, force, and coercion as they pertain to the bounded injury of sexualized violence—with that same humility of (un)knowing? What else sidles up? See Hong, "The Ghosts of Transnational American Studies," 35.

91. Hong, "The Ghosts of Transnational American Studies," 35.

92. Gopinath, *Unruly Visions*, 6.

93. Tompkins, *Racial Indigestion*, 3.

94. Reid-Pharr, *Archives of Flesh*, 6.

95. As Wendy Brown, in a trenchant analysis of Foucault, writes, "The state rises in importance with liberalism precisely through its provision of essential social repairs, economic problem solving, and the management of a mass population: in short, through those very functions that standard ideologies of liberalism and capitalism cast as self-generating in civil society and thus obscure as crucial state activities" (Brown, *States of Injury*, 17).

96. This migration is partly accomplished through the social fact of mass movement in the wake of the 1990s wars. In the aftermath of the Balkan conflicts, migration, emblematized by the reinvigoration of human trafficking as a framework that names sexualized exploitation as "the new slavery," becomes a means of managing the expectations and relation between freedom and low-wage or precarious labor as a piece of capital's ascent. Bodies and "sex" out of place collide with the emergent international law and governance order that is increasingly positioned as the site of authoritative, carceral address. Framed as a problem for the international community through the instruments and specificities of international law, the focus on war crimes shifts and expands outward. Unlike war crimes, crimes against humanity and genocide can occur during "peacetime." See Jaleel, "The Wages of Human Trafficking." See also Chuang, "Exploitation Creep"; Hua, *Trafficking Women's Human*

Rights; Shamir, "A Labor Paradigm for Human Trafficking"; and Suchland, *Economies of Violence.*

97. Halley notes these terminological shifts but does not analyze them. See Halley, "Rape at Rome," 7.

98. *Prosecutor v. Akayesu* (Trial Judgment), ICTR-96-4-T, International Criminal Tribunal for Rwanda, September 2, 1998.

99. *Prosecutor v. Kunarac* (Third Amended Indictment), IT-96-23-PT, International Criminal Tribunal for the former Yugoslavia, November 8, 1999.

100. *Prosecutor v. Kvočka* (Trial Judgment), IT-98-30/1-T, International Criminal Tribunal for the former Yugoslavia, November 2, 2001.

101. *Prosecutor v. Tadić* (Opinion and Judgment), IT-94-1-T, International Criminal Tribunal for the former Yugoslavia, May 7, 1997; *Prosecutor v. Mucić* ["Čelebići Camp"] (Trial Judgment), IT-96-21, International Criminal Tribunal for the former Yugoslavia, November 16, 1997.

102. Foucault, *The Archaeology of Knowledge*, 7.

103. See Philipose, "Feminism, International Law, and the Spectacular Violence of the 'Other.'" This account of the neocolonial origins of law does not fully consider how social movements and local struggle might mark or strategically repurpose it. See Falcón, *Power Interrupted*, for an ethnographic account of how indigenous and grassroots feminists in the Americas critically avail the UN's mechanisms for addressing racial justice.

104. Amar, *The Security Archipelago*; Atanasoski, *Humanitarian Violence*; Farris, *In the Name of Women's Rights*; Murphy, *The Economization of Life*; Puar, *Terrorist Assemblages*; Reddy, *Freedom with Violence.*

105. Ferguson, *Aberrations in Black*; Hong, *Death beyond Disavowal*; Lowe, *The Intimacies of Four Continents*; Melamed, *Represent and Destroy*; Reddy, *Freedom with Violence.*

106. Fischel, *Screw Consent*; Franke, "Theorizing Yes"; Gruber, "Consent Confusion"; Halley, "Rape at Rome"; Tuerkheimer, "Sex without Consent."

107. Duggan, *The Twilight of Equality?*; Gopinath, *Impossible Desires*; Muñoz, *Cruising Utopia*; Puar, *Terrorist Assemblages.*

108. Atanasoski, *Humanitarian Violence*; Rana, "The Racial Infrastructure."

109. Stoler, "On Degrees of Imperial Sovereignty," 133.

110. For a historical account, see Freedman, *Redefining Rape*; Haag, *Consent.*

111. See Rodríguez, "Keyword 6: Testimony." See also Bully Bloggers, http://bullybloggers.wordpress.com.

112. Lowe, *The Intimacies of Four Continents.*

113. UN Convention on the Prevention and Punishment of the Crime of Genocide, 1948.

114. See Musser, "Queering Sugar"; and Musser, "Consent, Capacity, and the Non-narrative."

115. Marx, *Capital*, 257.

116. See also Marcus, "Fighting Bodies, Fighting Words," 389. Marcus offers a critique of the feminist modeling of a rape on a "collapsed continuum." A continuum theory of sexual violence links language and rape in a way that can be taken to mean that representations of rape, obscene remarks, threats, and other forms of harassment should be considered equivalent to rape. Such a definition substitutes the remarks and threats that gesture toward a rape for the rape itself and thus contradicts the meaning of *continuum*, which requires a temporal and logical distinction between the various stages of a rape attempt. In a continuum theory that makes one type of action (a verbal threat) immediately substitutable for another type of action (sexual assault) the time and space between these two actions collapse and again rape has always already occurred.

117. Sara Meger writes that efforts to address wartime sexualized violence produce a political economy through securitization logics—"securitization produces *commodified* objects of security" (Meger, "The Fetishization of Sexual Violence," 149). In contrast, I locate the commodification process as internal to the notion of sexualized violence and rape itself—not simply in the context of war—and within the multitemporal circuits of race and empire.

118. Rosenberg and Villarejo, "Queer Studies and the Crises of Capitalism," 4.

119. Rubenfeld, "The Riddle of Rape," 1375. *State of Israel v. Kashour*, CrimC (Jer) 561/08, Nevo Legal Database (by subscription), July 19, 2010, para. 13, 15.

120. Rubenfeld, "The Riddle of Rape," 17.

121. Tuerkheimer, "Sex without Consent."

122. Dougherty, "No Way around Consent"; Falk, "Not Logic, but Experience"; Ramachandran, "Delineating the Heinous."

123. Fischel, *Screw Consent*, 173.

124. Rubenfeld, "The Riddle of Rape," 1372.

125. Gross, "Rape by Deception," 2.

126. Ratner, "Haifa Transgender Sex Scandal Ends."

127. Gross, "Rape by Deception," 5.

128. Beauchamp, *Going Stealth*, 2.

129. Beauchamp, *Going Stealth*, 9.

130. UN Convention on the Prevention and Punishment of the Crime of Genocide, 1948.

131. Rodríguez, "Racial/Colonial Genocide," 810.

132. Rodríguez, "Racial/Colonial Genocide," 810.

133. Mbembe, "Necropolitics"; Morgensen, *Spaces between Us*; Smith, "Not an Indian Tradition"; Wolfe, "Settler Colonialism and the Elimination of the Native."

134. Stoler, "On Degrees of Imperial Sovereignty," 137, 146.

135. Stoler, "On Degrees of Imperial Sovereignty," 146.

136. Ratner, "Haifa Transgender Sex Scandal Ends."

137. Ratner, "Haifa Transgender Sex Scandal Ends."

138. Beauchamp, *Going Stealth*, 5.

An early version of this chapter appeared as "Weapons of Sex, Weapons of War," *Cultural Studies* 27, no. 1 (2013): 115–35.

1. *Reuters*, "'Rape Epidemic' in Conflict Zones."

2. Batha, "Yazidi Girls Sold as Sex Slaves."

3. *Reuters*, "'Rape Epidemic' in Conflict Zones."

4. *Reuters*, "'Rape Epidemic' in Conflict Zones."

5. Note Sarah Deer's trenchant criticism of describing rape on tribal lands as an epidemic. Deer writes: "The connotations of the word allow society to absolve itself of blame. The word suggests that the problem is biological, that the problem originated independent of long-standing oppression. . . . A biological epidemic is not a crisis of human origin" (Deer, *The Beginning and End of Rape*, ix).

6. Kaldor, *New and Old Wars*, 95.

7. Mamdani, *When Victims Become Killers*.

8. Hansen, "Gender, Nation, Rape."

9. United Nations Security Council Resolution 1820 on Women, Peace, and Security, 2008, https://www.unwomen.org/en/docs/2008/6/un-security-council-resolution-1820.

10. For an explanation of the state and stakes of international law during the mid-1990s, see Bassiouni, "International Crimes."

11. Duggan and Hunter, *Sex Wars*, 1. See also Comella, "Revisiting the Feminist Sex Wars," 462.

12. Comella, "Revisiting the Feminist Sex Wars," 444.

13. This is not to suggest that US law absolutely determines or controls international law and its governing bodies, but to emphasize the conceptual travel of theories of sexualized violence, including those named as sex discrimination that "begin" in US civil law and carry on through global legal regimes.

14. Halley, "Rape at Rome," 67.

15. Farris, *In the Name of Women's Rights*; Abu-Lughod, *Do Muslim Women Need Saving?*; Amar, *The Security Archipelago*.

16. Reddy, *Freedom with Violence*; Puar, *Terrorist Assemblages*.

17. Halley, "Which Forms of Feminism?," 36.

18. Daniela Nadj argues that the attention to war rape "depoliticizes" gender by portraying sexual violence as a "group harm directed against an ethnic community, rather than as a gendered harm against the woman" (Nadj, "The Culturalisation of Identity," 649). But see Franke's ("Putting Sex to Work," 1173) explanation of how prosecutors framed indictments for individual acts of rape versus rapes occurring in "rape camps" through different charges. Neither example, however, is concerned with how conceptualizations of gender and injury correspond to, frustrate, or facilitate shifting geopolitical rearrangements of labor and property.

19. Halley sees this move to "coercion" as part of a melding of liberal and dominance feminist views, wherein "liberal feminism converts dominance

feminism's hyper-capacious understandings of domination into coercions and uses them *within the liberal legal paradigm* to justify feminist social-control initiatives and build them out into highly punitive [governance feminism] projects" (Halley, "Which Forms of Feminism?," 43). I build on it by looking beyond the genealogies of US feminisms and their internal parsing to consider transnational feminisms, global economic and political upheaval, and long-standing critiques of consent that do not fall cleanly into the genealogy of Western feminisms or the dominance versus "the rest" divide. This approach begins to reassess the making, meanings, and significance of feminist epistemologies, including legal ones, and in this way follows the makings and meanings of rape and other forms of sexualized violence beyond US categories and elite legal framings, which center particular understandings of sex/gender and centers them in ways that other perspectives do not always follow.

20. For a discussion on feminist carceral politics and militarized humanitarianism, see Bernstein, "Militarized Humanitarianism Meets Carceral Feminism"; and Bernstein, "The Sexual Politics of the 'New Abolitionism.'"

21. See Charlesworth, Chinkin, and Wright, "Feminist Approaches to International Law," 614, noting that "international law has thus far largely resisted feminist analysis."

22. For context, see Meron, "On a Hierarchy of International Human Rights"; and Meron, "Rape as a Crime under International Law."

23. See Gutman, "Rape Camps"; and Gutman, *A Witness to Genocide*.

24. Woodward, "Violence-Prone Area or International Transition?," 19.

25. See Almond, *Europe's Backyard War*.

26. Woodward, "Violence-Prone Area or International Transition?," 19–20.

27. The origin of the term *ethnic cleansing* is unclear, but several sources cite early usage in reference to minority ethnic Serbian populations and their experiences living in Kosovo. See Petrovic, "Ethnic Cleansing," 343: "Mass media reports discussed the establishment of 'ethnically clean territories' in Kosovo after 1981. At the time, it related to administrative and nonviolent matters and referred mostly to the behavior of Kosovo Albanians towards the Serbian minority in the autonomous province within the Socialist Federal Republic of Yugoslavia." See also Žarkov, *The Body of War*, 20–42, documenting the "rape protests" of the early 1990s, where ethnic Serbian women in Kosovo protested sexualized violence and were considered "nonfeminist" because of the ethnic dimensions of their protest.

28. Žarkov, *The Body of War*, 5.

29. Žarkov, *The Body of War*, 5–6.

30. Gagnon, *The Myth of Ethnic War*, 6; Todorova, *Imagining the Balkans*.

31. Bilic, *We Were Gasping for Air*; Broz, *Good People in an Evil Time*; Devic, "Anti-war Initiatives."

32. Vulliamy, *Seasons in Hell*. Subsequently, the report of the UN Commission of Experts to the Security Council (the Bassiouni Commission Report) would determine Logor Trnopoljie to be a concentration camp, functioning primarily as

a staging area for mass deportations of nonethnic Serbs. The report also describes Omarska and Keraterm as death camps for non-Serb men. The report specifically used the word *Logor*, derived from the German *Lager* (camp or storage area) to align the Prijedor camps with the Nazi regime and downplay less brutal meanings attending English uses of *camp*. See United Nations, "The Prijedor Report."

33. Gutman, "Rape Camps"; Allen, *Rape Warfare*, xii.

34. Krieger, *The Kosovo Conflict and International Law*, 82.

35. For a summary of the debates distinguishing genocide from ethnic cleansing, see Krieger, *The Kosovo Conflict and International Law*.

36. Darton, "Does the World Still Recognize a Holocaust?," 25.

37. Darton, "Does the World Still Recognize a Holocaust?," 25. For another *New York Times* account that details the massacre of Muslims by Croatian nationalists, see Burns, "Oct. 24–30." The article provides context for the Clinton administration's attempts to unite Croats and Muslims in a "united front" against the Serbs. See Cohen, "Croat-Muslim Link as Flimsy."

38. The humanitarian armed intervention that ultimately occurred proved controversial and precedent setting. See Chinkin, "Kosovo: A 'Good' or 'Bad' War?"; Finnemore, *The Purpose of Intervention*; Independent International Commission on Kosovo, *The Kosovo Report*.

39. Kinzer, "U.N. Official Warns Europe on Ethnic Strife."

40. Kinzer, "Ethnic Conflict Is Threatening."

41. See Mamdani, *When Victims Become Killers*; des Forges, *Leave None to Tell the Story*; Buss, "Sexual Violence, Ethnicity, and Intersectionality," 108; Jefremovas, *Brickyards to Graveyards*; and Jefremovas, "Contested Identities."

42. Jefremovas, "Treacherous Waters," 304.

43. Jefremovas, "Treacherous Waters," 304.

44. See Jefremovas. *Brickyards to Graveyards*; and Jefremovas, "Contested Identities." The Rwandan or even African sources that enter feminist legal academic literature on rape in war and the development of international law are scant. Mentions of Rwanda feel like footnotes to or a supporting cast member in a story that has already telegraphed its ending.

45. Hague Convention with Respect to the Laws and Customs of War on Land, October 18, 1907, art. 46, 36 Stat. 2277, TS no. 539.

46. Geneva Convention Relative to the Treatment of Prisoners of War, July 27, 1929, art. 3, 118 LNTS 343; Geneva Convention for the Amelioration of the Condition of the Wounded and Sick in Armed Forces in the Field, August 12, 1949, art. 12, 75 UNTS 31; Geneva Convention for the Amelioration of the Condition of the Wounded, Sick and Shipwrecked Members of the Armed Forces at Sea, August 12, 1949, art. 12, 75 UNTS 85; Geneva Convention Relative to the Treatment of Prisoners of War, August 12, 1949, art. 14, 75 UNTS 135.

47. Protocol Additional to the Geneva Conventions of August 12, 1949, and Relating to the Protection of Victims of International Armed Conflicts, June 8, 1977, 1125 UNTS 3; Protocol Additional to the Geneva Conventions of August,

12 1949, and Relating to the Protection of Victims of Non-international Armed Conflicts, June 8, 1977, 1125 UNTS 609. See also Sellers, "The Cultural Value of Sexual Violence"; and Copelon, "International Human Rights Dimensions."

48. Goldstone, "Prosecuting Rape as a War Crime," 279.

49. The ICTY formally dissolved in December 2017, and the ICTR in December 2015.

50. Buss, "Sexual Violence, Ethnicity, and Intersectionality," 109.

51. Halley, "Rape at Rome."

52. Halley, "Rape at Rome," 10.

53. See Copelon, "Surfacing Gender."

54. In 2008 the UN Security Council adopted Resolution 1820, which held that "rape and other forms of sexual violence can constitute war crimes, crimes against humanity or a constitutive act with respect to genocide."

55. United Nations, "Framework of Analysis for Atrocity Crimes," 1.

56. United Nations, "Framework of Analysis for Atrocity Crimes," 1.

57. United Nations, "Framework of Analysis for Atrocity Crimes," 1.

58. See Article 5(g) of the Statute of the International Criminal Tribunal for the Former Yugoslavia. http://www.icty.org/x/file/Legal%20Library/Statute /statute_sept09_en.pdf.

59. See Article 3(g) of the Statute of the International Tribunal for Rwanda. https://www.ohchr.org/en/professionalinterest/pages/statuteinternationalcriminal tribunalforrwanda.aspx.

60. Buss, "Sexual Violence, Ethnicity, and Intersectionality," 108. Italics added.

61. Article 7(1)(g) of the Rome Statute defines rape, sexual slavery, enforced prostitution, forced pregnancy, enforced sterilization, or any other form of sexual violence of comparable gravity as a crime against humanity. Article 8(b)(xxii) and 8(e)(vi) list rape, sexual slavery, forced prostitution, and any other form of sexual violence as a serious violation of common Article 3 of the four Geneva Conventions. Article 8 establishes sexual violence as a war crime in both conflicts of an international and noninternational character. See Rome Statute of the International Criminal Court, https://www.icc-cpi.int/resourcelibrary/official-journal /rome-statute.aspx.

62. Lewin, "The Balkans Rapes."

63. Lewin, "The Balkans Rapes."

64. Quoted in Lewin, "The Balkans Rapes."

65. A good deal of feminist legal scholarship takes this path, celebrating the feminist influence within international law. See Askin, "Prosecuting Wartime Rape and Other Gender-Related Crimes under International Law."

66. Askin, "Sexual Violence in Decisions and Indictments"; Copelon, "International Human Rights Dimensions of Intimate Violence"; Engle, "Feminism and Its (Dis)contents"; MacKinnon, "Defining Rape Internationally"; Halley, "Rape at Rome"; Spees, "Women's Advocacy in the Creation of the International Criminal Court."

67. See Romany, "Women as Aliens"; Chinkin, "Rape and Sexual Abuse of Women"; Copelon, "Recognizing the Egregious in the Everyday"; Copelon, "Women and War Crimes"; MacKinnon, "Rape, Genocide, and Women's Human Rights"; Oosterveld, "When Women Are the Spoils of War"; and Halley, "Rape at Rome."

68. While "sexual violence in conflict zones" might seem like "unwieldy bureaucratese for 'wartime rape,'" sexual violence as a legal term has come to reference a broad array of (gendered) crimes, including forced prostitution, forced pregnancy, forced abortion, female infanticide, sexual mutilation, and sexual humiliation. Heineman, "The History of Sexual Violence in Conflict Zones," 2.

69. MacKinnon, "Defining Rape Internationally."

70. Copelon, "International Human Rights Dimensions," 867.

71. Alternate frameworks for addressing gender, many of which strongly objected to radical and dominance ones, which had held some sway at prior UN conferences, were diverted by the presence of the Bosnian women, and sexualized violence came to supersede economic or distributional concerns. See Ong, "Strategic Sisterhood or Sisters in Solidarity?"

72. Copelon, "International Human Rights Dimensions," 867.

73. Copelon, "International Human Rights Dimensions," 867.

74. I explore some of the potential implications of this framing in chapter 3.

75. Rome Statute, Article 36(8)(b).

76. Article 7(3) of the Rome Statute provides the following definition of gender: "For the purposes of this Statute, it is understood that the term 'gender' refers to the two sexes, male and female, within the context of society. The term 'gender' does not indicate any meaning different from the above."

77. Halley, "Rape at Rome"; Engle, "Liberal Internationalism, Feminism, and the Suppression of Critique."

78. Echols, *Daring to Be Bad*.

79. MacKinnon, *Feminism Unmodified*, 3.

80. Duggan and Hunter, *Sex Wars*.

81. Gruber, "Rape, Feminism, and the War on Crime." For a counterstory of feminist antiracist and anticarceral organizing in the United States, see Thuma, *All Our Trials*.

82. Echols, *Daring to Be Bad*.

83. Vance, *Pleasure and Danger*; Potter, "Taking Back Times Square."

84. See Echols, *Daring to Be Bad*; Bumiller, *In an Abusive State*, 18.

85. MacKinnon, "International Gender Justice Dialogue."

86. MacKinnon, *Are Women Human?*, 48.

87. See Brown, *States of Injury*.

88. Harris, "Race and Essentialism in Feminist Legal Theory," 588.

89. Harris, "Race and Essentialism in Feminist Legal Theory," 591.

90. Harris, "Race and Essentialism in Feminist Legal Theory," 592.

91. Walters, "Introduction," 4.

92. Walters, "Introduction," 4.

93. Walters, "Introduction," 4.

94. Walters, "Introduction," 3.

95. Walters, "Introduction," 2.

96. Walters, "Introduction," 4.

97. Walters, "Introduction," 4.

98. Walters, "Introduction," 4.

99. Halley, "Rape at Rome," 6.

100. Halley, "Rape at Rome," 6.

101. Halley, "Rape at Rome," 90; Engle, "Feminism and Its (Dis)contents," 798.

102. Copelon, "Surfacing Gender," 199.

103. Atanasoski, *Humanitarian Violence*, 20.

104. Nash, *Black Feminism Reimagined*, 82.

105. Nash, *Black Feminism Reimagined*, 91.

106. See Alvarez et al., "Encountering Latin American and Caribbean Feminisms," for a detailed description of how the rise of international NGOs and UN conferences on gender issues shifted the course of feminisms in the Americas. See Halley, "Rape in Berlin," for the role of feminist NGOs in the formation and operations of the International Criminal Tribunals and the International Criminal Court.

107. For a thorough discussion of how this consensus manifested in negotiations around the Rome Statute, see Halley, "Rape at Rome."

108. MacKinnon, "Reflections on Sex Equality under Law." See also *Meritor Savings Bank v. Vinson*, 477 U.S. 57 (1986) (establishing that sexual harassment in an employment environment is sex discrimination) and *California Fed. Savings & Loan Association v. Guerra*, 479 U.S. 272 (1987) (establishing that paid pregnancy leave is not discrimination on the basis on sex).

109. MacKinnon, "From Practice to Theory," 13. Note that a presentation and circulation of an early draft there netted a fairly scathing open letter from the Women of Color Collective at Yale Law School. See "Open Letters to Catharine MacKinnon." See also Mahoney, "Whiteness and Women."

110. MacKinnon, "From Practice to Theory," 15.

111. MacKinnon, "From Practice to Theory," 22.

112. MacKinnon, "From Practice to Theory," 13–14.

113. See Nash, *Black Feminism Reimagined*, for an in-depth analysis of the relationships between Black feminist labor and feminist methodologies.

114. Harris, "Race and Essentialism in Feminist Legal Theory," 583.

115. Atanasoski, *Humanitarian Violence*, 179.

116. Suchland, "Is Postsocialism Transnational?," 839.

117. Brown, *States of Injury*.

118. Suchland, "Is Postsocialism Transnational?," 838. For an illuminating summary of the development and continuing promises and challenges of transnational feminism, see Blackwell, Briggs, and Chiu, "Transnational Feminisms Roundtable."

119. Quoted in Žarkov, *The Body of War*, 137.

120. Quoted in Žarkov, *The Body of War*, 137.

121. The conjoining of sexual and racial violence, radical feminism, and the US experience of slavery resonates throughout late twentieth-century feminist legal efforts to prosecute mass rape as well as human trafficking and "sexual slavery." The convolutions in consent and coercion that occur in human trafficking law are beyond the scope of the book, but see Chuang, "Exploitation Creep"; Jaleel, "The Wages of Human Trafficking"; and Oosterveld, "Sexual Slavery and the International Court." See also Hua, *Trafficking Women's Rights*; and Suchland, *Economies of Violence*.

122. See Kajevska, *Feminist Activism at War*, 3. Kajevska notes that *nationalist* was an "ascribed" description whose meanings differed based on geographic location—what *nationalist* signified in Belgrade, she argues, differed from what the word meant in Zagreb. Feminist struggles for legitimacy, she argues, define the debate.

123. Allen, *Rape Warfare*, xiii; Batinic, "Feminism, Nationalism, and War."

124. *Kadic v. Karadzic*, 70 F.3d 232 (2d Cir. 1995), *cert. denied* 518 U.S. 1005 (1996). See chapter 2 for a discussion of this case.

125. Allen, *Rape Warfare*, 9. See also Askin, "The ICTY at Ten"; and MacKinnon, *Are Women Human?*, 37.

126. MacKinnon, *Are Women Human?*, 183. MacKinnon counters accusations of deploying gender in the service of nationalisms with the following: "I have never heard Native Americans called nationalists for objecting to being subjected to genocide and wanting their own nations back" (172).

127. This article was subsequently expanded and published in Alexandra Stiglmayer's edited collection, *Mass Rape*.

128. MacKinnon, "Turning Rape into Pornography," 75.

129. MacKinnon, *Are Women Human?*, 189.

130. MacKinnon, "Turning Rape into Pornography," 73.

131. Tripp, "Challenges in Transnational Feminist Mobilization," 3.

132. Copelon, "Surfacing Gender," 199.

133. Engle, "Feminism and Its (Dis)contents."

134. Engle, "Feminism and Its (Dis)contents."

135. MacKinnon, *Are Women Human?*

136. Balkan nonnationalist antiwar feminists should not have the last word on the issue of nationalism, war, and ethnoreligious difference in the conflict. As Žarkov has written, many nonnationalist feminists in the former Yugoslavia arrive at an antiwar position through a general tendency to disavow ethnic difference in favor of gender universalism.

137. Kesic, "A Response to Catharine MacKinnon's Article"; Batinic, "Feminism, Nationalism, and War."

138. Kajevska, *Feminist Activism at War*.

139. Batinic, "Feminism, Nationalism, and War," 9–10.

140. Kesic, "A Response to Catharine MacKinnon's Article"; Žarkov, *The Body of War*.

141. Žarkov, "Gender, Orientalism and the History of Ethnic Hatred," 144. See also Buss, "Women at the Borders."

142. Nash, *Black Feminism Reimagined*, 82.

143. Soto, "Transnational Knowledge Projects and Failing Racial Etiquette," 70. Karla F. C. Holloway confirms: "I suspect that the attention to the global and the transnational, as much as it is a version of an absorbed interest in the other extending from the body of U.S. feminisms, it additionally manifests a profound and troubling discomfort with the local" (Holloway, "'Cruel Enough to Stop the Blood,'" 2).

144. "It is also gratifying to see that, in bringing their analyses to the realm of international human rights, feminists have avoided some of the conceptual and procedural errors that marred their earlier approach to similar problems. Russell-Brown notes, for example, that Catharine MacKinnon has highlighted the intersectional character of the genocidal rape of Muslim women in the former Yugoslavia: this rape is both ethnically based and a form of genocide directed specifically at women" (Abrams, "Feminists in International Human Rights," 391). See Russell-Brown, "Rape as an Act of Genocide," 350.

145. MacKinnon, "Crimes of War, Crimes of Peace," 67.

146. Brown, *States of Injury*.

147. The Convention on Genocide defines genocide as a form of reproductive violence, including acts that "impos[e] measures intended to prevent births within the group" and the "forcib[le] transfe[r] of children of the group to another group" (UN Convention on the Prevention and Punishment of the Crime of Genocide, 1948, 2(e)). For a full discussion of how rape is theorized as genocide in the 1990s, see Engle, "Feminism and Its (Dis)contents"; and Carpenter, "Surfacing Children."

148. Puar, *Terrorist Assemblages*, xi.

149. Puar, *Terrorist Assemblages*, 161.

150. MacKinnon, *Are Women Human?*, 205.

151. Other US legal feminists specializing in international human rights law, including Rhonda Copelon and Celina Romany on behalf of the Center for Constitutional Rights, were involved in a separate civil action, *Doe v. Karadzic* (461 [S.D.N.Y. 1997], No. 93-Civ-1163), seeking damages for people, not solely women, who suffered at the hands of the defendant and his subordinates. When these cases were collectively dismissed at the district level, they were procedurally, routinely consolidated on appeal under the caption *Kadic v. Karadzic*. I discuss the consequences of this consolidation in chapter 3.

152. *Kadic v. Karadzic*, 242.

153. *Prosecutor v. Akayesu*, para. 688.

154. *Akayesu*, para. 597.

155. *Akayesu*, para. 688.

156. MacKinnon, *Are Women Human?*, 244.

157. MacKinnon, *Are Women Human?*, 244.

158. MacKinnon, *Are Women Human?*, 244.

159. MacKinnon, *Are Women Human?*, 239.

160. Wood, "Variation in Sexual Violence during War."

161. Buss, "Sexual Violence, Ethnicity, and Intersectionality."

162. In contrast, international relations and political science scholarship are often preoccupied with the perceived subsumption of "women's issues" by "race" (made mass by the charge of genocide) and the lack of recognition of the individual woman's pain inherent in charges of genocide. See Nadj, "The Culturalisation of Identity."

163. See Sharlach, "Gender and Genocide in Rwanda," 387–99.

164. In chapter 3, I elaborate how the recognition of mass injury is only made possible by assigning individual (and not corporate) blame, requiring individual criminal legal liability for crimes that had once been thought to govern only the behavior of states.

165. For feminist legal scholar Doris E. Buss, the genocidal rape narrative "impacts what is known and knowable about the Rwandan genocide. . . . The narrative of rape as an instrument of the genocide makes it difficult to ask why the rapes happened, how the rapes might have been connected to various social relations and structures that pre-dated the genocide, and what women did to negotiate and resist sexual violence" (Buss, "Rethinking 'Rape as a Weapon of War,'" 147–48).

166. Atanasoski, *Humanitarian Violence*, 180–81.

167. Atanasoski, *Humanitarian Violence*, 180–81.

168. Li, *The Universal Enemy*.

169. "In this connection, former U.S. secretary of state Madeleine Albright stated, "This will be no victor's tribunal. The only victor that will prevail in this endeavor is the truth." Quoted in Atanasoski, *Humanitarian Violence*, 171.

170. Engle, "Feminism and Its (Dis)contents," 798. See *Prosecutor v. Kunarac* (Third Amended Indictment), IT-96-23-PT, International Criminal Tribunal for the former Yugoslavia, November 8, 1999.

171. Slye, "The Dayton Peace Agreement," 463.

172. Slye, "The Dayton Peace Agreement," 463.

173. Orford, *International Authority*, 98–99. See also Orford, *Reading Humanitarian Intervention*.

174. See Gettleman, "Symbol of Unhealed Congo"; Gettleman, "Clinton Presses Congo on Minerals"; and Gettleman, "Clinton Presents Plan."

175. Eichstadt, *Consuming the Congo*; Meger, "Rape in Contemporary Warfare."

176. Halley et al., preface to *Governance Feminism*, x.

177. Williams, *The Divided World*.

178. For examples of situated local engagement with law and rights and the variability of their impact across geographies and scales of law, see Amar, "Turning

the Gendered Politics of the Security State Inside Out?"; Jain and Das Gupta, ""Law, Gender Identity, and the Uses of Human Rights"; and Merry, *Human Rights and Gender Violence.*

Chapter Two / States of War, Men as State

1. The scope of violence suffered in those conflicts has been officially documented by the Guatemalan Comisión para el Esclarecimiento Histórico and the Peruvian Comisión de Verdad and Reconciliación. The commissions found, respectively, that approximately 88.7 percent of raped women in Guatemala were indigenous, and in Peru, 75 percent were Quechua speakers. The commissions established that soldiers received orders to rape, torture, and kill as part of a recognized strategy of group consolidation and nation-building. See Franco, "Rape: A Weapon of War," 24; and Boesten, "Analyzing Rape Regimes."

2. An agreement with the UN to prosecute serious crimes in Guatemala was not formalized until the end of 2006 with the creation of the International Commission against Impunity in Guatemala, an independent body convened to assist the Procuraduría General de la Nación (Public Prosecutor's Office), the Policía Nacional Civil (National Civilian Police), and other national institutions in the prosecution of difficult cases. International involvement was premised on the express goal of strengthening the national judicial system. See Roht-Arriaza, "Prosecuting Genocide in Guatemala," 9.

3. Copelon, "Surfacing Gender," 244–45.

4. Copelon, "Recognizing the Egregious in the Everyday," 295–96.

5. My thinking about silence has been informed by work in Asian American studies. See Kang, *Compositional Subjects*; Chuh, "Discomforting Knowledge"; and Yoneyama, *Cold War Ruins.*

6. See Castillo, *Multiple Injustices*; Sieder, "Contested Sovereignties."

7. "For the purposes of this Convention, the term 'torture' means any act by which severe pain or suffering, whether physical or mental, is intentionally inflicted on a person for such purposes as obtaining from him or a third person information or a confession, punishing him for an act he or a third person has committed or is suspected of having committed, or intimidating or coercing him or a third person, or for any reason based on discrimination of any kind, when such pain or suffering is inflicted by or at the instigation of or with the consent or acquiescence of a public official or other person acting in an official capacity. It does not include pain or suffering arising only from, inherent in or incidental to lawful sanctions." UN Human Rights, Office of the High Commissioner, Convention against Torture and Other Cruel, Inhuman, or Degrading Treatment or Punishment, UN General Assembly resolution 39/46, December 10, 1984, https://www.ohchr.org/en/professionalinterest/pages/cat.aspx.

8. See, e.g., the UN Convention against Torture.

9. Stoler, "On Degrees of Imperial Sovereignty," 127–28.

10. I approach their texts as part of an expanded legal archive and as soft forms of lawmaking that shape how sexualized violence may be conceptualized in ways that conform to existing law and doctrine while also reworking them.

11. Here, I use *settler/colonial* to note the ongoing debates in the Americas over the appropriateness of the term *settler colonialism* in different locations and contexts.

12. A different project could, for example, focus on US imperial engagements in very specific regions or contexts. Another could decenter US engagement entirely or examine that engagement through other imperial formations, including Portuguese and Spanish ones. I focus on US empire here to better illustrate elite legal feminism's relationship to the rearrangements of US law and power at the end of Soviet empire.

13. McClintock, *Instruments of Statecraft, 329.*

14. McClintock, *Instruments of Statecraft.*

15. Grandin, *Empire's Workshop*, 91.

16. Grandin, *Empire's Workshop*, 91.

17. McClintock, *Instruments of Statecraft*, 330.

18. McClintock, *Instruments of Statecraft*, xviii–xix.

19. Grandin, "The Latin American Exception."

20. Gagnon, *The Myth of Ethnic War,* 8–9. Scholars locate the roots of the Balkan conflict as a political destabilization strategy that mobilizes "Yugoslav elite policies of violence along ethnic lines." Gagnon, *The Myth of Ethnic War*, 8. For Gagnon, ethnic conflict is produced in a cosmopolitan society by rendering ethnicity as bounded and fixed during a fiscal crisis precipitated by the US withdrawal of aid to the nonaligned federated country in the wake of communism's fall. See also Grandin, *Empire's Workshop*; Friedman, *Seeking Rights from the Left.*

21. See Alvarez et al., "Encountering Latin American and Caribbean Feminisms," for a detailed description on how the rise of international NGOs and UN conferences on gender issues shifted the course of feminisms in the Americas.

22. Hobson, *Lavender and Red*, 7.

23. Hobson, *Lavender and Red*, 7.

24. Hobson, *Lavender and Red*, 7.

25. Hobson, *Lavender and Red*, 7.

26. Copelon, "International Human Rights Dimensions of Intimate Violence."

27. Rhonda Copelon, Patrick Cotter, Jennifer Green, and Beth Stephens authored a self-explanatory proposal, "Affecting the Rules for the Prosecution of Rape and Other Gender-Based Violence before the International Criminal Tribunal for the Former Yugoslavia: A Feminist Proposal and Critique," that ultimately shaped tribunal operations.

28. For a full account of the controversy, see Batinic, "Feminism, Nationalism, and War." In Toronto, in March 1993, copies of a fax denouncing the MADRE Mother Courage II tour and two of its speakers, Vesna Kesnic and Lepa Mladje-

novic (a member of Women in Black), were distributed at one of the tour's stops. The feminist groups who authored the fax (the Kareta Feminist Group, Biser, Zene BiH, and Bedem Ijubavi Women's Group) opposed framing rape as a "weapon of war," insisting instead that Bosnian, Croat, and Muslim women were the victims of Serbian-led genocide. To view a copy of the fax, see "Fax: Response to the MADRE Courage Tour on Rape," March 23, 1993, http://k.mihalec.tripod.com/fax.htm.

29. Duarte, "From the Margins of Latin American Feminism," 155.

30. Duarte, "From the Margins of Latin American Feminism," 156.

31. Duarte, "From the Margins of Latin American Feminism," 156, citing Gisela Espinosa.

32. Sternbach et al., "Feminisms in Latin America"; Halley, "Rape at Rome."

33. Duarte, "From the Margins of Latin American Feminisms," 157.

34. Duarte, "From the Margins of Latin American Feminisms," 157; Castro, "Engendering Powers."

35. I use the term *political subject* to mark an important moment for heterogeneous struggles for collective determination while emphasizing the terms and substance of that entrance into law and governance as historically conditioned. Acknowledging indigenous feminisms as epistemological contributions need not posit a unified position or an idealized one. As Rosalva Aída Hernández Castillo writes, "Recognizing indigenous women's theorizations and learning from their emancipatory potential does not imply an idealization of contemporary indigenous cultures. . . . [R]ecognizing the historical and political heterogeneity underlying indigenous women's movements that demand rights and the use of laws as tools for struggle is [instead] a first step toward the construction of political alliances." Following Castillo, what such recognition creates is an opportunity for testing and trying ways to pose questions or issues that could not otherwise have been broached, including, as this book argues, epistemological contributions—however adulterated or obscured—to feminist law making. See Castillo, *Multiple Injustices*, 16.

36. Castillo, *Multiple Injustices*, 3.

37. Castillo, *Multiple Injustices*, 3.

38. Castillo, *Multiple Injustices*, 4.

39. Duarte, "From the Margins of Latin American Feminisms," 163, citing Rivera, *El Andar de las Mujeres Indígenas*, 19.

40. Copelon, "End Torture, End Domestic Violence." The Furies were a US communal lesbian separatist collective that existed between 1971 and 1973. For good reading about them, see Echols, *Daring to Be Bad*, 234–42. Catharine MacKinnon also credits her turn to the international to feminist organizing: "right after Vukovar [city in eastern Croatia] fell, Bosnian and Croatian women's request to work with them took my work international, as it has remained" (MacKinnon, *Are Women Human?*, vii). I discuss the progression of MacKinnon's work in relation to the genocidal rape debates more thoroughly in chapter 1.

41. Alvarez et al., "Encountering Latin American and Caribbean Feminisms," 540.

42. Alvarez et al., "Encountering Latin American and Caribbean Feminisms," 540.

43. Alvarez et al., "Encountering Latin American and Caribbean Feminisms," 540.

44. One such *desencuentros* occurred in 1990 at San Bernardo, when indigenous women organized a workshop in opposition to the impending 500-year celebration of Columbus's "discovery" of the Americas, where they proposed to proclaim October 11 Indigenous Women's Day. See Alvarez et al., "Encountering Latin American and Caribbean Feminisms," 566. See Castro, "Engendering Powers."

45. Rodríguez, "Fifth Feminist Conference."

46. It is worth noting that US legal feminist engagement with international law and governance, including UN forums, might be understood as part of what Sylvanna M. Falcón characterizes as a "UN agenda on women . . . dominated by feminist politics steeped in Western-centric ideologies that represent interests different from those of feminists from the anti-racism forums." As she notes, "most white feminists from the United States neglected to support the 2001 [World Conference against Racism], but gave strong support to the 1995 UN Conference on Women in Beijing." Falcón, *Power Interrupted*, 8.

47. UN Convention against Torture.

48. Copelon, "Recognizing the Egregious in the Everyday," 297.

49. Copelon, "Recognizing the Egregious in the Everyday," 295–96.

50. Copelon, "Recognizing the Egregious in the Everyday," 295–96.

51. Gruber, *The Feminist War on Crime*, 59. This occurred despite vibrant, contemporaneous organizing by antiracist queer feminists that was decidedly anticarceral, that refuted in absolute terms the "hegemonic story" that "crime-control approach" and "incarceration [are] necessary to end gender violence." Antiracist queer organizing instead located the lion's share of violence against poor women and queers of color as issuing not from their homes but from the state—particularly the criminal justice system—itself (Thuma, *All Our Trials*, 163). State abandonment and rape enablement, from this perspective, occurs not when laws aren't tough on crime, but when incarcerated women, like Joan Little in 1974, are charged with murder for defending themselves against the guards who attempt to rape them. When Little's defense campaign portrays her as a "political prisoner," it is not indicting the state for failing to be tough on crime (Thuma, *All Our Trials*, 27).

52. Copelon and Romany were no strangers to the diplomatic and discursive potentials of international law, torture, and human rights. Copelon, a founding member of the City University of New York Law School, in 1991 cofounded with Romany that school's International Women's Human Rights Clinic (IWHR). The IWHR subsequently produced amicus briefs for the ICTY and ICTR that advanced the recognition of rape as a crime of genocide and torture under international law and influenced the Rome Statute's uptake of prohibitions against

gender crimes. Under the direction of Copelon and Romany, the IWHR also collaborated with international bodies and organizations, including the United Nation's Committee against Torture, to further the recognition of domestic violence and other gender crimes as constitutive of torture under the UN Convention against Torture. In 1980, Copelon was a key member of a team of Center for Constitutional Rights attorneys whose innovative application of the Alien Torts Statute in a case involving torture in Paraguay opened some international human rights violations to civil prosecution in US federal courts, paving the way for the first charges of rape as genocide in an influential US federal court (see chapter 3).

53. Copelon, "End Torture, End Domestic Violence."

54. Copelon, "Recognizing the Egregious in the Everyday," 339. The association of torture with sexualized violence is not new. In fact, an inverse relationship between torture and sexualized violence (where sexualized violence makes torture visible) might be noted in the French Algerian War. The abuse of Djamila Boupacha, an Algerian National Liberation Front militant, by the French army in 1960 garnered international attention precisely through the interplay of gender, nationalism, and sexualized violence. What I am interested in here is the immediate work of elite legal feminists who are finding their footing in international human rights law when international law—including international criminal law—consolidates as a premier site of justice.

55. Copelon, "End Torture, End Domestic Violence." For a critique of the collapse of domestic violence into rape, see Deer, *The Beginning and End of Rape*.

56. Copelon, "End Torture, End Domestic Violence."

57. Copelon, "End Torture, End Domestic Violence."

58. Copelon, "Recognizing the Egregious in the Everyday," 307, 296.

59. Copelon, "Recognizing the Egregious in the Everyday," 299.

60. Copelon, "Recognizing the Egregious in the Everyday," 299.

61. Cherniavsky, "On (the Impossibility of) Teaching Gayle Rubin," 90.

62. Cherniavsky, "On (the Impossibility of) Teaching Gayle Rubin."

63. Byrd, *The Transit of Empire*, xii.

64. As MacKinnon wryly notes about the status of international human rights: "A right is also something only an entity with the power of a nation can violate; it is a duty of government not to interfere with civil and political liberties as they socially exist. The role of international law has been largely, in Isaiah Berlin's sense, negative. It could be more, but it fosters human rights less by mandating governmental intervention than by enforcing governmental abstinence. In other words, if your human rights are going to be violated, pray it is by someone who looks like a government, and that he already acted, and acted wrong" (MacKinnon, "Crimes of War, Crimes of Peace," 59, 69). The next chapter discusses the subsequent rise of individual liability across bodies of international law.

65. Thongchai Winichakul, quoted in Stoler, "On Degrees of Imperial Sovereignty," 136.

66. Williams, *The Divided World*.

67. *Mujer/Fempress* no. 117, July 1991, cited in Radcliffe, "Women's Place/El Lugar de Mujeres," 109.

68. See Ritchie, *Arrested Justice*.

69. Copelon, "Recognizing the Egregious in the Everyday," 299. While Copelon theorizes a legal kinship between torture and domestic violence through indigenous and women of color feminisms at Encuentros, she only mentions Argentina in a footnote as part of an internal citation when she mobilizes US feminist Judith Herman's work on trauma to make a case for its close connection to torture (Copelon, "Recognizing the Egregious in the Everyday," 313n62).

70. Copelon, "Recognizing the Egregious in the Everyday," 309.

71. Copelon, "Women and War Crimes," 63.

72. Copelon, "Recognizing the Egregious in the Everyday," 297. In a 1990 speech, MacKinnon framed state failures to guard against domestic abuse as "torture on the basis of sex." MacKinnon, *Are Women Human?*, 17.

73. The social contract derives from liberal European moral and political philosophy. It seeks to explain, justify, and legitimate state authority over individuals. Developed by thinkers like Thomas Hobbes, Hugo Grotius, Samuel von Pufendorf, John Locke, Immanuel Kant, and Jean-Jacques Rousseau, the basis of the social contract is the notion that individuals consent to the curtailment of some rights in exchange for state protection.

74. Reddy, *Freedom with Violence*, 8.

75. Reddy, *Freedom with Violence*, 8.

76. Romany, "Women as Aliens," 97.

77. Romany, "Women as Aliens," 90.

78. Arondekar and Patel, "Area Impossible," 156.

79. The sexual state form might be read productively alongside Tadiar, "Sexual Economies of the Asia-Pacific" as a way to extend the discussion of sexual, racial, and gendered fantasy at play within economic imaginaries. The sexual state form also extends discussions of "national differentiation as sexual differentiation" to consider how criticisms of state governance build out into impermissible sexual behaviors, if not sexualities. See also Puar, *Terrorist Assemblages*, 98–99.

80. Driskill et al., introduction to *Queer Indigenous Studies*, 19. See also Smith, "Queer Theory and Native Studies"; and Morgensen, *Spaces between Us*.

81. 8 I.L.M. 294 (1989), holding under Article 1(1) of the American Convention on Human Rights that the Honduran government was responsible for politically motivated disappearances, regardless of whether or not they were overtly carried out by government officials.

82. Romany, "Women as Aliens," 112.

83. As Romany writes, "In unveiling the genealogy of liberalism and its construction of the human rights field within international law, a feminist critique must expose the male supremacy within that construction. This is essential to recognizing the emancipatory potential of liberalism and to pushing liberalism's

main political tenets to their conclusions" (Romany, "Women as Aliens," 90–91). In this way, each echo—or at least are unassumingly hospitable to—dominance feminist configurations of sex, gender, and violence, even as neither feminist seems to entirely embrace MacKinnon's view of sex as domination (see chapter 1).

84. Mitchell, "Society, Economy, and the State Effect," 90.

85. Volpp, "The Indigenous as Alien," 802. See also Pateman, *The Sexual Contract*; and Mills, *The Racial Contract*.

86. Volpp, "The Indigenous as Alien," 802.

87. Volpp, "The Indigenous as Alien," 802.

88. Sieder, "Sexual Violence and Gendered Subjectivities."

89. Sieder, "Contested Sovereignties," 164.

90. Sieder, "Contested Sovereignties," 165.

91. Byrd, *The Transit of Empire*.

92. Smith, "Queer Theory and Native Studies"; Vimalassery, Pegues, and Goldstein, "Introduction."

93. Stoler, "On Degrees of Imperial Sovereignty," 137.

94. Stoler, "On Degrees of Imperial Sovereignty," 137.

95. Nobel Women's Initiative, "From Survivors to Defenders."

96. Indigenous scholars and scholars of indigenous law stress how modes of indigenous epistemologies and modes of governance—varied as they are—can challenge settler/colonial dynamics of possession, property ownership, and rationality by understanding "contract" as consensual, community-negotiated processes, instead of individualized and competitive binding agreements. See Barker, *Sovereignty Matters*; Goldstein, *Formations of United States Colonialism*.

Chapter Three / My Own Private Genocide

1. The MCA was spurred by the US Supreme Court's June 2006 decision in *Hamdan v. Rumsfeld* (548 US 557). The court's decision denounced Bush's prior system for trying suspects in military commissions (then called Combatant Status Review Tribunals), finding them neither authorized by federal law, required by military necessity, nor compatible with the prescriptions of the Geneva Conventions. *Hamdan* held that military commissions set up by the Bush administration to try detainees at Guantánamo Bay detention camp lacked "the power to proceed because its structures and procedures violate[d] both the Uniform Code of Military Justice and the four Geneva Conventions signed in 1949." The Geneva Conventions are a series of treaties that form the basis of international humanitarian law, or how people in wars should be treated. Specifically, the conventions standardize the treatment of civilians, prisoners of war, and soldiers. The MCA also granted the president the authority in interpret the meaning of the Geneva Conventions, including, as legal scholar Erwin Chemerinsky notes, definitions of torture. MCA §6(a)(3)(A) states that: "The President has the authority for the United States to interpret the meaning and application of the Geneva Conventions." Further,

"There is no requirement that the President publish this definition in the federal registry or anywhere else." Chemerinsky, "Presidential Powers," 913.

2. Barack Obama dropped this terminology in 2009. See US Department of Justice, "Department of Justice Withdraws 'Enemy Combatant' Definition."

3. Per the Center for Constitutional Rights, the term is an amalgamation of several legal categories, forged in an effort to work around the Geneva Conventions without explicitly denouncing them. Prior versions of the MCA contained much narrower definitions of "unlawful enemy combatant." Contestations around the meaning of the term are evident in the legislative record. An earlier version defined an "unlawful enemy combatant" as a person affiliated with a terrorist organization who engaged in or supported hostile actions against the United States, while a version of a rival Senate bill limited the definition of "unlawful enemy combatant" to those actually engaged in hostilities. See Center for Constitutional Rights, "FAQs: The Military Commission Act of 2006."

4. See Center for Constitutional Rights, "FAQs: The Military Commission Act of 2006." See also American Association of International Law, "The Military Commissions Act of 2006."

5. MCA §950v(21), defines rape as "forcibly or with coercion or threat of force wrongfully invad[ing] the body of a person by penetrating, however slightly, the anal or genital opening of the victim with any part of the body of the accused, or with any foreign object"; sec. 6(b).

6. See *Prosecutor v. Akayesu* (Trial Judgment), ICTR-96-4-T, International Criminal Tribunal for Rwanda, September 2, 1998.

7. MCA §950v(22), defines sexual assault or abuse as "forcibly or with coercion or threat of force engag[ing] in sexual contact with one or more persons, or caus[ing] one or more persons to engage in sexual contact"; sec. 6(b).

8. See MCA §950v(b) (11), "TORTURE.—(A) OFFENSE.—Any person subject to this chapter who commits an act specifically intended to inflict severe physical or mental pain or suffering (other than pain or suffering incidental to lawful sanctions) upon another person within his custody or physical control for the purpose of obtaining information or a confession, punishment, intimidation, coercion, or any reason based on discrimination of any kind, shall be punished, if death results to one or more of the victims, by death or such other punishment as a military commission under this chapter may direct, and, if death does not result to any of the victims, by such punishment, other than death, as a military commission under this chapter may direct." Within law, torture can be a contentious issue. Generally, the accused must knowingly inflict pain for a prohibited purpose for their actions to be considered torture. During the Bush administration, the specific intent requirement was at times interpreted to mean that "if the accused knowingly causes pain or suffering but had some other objective for which pain and suffering was merely incidental, such as extracting information, he lacks the requisite 'specific intent'" to be found responsible for an act of torture (Hathaway, Nowlan, and Spiegel, "Tortured Reasoning," 793).

9. *New York Times*, "Turning Back the Clock on Rape." Copelon long argued that torture did not require specific intent under international law: "The intent required under the international torture conventions is simply the general intent to do that act which clearly or foreseeably causes terrible suffering" (Copelon, "Recognizing the Egregious in the Everyday," 325). Others see it differently: "Purpose need not be read into the requirement that pain or suffering be 'intentionally inflicted' because it is explicitly provided for in the further requirement that the pain or suffering be inflicted for a prohibited 'purpose'" (Hathaway, Nowlan, and Spiegel, "Tortured Reasoning," 802).

10. *New York Times*, "Turning Back the Clock on Rape." See also the Center for Constitutional Rights, "FAQs: The Military Commission Act of 2006."

11. *New York Times*, "Turning Back the Clock on Rape."

12. 18 U.S.C. §2331.

13. Butler, *Frames of War*, 125.

14. Butler, *Frames of War*, 125.

15. For a detailed account of the US practice of torture, see Hajjar, "American Torture"; and Hajjar, "From Nuremberg to Guantánamo."

16. Puar, *Terrorist Assemblages*, 49.

17. I use *sex/gender* to acknowledge historical work locating these terms and the divisions between them within projects of racial management. See Gill-Peterson, *History of the Transgender Child*; Schuller, *The Biopolitics of Feeling*; and LaFleur, *The Natural History of Sexuality in Early America*.

18. Greppi, "The Evolution of Individual Criminal Responsibility under International Law"; Schabas, "Theoretical and International Framework."

19. Schabas, "Theoretical and International Framework," 918.

20. Schabas, "Theoretical and International Framework," 918.

21. Schabas offers a very serviceable summary of the motivating distinctions between international and noninternational conflict: "The definition of non-international armed conflict is intricately bound up with the existence of organized non-State armed groups. These are the 'non-State actors' in the title of this Article. Common Article 3 of the Geneva Conventions, at least explicitly, imposes no such requirement, but the other two instruments insist, for their application, upon the presence of 'non-State actors' with a certain level of organizational capacity. The requirements in the Additional Protocol are somewhat higher than those of the Rome Statute, in that in the former case, the non-State actor must actually control territory. It must be 'State-like,' even if it lacks all of a sovereign State's attributes, and does not enjoy recognition by other States, or membership in international organizations. At the low end of non-international armed conflict, the definition hinges upon the intensity of the conflict, rather than upon the level of organization or territorial control of its non-State participants" (Schabas, "Theoretical and International Framework," 915–16).

22. *Prosecutor v. Tadić* (Opinion and Judgment), IT-94-1-T, International Criminal Tribunal for the former Yugoslavia, May 7, 1997.

23. "That certain violations of international humanitarian law might incur individual criminal liability was first established at Nuremberg, in 1946. These 'violations of the laws and customs of war' reflected prohibitions in the 1907 Convention (IV) Respecting the Laws and Customs of War By Land ('Hague Convention'), but were also considered to form part of customary international law. Because the entire concept of legal regulation of non-international armed conflict was in its infancy, it was not considered that there could be international criminal liability for violations of humanitarian law in non-international armed conflict. In 1949, when the Geneva Conventions were adopted, certain rules concerning international criminal liability were codified. This is the 'grave breach' regime, as it is known in the Conventions. . . . [It] establishes obligations upon States to prosecute or extradite (aut dedere aut judicare) in the case of certain particularly serious violations. Because it was generally believed that common Article 3 was the only provision in those instruments that governed non-international armed conflict, the prevailing view was that the grave breach system simply did not apply in such cases. In other words, there were no 'international crimes' in non-international armed conflicts. Proposals to extend the grave breach system to non-international armed conflict were rejected by those who negotiated the Additional Protocol" (Schabas, "Theoretical and International Framework," 914–15).

24. Since the Nuremberg trials, international criminal law might be argued to have been a mechanism to hold individuals acting in the service of states (not necessarily states themselves) accountable for war crimes, but what I mark here is the movement beneath the idea of individual criminal liability of how war is conducted and what international armed violence means. For a detailed account of individual liability and international criminal law, see Van Sliedregt, *Individual Criminal Responsibility*; and Portman, *Legal Personality in International Law*.

25. In Copelon's ("Gender Crimes as War Crimes," 229) account, this treatment of sexualized violence (prosecuted as inhumane acts or crimes against humanity and cruel treatment, or as a violation of the laws and customs of war) differed sharply from concurrent cases involving the sexualized violation of women and further galvanized feminist actions in international criminal lawmaking.

26. Schabas, "Theoretical and International Framework," 933.

27. Oosterveld, "The Definition of 'Gender,'" 58.

28. Oosterveld, "The Definition of 'Gender,'" 65.

29. See Texas Archival Resources Online, historical note, in "Women's Caucus for Gender Justice's Documentary Footage for *If Hope Were Enough*," accessed February 17, 2021, https://legacy.lib.utexas.edu/taro/hrdi/00005/hrdi-00005.html. See Spees, "Women's Advocacy in the Creation of the International Criminal Court."

30. Texas Archival Resources Online, historical note.

31. Rome Statue, Article 7(3).

32. Oosterveld, "The Definition of 'Gender,'" 57–58.

33. Butler, *Frames of War*, 102.

34. Other areas of international law and governance, including the UN and various human rights efforts, have taken a different approach. The UN General Assembly, for example, has repeatedly called on states to protect the right to life of all persons and to investigate violence stemming from sexual orientation and gender identity. Yet this chapter asks what work the exclusion in the Rome Statute performs because it understands that when law is fractured in aims, it is nonetheless successful in its production of the violences and freedoms that justify its existence and efforts. The principles and aims of international human rights and humanitarian and criminal law infuse each other in a productive tension. See, for example, UN General Assembly, Extrajudicial, Summary or Arbitrary Executions, UN Resolution A/RES/67/16(6)(b), urging states: "To ensure the effective protection of the right to life of all persons under their jurisdiction, to investigate promptly and thoroughly all killings, including those targeted at specific groups of persons, such as racially motivated violence leading to the death of the victim, killings of persons belonging to national or ethnic, religious and linguistic minorities or because of their sexual orientation or gender identity."

35. 28 U.S.C. §1350 (1994).

36. Chowdury, "*Kadic v. Karadzic*," 109.

37. Perluss and Hartman, "Temporary Refuge." For a fuller discussion of the complex interactions of customary law and domestic remedies for human rights violations with a specific focus on the ATS and *Filártiga*, see Stephens, "Translating *Filártiga*."

38. Stephens, "Individuals Enforcing International Law"; Ochoa, "Access to U.S. Federal Courts."

39. Davis, *Justice across Borders*, 18.

40. *Filártiga v. Peña-Irala*, 630 F.2d 876 (2d Cir. 1980).

41. *Filártiga*, 879–80.

42. White, *Breaking Silence*, 213; Davis, *Justice across Borders*, 18. Weiss and Copelon later represented plaintiffs in the ATS suit *Doe v. Karadzic*, 461 (S.D.N.Y. 1997), 93-Civ-1163. In the Anglo-American legal tradition, as US Second Circuit judge Pierre N. Leval ("Beyond *Kiobel*," 2) explains, the law of nations referred to "(1) violations of safe conduct; (2) interference with the rights of ambassadors; and (3) piracy, which was of intense concern among nations, because of the threat piracy represented to trade among nations and the huge amounts nations invested in vessels that were vulnerable." Yet, as Leval continues, "The content and scope of the Law of Nations underwent a sea change in response to the Nazi atrocities of World War II. The Nuremberg trials were premised on the proposition that the civilized world does not tolerate a small nucleus of heinous conduct, including genocide and slavery, and that such conduct, like piracy, violates the customary international law, even when practiced by a sovereign upon its own citizens." This history evinces the movement from the law of nations as describing relations between nations to "matters of human rights or issues of a sovereign's treatment of

its own citizens" and, as importantly, the civilizing and sorting dimensions of the law of nations as a project of global racial management.

43. For a detailed account of the case's procedural history, see Koh, "*Filártiga v. Peña-Irala.*" See also Aceves, *The Anatomy of Torture.*

44. *Filártiga*, 878.

45. Posner, "Kadic v. Karadzic," 660.

46. See *Kiobel v. Royal Dutch Petroleum Co.* (2013 U.S. LEXIS 3159). On April 17, 2013, in a unanimous decision, the US Supreme Court held that the ATS does not afford jurisdiction to Nigerian human rights victims who were harmed when Shell Oil assisted the Nigerian government in perpetrating human rights abuses. See Leval, "Beyond *Kiobel*" for an analysis of ATS litigation in the aftermath of that decision.

47. The CCR's emphasis on torture as a violation of international customary law also helped vault the issue to the forefront of domestic politics and legislation, culminating in the 1992 passage of the Torture Victim Protection Act of 1991 (TVPA). The passage of the TVPA in turn complemented and strengthened feminist efforts to harness disapprobation of torture as a vehicle for achieving recognition of rape, domestic violence, forced pregnancies, and other sex and gender crimes in the purview of international human rights law.

48. *Kadic v. Karadzic*, 70 F.3d 232 (2d Cir. 1995), *cert. denied* 518 U.S. 1005 (1996).

49. Zimmerman, "Impressions of Karadžić."

50. *Kadic*, 237.

51. *Kadic*, 239.

52. *Kadic* citing *Klinghoffer v. S.N.C. Achille Lauro*, 937 F.2d 44, 47 (2d Cir. 1991).

53. *Doe*, 741.

54. *Kadic*, 239.

55. *Kadic*, 239.

56. *Kadic*, 236–37.

57. *Kadic*, 236.

58. *Kadic*, 236–37.

59. *Kadic*, 242.

60. *Kadic*, 239. See Ochoa, "Access to U.S. Federal Courts"; Kunstle, "*Kadic v. Karadžić*," 319.

61. Green, quoted in Irwin, "Civil Actions Offer Some Closure."

62. MacKinnon, quoted in Irwin, "Civil Actions Offer Some Closure."

63. Quoted in Irwin, "Civil Actions Offer Some Closure."

64. Green, quoted in Irwin, "Civil Actions Offer Some Closure."

65. *Doe.*

66. MacKinnon, *Are Women Human?*, 205.

67. For a contemporary critique of the denial of summary judgment in *Doe* and *Kadic*, see Brandt, "*Doe v. Karadzic.*"

68. MacKinnon, *Are Women Human?*, 206–7.

69. MacKinnon, *Are Women Human?*, 207.

70. MacKinnon, *Are Women Human?*, 208.

71. MacKinnon, *Are Women Human?*, 207.

72. Danner and Martinez, "Guilty Associations," 75.

73. Danner and Martinez, "Guilty Associations," 78.

74. Danner and Martinez, "Guilty Associations," 78.

75. Danner and Martinez, "Guilty Associations," 90.

76. Danner and Martinez, "Guilty Associations," 89. Jens David Ohlin further complicates assignations of guilt for collective crimes by problematizing the theory of joint criminal enterprise. See Ohlin, "Three Conceptual Problems." Mirjan R. Damaska similarly explores the "shadow side" of command responsibility. Each emphasizes the divide between assigning criminal liability and the demonstrable degree of actors' personal culpability under international criminal law. See Damarska, "The Shadow Side of Command Responsibility."

77. For a discussion of joint criminal enterprise and rape, see Sellers, "The Prosecution of Sexual Violence in Conflict," 14–16.

78. Danner and Martinez, "Guilty Associations," 80–89. Further, legal configurations of blame that assume some degree of coherence, strategy, and control produce a model of crime—and sexualized violation—as essentially rational and able to be deterred through prosecutions or appeals. As international relations scholars Chris Dolan, Maria Eriksson Baaz, and Maria Stern write, "This view does not readily accommodate the possibility that warring could itself unleash or produce particular manifestations of the sexual that, while conflict-related, are not necessarily dependent on juridical notions of 'command responsibility' and 'joint criminal enterprise', in so far as this possibility threatens the politically important stance that sexual violence is not inevitable and can be brought to an end" (Dolan, Eriksson Baaz, and Stern, "What Is Sexual about Conflict-Related Sexual Violence?," 1158). I extend this observation to emphasize how the reliance on strategy and coordination in law as evidence of culpability can be an individualizing framing of sex and violence that further occludes the reproduction of settler/empire and the work of rape.

79. Lee, "Introduction," 8.

80. The jurisdictional requirements and debates surrounding individual legal liability and corporations in particular are complex and beyond the scope of this book. For example, corporations have been prosecuted under human rights and civil torts law; while corporate officials have been prosecuted by the ICC, corporations as juridical persons have not. See Scheffer, "Corporate Liability under the Rome Statute," 38.

81. Freeman, "Time Binds," 63.

82. See UNFPA, "From Conflict and Crisis to Renewal."

83. Bush, "President Bush Signs Military Commissions Act of 2006."

84. Center for Constitutional Rights, "FAQs: The Military Commission Act of 2006."

85. In 2008, *Boumediene v. Bush* (553 US 723) would find that detainees possessed a right to habeas corpus under US federal law, concluding that Section 7

of the MCA was an unconstitutional suspension of habeas. The plaintiff, Lakhdar Boumediene, a detainee at the US Guantánamo Bay detention camps, was a citizen of Bosnia and Herzegovina.

86. Puar and Rai, "Monster, Terrorist, Fag," 123.

87. Puar and Rai, "Monster, Terrorist, Fag," 123.

88. The notion of necropolitics facilitates an understanding of unending war technologies that "are less concerned with inscribing bodies within disciplinary apparatuses as inscribing them, when the time comes, within the order of the maximal economy now represented by the 'massacre'" (Mbembe, "Necropolitics," 34). The massacre can occur because wars are not fought not by sovereign states but by "armed groups acting behind the mask of the state against armed groups that have no state but control very distinct territories; both sides having as their main targets civilian populations that are unarmed or organized into militias" (35). Mbembe is clear that these martial arrangements stem from economic ones, emerging at the end of the twentieth century in Africa "in direct relation to the erosion of the postcolonial state's capacity to build the economic underpinnings of political authority and order" (31).

89. Roy, *The Failure of Political Islam*, 154.

90. Li, "Jihad in a World of Sovereigns," 375.

91. Li, "Jihad in a World of Sovereigns," 376.

92. Rana, "The Racial Infrastructure," 113.

93. Rana, "The Racial Infrastructure," 113.

94. Abu-Lughod, *Do Muslim Women Need Saving?*; Farris, *In the Name of Women's Rights*.

95. UNFPA, "From Conflict and Crisis to Renewal," i.

96. UNFPA, "From Conflict and Crisis to Renewal," ii.

97. UNFPA, "From Conflict and Crisis to Renewal," iii.

98. UN Security Council Resolution 1820 on Women, Peace, and Security, 2008, accessed February 17, 2021, https://www.unwomen.org/en/docs/2008/6/un-security-council-resolution-1820.

99. Resolution 1820 inscribes wartime sexual violence as a weapon of war and a violation of human rights, while simultaneously reaffirming the resolve expressed in the 2005 World Summit Outcome document to eliminate all forms of violence against women and girls. This includes ending impunity and ensuring the protection of civilians, in particular women and girls, during and after armed conflicts, in accordance with the obligations states have undertaken under international humanitarian law and international human rights law. UN Security Council Resolution 1820.

100. UNFPA, "From Conflict and Crisis to Renewal," 4.

101. Foucault, *Security, Territory, Population*, 252.

Chapter Four / Two Title IXs

This chapter is a reworking of "Two Title IXs: Empire and the Transnational Production of 'Welcomeness' on Campus," *Critical Ethnic Studies Journal* 6, no. 1 (2020): https://manifold.umn.edu/read/two-title-ixs-empire-and-the -transnational-production-of-welcomeness-on-campus/section/8503d2e2-7157 -44cb-9a20-730cb279fb99.

1. These opening two scenes are fictional amalgamations generated from a number of sources that I examined over the course of my research. These scenes have been crafted to express recurring patterns; they do not record discrete events. Any resemblance to singular and actual incidents, locations, or persons is entirely coincidental.

2. Oxford English Dictionary Online, s.v. "welcome," accessed February 18, 2021, https://www.oed.com/view/Entry/226941?rskey=Ly8LKb&result=1.

3. West, "Sex, Law and Consent," 5.

4. Lieberwitz et al., "The History, Uses, and Abuses of Title IX."

5. Halley, "The Move to Affirmative Consent"; Gersen and Suk, "The Sex Bureaucracy," 881.

6. See Fineman, "The Vulnerable Subject," 18–19. As Fineman writes, "Vulnerability theory supplements antidiscrimination approaches in that it is not initially concerned with exclusion and inequality but on the nature of the institutions, their functions, and the relationships contained within them."

7. For a summary of the legal theory, see Fischel, *Screw Consent*.

8. Musser, "Queering Sugar"; Musser, "Consent, Capacity, and the Non-narrative."

9. See Davis, "Rape, Racism and the Myth of the Black Rapist"; Hartman, *Scenes of Subjection*; Morgan, "Accounting for 'The Most Excruciating Torment'"; Chuh, "Discomforting Knowledge"; and Hanssens et al., "A Roadmap for Change."

10. Gersen and Suk, "The Sex Bureaucracy."

11. Agtuca, *Safety for Native Women*, 51.

12. See Owens, "Keyword 7"; and Freedman, *Redefining Rape*.

13. Byrd et al., "Predatory Value," 3.

14. For a discussion of how feminism putatively undid in loco parentis as an animating legal doctrine, see Wiegman, Lubiano, and Hardt, "In the Afterlife of the Duke Case," 8. They write: "In the course of these multiple and sweeping demands, students dismantled much of the prior edifice of the in loco parentis logic. Simple things such as parents receiving grades were replaced with the authority of students to represent themselves as legitimately adult subjects of the institution."

15. "The Violence Against Women Act brought unprecedented recognition and resources to the issue [of violence against women] . . . [T]he 1994 legislation made it a federal crime to cross state lines in order to commit domestic violence or to violate a protection order. It required states to give full faith and credit to protection orders issued by other states. It authorized federal grants to increase

the effectiveness of police, prosecutors, judges, and victim services agencies. It provided funding for a national toll-free domestic violence hot line. It increased federal financial support for battered women's shelters. It reformed immigration law to help immigrant women escape their abusers without being forced to leave the country. It amended the Federal Rules of Evidence to extend rape shield protection to civil as well as criminal cases. It provided federal leadership for efforts to expand research and record-keeping on violence against women." Aleinikoff et al., "Welcoming Remarks and Panel One," 511, 522.

16. Thuma, "Lessons in Self Defense."

17. 42 U.S.C. §13981(c) (2012).

18. Schmidt, "What Killed the Violence against Women Act's Civil Rights Remedy," 516–17. "[MacKinnon] drew on her anti-pornography ordinance but encouraged expanding it to all acts of violence against women. Specifically, she advised that '[i]f Biden wants to do something for women, he should recognize rape and battering as federal sex discrimination claims.'" The Implementation of the Violence against Women Act Provisions of the Violent Crime Control and Law Enforcement Act (Public Law 103–322), Hearing before the S. Comm. on the Judiciary, 103d Cong. 54 (1994) (statement of Sen. Joseph R. Biden, Chairman, S. Comm. on the Judiciary).

19. Typically, criminal charges must be proven beyond a reasonable doubt, while civil cases employ a variety of less stringent standards.

20. See Goldscheid, "Elusive Equality," noting administrative and practical barriers to VAWA's effectiveness; and Schmidt, "What Killed the Violence against Women Act's Civil Rights Remedy?"

21. Post and Siegel, "Equal Protection by Law," 443.

22. Post and Siegel, "Equal Protection by Law," 443. In *Kimel*, a case of age discrimination, decided concurrently, the Court concluded that Congress's enforcement powers under the Fourteenth Amendment did not allow for an abrogation of state authority per the Eleventh Amendment, where the alleged discrimination was rationally based on age.

23. 379 US 241, 250–52 (1964).

24. Cacho, "Civil Rights, Commerce, and US Colonialism," 65.

25. Note, too, that the majority opinion also dismisses the federal civil remedy under "the time-honored principle that the Fourteenth Amendment, by its very terms, prohibits only state action. [T]he principle has become firmly embedded in our constitutional law that the action inhibited by the first section of the Fourteenth Amendment is only such action as may fairly be said to be that of the States. That Amendment erects no shield against merely private conduct, however discriminatory or wrongful." *United States v. Morrison*, 529 U.S. 598 (2000): 21 quoting *Shelley v. Kraemer*, 334 U. S. 1, 13, and n. 12 (1948).

26. *United States v. Morrison*, 120 S. Ct. 1740, 1754.

27. Legal feminist investments in carceral strategies depends on the marginalization of the abolitionist and decolonial traditions of feminist activism

and scholarship. Unfortunately, these studied omissions describe much of the legal feminist scholarship on Title IX. Nancy Chi Cantalupo, characterizing the difference between criminal and civil frameworks for addressing sexualized violence through a lineage of feminism that privileges elite legal and collegiate feminist activisms, writes that criminal frameworks "keep the abstract community as a whole safe from violence, which it achieves, in part, by incarcerating criminal actors while at the same time providing safeguards to avoid punishing innocent defendants. As a result, criminal cases are structured as adversarial proceedings between a defendant and the whole community, represented by the state's prosecutor. Moreover, because defendants face potential incarceration, death, and the loss of legal rights, the state must meet high procedural standards designed to protect defendants' liberty against unjust exercises of the government's immense power to punish. Therefore, the criminal system is primarily focused on the defendant's, not the victim's, rights." See Cantalupo, "For the Title IX Civil Law Movement."

28. Melamed, "The Spirit of Neoliberalism," 2.

29. Atanasoski, *Humanitarian Violence*, 3.

30. Atanasoski, *Humanitarian Violence*, 12.

31. Atanasoski, "'Race' toward Freedom," 213.

32. Atanasoski, *Humanitarian Violence*, 17. For a parsing of the false divide between "secular" and "religious," see Butler, *Frames of War*.

33. Reddy, *Freedom with Violence*, 17.

34. I elaborate this notion through the idea of the sexual state form. See chapter 2.

35. Halley, "Rape at Rome," 8.

36. MacKinnon, *Are Women Human?*, 238. Article 5 of the ICTY statute codifies rape as a crime against humanity, while Article 3 of the ICTR statute does the same. Article 7 of the ICC statute empowers the prosecution of rape, sexual slavery, enforced prostitution, forced pregnancy, enforced sterilization, or any other form of sexual violence of comparable gravity as crimes against humanity.

37. Halley, "Rape at Rome."

38. Engle, "Feminism and Its (Dis)contents."

39. Copelon et al., "Affecting the Rules." Consider, too, that the infamous Antioch College affirmative consent policy emerges in this moment. See *New York Times*, "'Ask First' at Antioch."

40. Dowds, "Conceptualizing the Role of Consent"; Schomberg and Peterson, "Genuine Consent to Sexual Violence under International Criminal Law." As Halley writes, "The ICTY very briefly adopted the no-consent-defense position, only to shift rapidly to a complex of rules that presume non-consent from the coercive circumstances and that allow defendants to offer their proof on the issue only after it had been found to be probative in an in camera hearing [in private chambers] and to be devoid of any admissions by the complaining witness" (Halley, "Rape at Rome," 99). For more on the innerworkings of the ICC, see also Pace and Schense, "Coalition for the International Criminal Court."

41. An endpoint, as I discuss in chapters 1 and 3, is renewed and expanded racialized demands for state accountability, justifying if not requiring criminal legal or military redress by transforming the relationship between (and the meaning of) state sovereignty and sexual consent as first articulated in response to the dissolution of the former Yugoslavia.

42. *Prosecutor v. Akayesu*, ICTR-96-4-T (1998); *Prosecutor v. Kunarac*, T-96-23 and IT-96-23/1-A (2001).

43. Rome Statute, Article 7.

44. UN, "Crimes against Humanity," accessed February 29, 2021, https://www.un.org/en/genocideprevention/crimes-against-humanity.shtml.

45. "Because facts of sexual violence were indicted under this existing legal definition of genocide [as part of an intentional campaign to destroy a people on an ethnic basis], rape was not defined in this connection; the kind of sexual violence that causes genocide is defined by whatever causes serious bodily or mental harm" (MacKinnon, *Are Women Human?*, 239).

46. *Prosecutor v. Akayesu*, 688.

47. *Prosecutor v. Akayesu*, 688.

48. MacKinnon, *Are Women Human?*, 239.

49. MacKinnon, *Are Women Human?*, 238.

50. *Prosecutor v. Akayesu*, 596.

51. *Prosecutor v. Akayesu*, 596.

52. MacKinnon, *Are Women Human?*, 238.

53. MacKinnon, *Are Women Human?*, 238.

54. For example, see the mobilization of international rights standards, sprung from the grounds of war, in the service of US civil law: "The treatment of sexual harassment victims by their schools, and of schools by courts, under the institutional liability standard of deliberate indifference for damages in private suits is inconsistent with Title IX's guarantee of equal educational outcomes on the basis of sex. Replacing deliberate indifference with the international human rights liability standard of due diligence would shift power into the hands of survivors, guarantee institutional accountability, ending current impunity for sexual abuse in schools, and promote change toward sex equality in education" (MacKinnon, "In Their Hands," 2038). I am not commenting on the desirability of a due diligence standard, only noting the interplay between different bodies of law.

55. The collapse of the broad category of sex discrimination to the narrow notion of rape or sexual assault within Title IX is also part of a larger problem with contemporary legal theorizations of sexual consent. As legal scholar Aya Gruber writes about affirmative consent models, "The prohibition of a broad category of sex (sex without a yes) somewhat surreptitiously evolved under the banner of preventing a narrower, less controversial category (compelled or aversive sex)" (Gruber, "Consent Confusion," 420). See also Marcus. "Fighting Bodies, Fighting Words."

56. Note that the legislation did not initially include the phrase "sexual harassment," but was instead an attempt to secure a range of educational opportunities

for women, including access to higher education, athletics, career training and education, education for pregnant and parenting students, employment, the learning environment, math and science education, standardized testing, and technology. 118 Cong. Rec. 5803 (February 28, 1972).

57. See US Department of Justice, "Sexual Assault," https://www.justice.gov /ovw/sexual-assault.

58. What constitutes a "yes" is a separate question. The ambiguity of what is meant by consent, affirmative or otherwise, matters because it marks a shift in the relationship between acceptable and coercive sex. See Gruber, "Consent Confusion," 418, which explores how conceptual ambiguities allow people "to come to wholly different conclusions about how consent and affirmative consent standards actually impact legal decisions and human behavior." See also Ferzan and Westen, "How to Think." They note multiple unmarked usages of consent. Furthermore, coercion, as Ferzan and Westen argue, can revivify the resistance requirement by serving as substitute for force. Welcomeness sidesteps it because welcomeness is entirely subjective: the proof is in the feeling, not the action, not the word.

59. For example, a 2015 Model Penal Code draft seeking to update criminal sexual consent provisions states plainly, "If the actor honestly and sincerely believes a sexual overture is welcomed, there should not be liability even if the other person in fact found the date insufferable, and yet continued to be politely accommodating" (quoted in Gruber, "Consent Confusion," 428).

60. See Model Penal Code §2.02(2)(c) cmt. 5 at 244 (American Law Institute, 1962).

61. *Meritor Savings Bank FSB v. Vinson*, 477 US 57, 1986.

62. MacKinnon, *Women's Lives, Men's Laws*, 244.

63. Halley, "The Move to Affirmative Consent," 261; Lieberwitz et al., "The History, Uses, and Abuses of Title IX."

64. US Department of Justice Civil Rights Division to President Robert G. Frank of the University of New Mexico, April 22, 2016, https://www.justice.gov /opa/file/843901/download.

65. US Department of Justice Civil Rights Division and US Department of Education Office for Civil Rights to President Royce Engstrom of the University of Montana, May 9, 2013, http://www.justice.gov/sites/default/files/opa/legacy /2013/05/09/um-ltr-findings.pdf; emphasis added.

66. Halley, "The Move to Affirmative Consent," 260. At the time of this writing, this guidance has been suspended by Betsy DeVos, but a controlling interpretation has yet to be established.

67. See also Marcus, "Fighting Bodies, Fighting Words," 389. Marcus offers a critique of the feminist modeling of a rape on a "collapsed continuum." A continuum theory of sexual violence links language and rape in a way that can be taken to mean that representations of rape, obscene remarks, threats, and other forms of harassment should be considered equivalent to rape. Such a definition substitutes the remarks and threats that gesture toward a rape for the rape itself and thus

contradicts the very meaning of *continuum*, which requires a temporal and logical distinction between the various stages of a rape attempt. Instead, the "collapsed continuum" makes one type of action (a verbal threat) immediately substitutable for another type of action (sexual assault), the time and space between these two actions collapse, and once again rape has always already occurred.

68. Kipnis, *Unwanted Advances*; Halley, "The Move to Affirmative Consent"; Lieberwitz et al., "The History, Uses, and Abuses of Title IX."

69. Cantalupo, "For the Title IX Civil Rights Movement," 281.

70. See Fischel, *Screw Consent*. Fischel does not look at actual Title IX cases—what few are publicly available—and I would suggest that it is difficult to definitively state how consent is understood in practice beneath prevailing and opaque regimes of nondisclosure.

71. Halley, "The Move to Affirmative Consent," 260.

72. Halley, "The Move to Affirmative Consent," 260.

73. MacKinnon, "Defining Rape Internationally," 940.

74. MacKinnon, "Defining Rape Internationally," 941.

75. MacKinnon, "Rape Redefined."

76. Bazelon, "The Return of the Sex Wars."

77. Janet Halley, Deborah Tuerkheimer, and Stu Marvel outline these legal disputes eloquently in their work on the discrepancies between criminal notions of sexualized violence and campus ones. While colleges and US society at large have moved toward understanding consent or even welcomeness as the critical diagnostic of sexualized violation, in Tuerkheimer's words, "the Model Penal Code [a project of the American Law Institute that attempts to standardize penal law across the United States] and a majority of states still retain a force requirement, effectively consigning most rape—that is, non-stranger rape—to a place beyond law's reach" (Tuerkheimer, "Rape on and off Campus," 1). See Halley, "The Move to Affirmative Consent"; and Marvel, "The Vulnerable Subject of Rape Law."

78. Harris, "Race and Essentialism in Feminist Legal Theory."

79. Jaleel, "Weapons of Sex, Weapons of War."

80. Schultz, "Reconceptualizing Sexual Harassment, Again."

81. MacKinnon, "Rape Redefined," 474.

82. Fanon, *Black Skin, White Masks*, 120.

83. McKittrick, *Demonic Grounds*; Weheliye, *Habeas Viscus*; Spillers, "Mama's Baby, Papa's Maybe"; Beauchamp, *Going Stealth*; Snorton, *Black on Both Sides*.

84. Deer, *The Beginning and End of Rape*; Smith, *Conquest*.

85. Deer, *The Beginning and End of Rape*.

86. Thuma, *All Our Trials*, 25.

87. De Finney et al., "Refusing Band-Aids," 31.

88. Thuma, *All Our Trials*, 7.

89. Bernstein, "Carceral Politics as Gender Justice?"

90. Modulations in the meaning of rape, sexual harassment, and sexual assault depend on the structures and bodies of law that they may be mobilized beneath but also on the territory of the nation-state, whose economic health, as Chandan Reddy and Lisa Marie Cacho write, is tethered to the concept of civil rights and whose existence and health rests on relations of predatory racial capitalism and settler colonial expropriation. Reddy, *Freedom with Violence*; Cacho, "Civil Rights, Commerce, and US Colonialism."

91. Violence against Women Reauthorization Act of 2013, Pub. L. No. 113-4, §304(a)(1)(B)(iii), 127 Stat. 54, 89 (codified as amended at 20 U.S.C. §1092(f)(1) (F)(iii)).

92. Violence against Women Act, 79 *Federal Register* 79 (October 20, 2014): 62,752, 62,764.

93. Gersen and Suk, "The Sex Bureaucracy," 10.

94. Gersen and Suk, "The Sex Bureaucracy," 895–96, quoting Violence against Women Act at 62, 756.

95. Gersen and Suk, "The Sex Bureaucracy," 907–8.

96. Suk, "'The Look in His Eyes,'" 171.

97. See Gillette and Galbraith, "President Signs 2013 VAWA."

98. Deer, *The Beginning and End of Rape*, xiv.

99. Deer, *The Beginning and End of Rape*, xiv.

100. A recent study by the National Institute of Justice—one of the first national reports to include significant research on the perpetrators of "intimate violence"—showed that most were nonnative and largely identified as white. The author of the study, André B. Rosay, director of the Justice Center for the University of Alaska, noted that by far the most glaring result was that almost every victim experienced some sort of interracial violence. See Rosay, "Violence against American Indian and Alaska Native Women and Men."

101. Reyesno Task Force, as quoted in Doyle, *Campus Sex, Campus Security*, 15–16.

102. Reyesno Task Force, as quoted in Doyle, *Campus Sex, Campus Security*, 16.

103. Reyesno Task Force, as quoted in Doyle, *Campus Sex, Campus Security*, 16.

104. "The Chancellor was worried about being 'in violation' of Title IX. . . . Anxiety about the university's legal exposure, especially where sex is concerned (in all senses of the word 'sex') registers on every campus as a background hum" (Doyle, *Campus Sex, Campus Security*, 17).

105. Doyle, *Campus Sex, Campus Security*, 16.

106. Doyle, *Campus Sex, Campus Security*, 10.

107. Boggs et al., "Abolitionist University Studies"; Cottom, *Lower Ed*; Ferguson, *The Reorder of Things*; Harney and Moten, *The Undercommons*; Kamola, *Making the World Global*; Schwartz-Weinstein, "Not Your Academy"; the contributions in Harris et al., *Slavery and the University*.

108. Nash, "Pedagogies of Desire," 201.

Epilogue

1. Melamed and Reddy, "Using Liberal Rights to Enforce Racial Capitalism."
2. Melamed and Reddy, "Using Liberal Rights to Enforce Racial Capitalism."
3. Melamed and Reddy, "Using Liberal Rights to Enforce Racial Capitalism."
4. Jordan, "Poem about My Rights."
5. Farris and Rotenberg, "Introduction," 6. These consequences include the narrow feminisms of "non-emancipatory agendas, such as neoliberalism and right-wing xenophobic politics" advanced through the language of rights.
6. Quoted in Holmes, "Carceral Feminisms, Femonationalism, and Quarantine."
7. Jakobsen, "Perverse Justice," 22; Ritchie, *Arrested Justice*, 138–40.
8. Spade, "Their Laws Will Never Make Us Safer," 158.
9. Farris, *In the Name of Women's Rights*; Al-Ali, "Sexual Violence in Iraq," 16.
10. Farris, *In the Name of Women's Rights*.
11. TallBear, "Making Love and Relations," 161.
12. Jordan, "Poem about My Rights."
13. Jordan, "Poem about My Rights."
14. Jordan, "Poem about My Rights."
15. As Wendy Brown writes, "Freedom's relationship to identity—its promise to address a social injury or marking that is itself constitutive of identity—typically yields the paradox in which the first imaginings of freedom are always constrained by and potentially even require the very structure of oppression that freedom emerges to oppose" (Brown, *States of Injury*, 7).
16. Muñoz, *Cruising Utopia*, 189.
17. Melamed and Reddy, "Using Liberal Rights to Enforce Racial Capitalism."
18. Puar, *Terrorist Assemblages*, xxiii.
19. Mingus, "Transformative Justice."
20. Mingus, "Transformative Justice."
21. Wiegman, *Object Lessons*, quoted in Muñoz, *Cruising Utopia*, 208.
22. Blackwell, Briggs, and Chiu, "Transnational Feminisms Roundtable," 6.
23. Mingus, "Transformative Justice."
24. Here, I am instructed by phenomenal work on reproductive labor and the legacies of slavery. See Spillers, "Mama's Baby, Papa's Maybe"; Hartman, "The Belly of the World"; Morgan, *Laboring Women*; Tadiar, *Things Fall Away*; Tadiar, "Life-Times of Disposability within Global Neoliberalism"; and Weinbaum, *The Afterlife of Reproductive Slavery*.
25. Moten, "The Subprime and the Beautiful," 239.
26. McDuff, Pernell, and Saunders, "Open Letter to the Anti-rape Movement."

Bibliography

Abrams, Kathryn. "Feminists in International Human Rights: The Changer and the Changed." *Berkeley Journal of International Law* 21, no. 2 (2003): 390–94.

Abu-Lughod, Lila. *Do Muslim Women Need Saving?* Cambridge, MA: Harvard University Press, 2013.

Abu-Odeh, Lama. "Holier Than Thou? The Anti-imperialist versus the Local Activist." *Open Democracy*, May 4, 2015. https://www.opendemocracy.net /en/5050/holier-than-thou-antiimperialist-versus-local-activist/.

Aceves, William J. *The Anatomy of Torture: A Documentary History of* Filartiga v. Pena-Irala. Leiden: Brill, 2007.

Agtuca, Jacqueline. *Safety for Native Women: VAWA and American Indian Tribes.* Lame Deer, MT: National Indigenous Women's Resource Center, 2014.

Al-Ali, Nadje. "Sexual Violence in Iraq: Challenges for Transnational Feminist Politics." *European Journal of Women's Studies* 25, no. 1 (2018): 10–27.

Aleinikoff, Alex, Irasema Garza, Lynn Hecht Schafran, Victoria Nourse, Sally Goldfarb, Patricia Reuss, Hilary Shelton, and Helen Neubourne. "Welcoming Remarks and Panel One: Present at the Creation: Drafting and Passing the Violence against Women Act (VAWA)." *Georgetown Journal of Gender and Law* 11, no. 11 (2010): 511–32.

Allen, Beverly. *Rape Warfare: The Hidden Genocide in Bosnia-Herzegovina and Croatia.* Minneapolis: University of Minnesota Press, 1996.

Almond, Mark. *Europe's Backyard War: The War in the Balkans.* London: Heineman, 1994.

Alvarez, Sonia E., Elisabeth Jay Friedman, Ericka Beckman, Maylei Blackwell, Norma Chinchilla, Nathalie Lebon, Marysa Navarro, and Marcela Ríos Tobar. "Encountering Latin American and Caribbean Feminisms." *Signs: Journal of Women in Culture and Society* 28, no. 2 (2003): 537–79.

Amar, Paul. *The Security Archipelago: Human-Security States, Sexuality Politics, and the End of Neoliberalism.* Durham, NC: Duke University Press, 2013.

Amar, Paul. "Turning the Gendered Politics of the Security State Inside Out? Charging the Police with Sexual Harassment in Egypt." *International Feminist Journal of Politics* 13, no. 3 (2011): 299–338.

American Association of International Law. "The Military Commissions Act of 2006: Examining the Relationship between the International Law of Armed Conflict and US Law." *Insights* 10, no. 30 (2006). https://www .asil.org/insights/volume/10/issue/30/military-commissions-act-2006 -examining-relationship-between.

Amin, Kadji. *Disturbing Attachments: Genet, Modern Pederasty, and Queer History.* Durham, NC: Duke University Press, 2017.

Amin, Kadji. "Haunted by the 1990s: Queer Theory's Affective Histories." *Women's Studies Quarterly* 44, nos. 3–4 (2016): 173–89.

Arondekar, Anjali, and Geeta Patel. "Area Impossible: Notes toward an Introduction." *GLQ: A Journal of Lesbian and Gay Studies* 22, no. 2 (2016): 151–71.

Arvin, Maile, Eve Tuck, and Angie Morrill. "Decolonizing Feminism: Challenging Connections between Settler Colonialism and Heteropatriarchy." *Feminist Formations* 25, no. 1 (2013): 8–34.

Askin, Kelly D. "The ICTY at Ten: A Critical Assessment of the Major Rulings of the International Criminal Tribunal over the Past Decade: Reflections on Some of the Most Significant Achievements of the ICTY." *New England Law Review* 37, no. 4 (2003): 903–14.

Askin, Kelly D. "Prosecuting Wartime Rape and Other Gender-Related Crimes under International Law: Extraordinary Advances, Enduring Obstacles." *Berkeley Journal of International Law* 21, no. 2 (2003): 288–349.

Askin, Kelly D. "Sexual Violence in Decisions and Indictments of the Yugoslav and Rwandan Tribunals: Current Status." *American Journal of International Law* 93, no. 1 (1999): 97–123.

Atanasoski, Neda. *Humanitarian Violence: The US Deployment of Diversity*. Minneapolis: University of Minnesota Press, 2013.

Atanasoski, Neda. "'Race' toward Freedom: Post–Cold War US Multiculturalism and the Reconstruction of Eastern Europe." *Journal of American Culture* 29, no. 2 (2006): 213–26.

Baik, Crystal Mun-hye. *Reencounters: On the Korean War and Diasporic Memory Critique*. Philadelphia: Temple University Press, 2019.

Barker, Joanne, ed. *Sovereignty Matters: Locations of Contestation and Possibility in Indigenous Struggles for Self-Determination*. Lincoln: University of Nebraska Press, 2005.

Bassiouni, M. Cherif. "International Crimes: *Jus Cogens* and *Obligatio Erga Omnes*." *Law and Contemporary Problems* 59, no. 4 (1997): 63–74.

Batha, Emma. "Yazidi Girls Sold as Sex Slaves Create Choir to Find Healing." *Reuters*, February 6, 2020. https://www.reuters.com/article/us-iraq-yazidi-women-music/yazidi-girls-sold-as-sex-slaves-create-choir-to-find-healing-idUSKBN20103A.

Batinic, Jelena. "Feminism, Nationalism, and War: The 'Yugoslav Case' in Feminist Texts." *Journal of International Women's Studies* 3, no. 1 (2001): 1–23.

Bazelon, Emily. "The Return of the Sex Wars." *New York Times Magazine*, September 12, 2015. https://www.nytimes.com/2015/09/13/magazine/the-return-of-the-sex-wars.html.

Beauchamp, Toby. *Going Stealth: Transgender Politics and US Surveillance Practices*. Durham, NC: Duke University Press, 2018.

Bernstein, Elizabeth. "Carceral Politics as Gender Justice? The 'Traffic in Women' and Neoliberal Circuits of Crime, Sex, and Rights." *Theory and Society* 41, no. 3 (2012): 233–59.

Bernstein, Elizabeth. "Militarized Humanitarianism Meets Carceral Feminism: The Politics of Sex, Rights, and Freedom in Contemporary Anti-trafficking Campaigns." *Signs: Journal of Women in Culture and Society* 36, no. 1 (2010): 45–72.

Bernstein, Elizabeth. "The Sexual Politics of the 'New Abolitionism.'" *differences: A Journal of Feminist Cultural Studies* 18, no. 3 (2007): 128–51.

Best, Stephen M. *The Fugitive's Properties: Law and the Poetics of Possession*. Chicago: University of Chicago Press, 2004.

Bhandar, Brenna. *Colonial Lives of Property: Law, Land, and Racial Regimes of Ownership*. Durham, NC: Duke University Press, 2018.

Bhandar, Brenna. "Property, Law, and Race: Modes of Abstraction." UCLA *Law Review* 4, no. 1 (2014): 203–18.

Bilic, Bojan. *We Were Gasping for Air*. Baden, Germany: Nomos Verlagsgesellschaft, 2012.

Blackwell, Maylei, Laura Briggs, and Mignonette Chiu. "Transnational Feminisms Roundtable." *Frontiers: A Journal of Women Studies* 36, no. 3 (2015): 1–24.

Block, Sharon. *Rape and Sexual Power in Early America*. Chapel Hill: University of North Carolina Press, 2006.

Boesten, Jelke. "Analyzing Rape Regimes at the Interface of War and Peace in Peru." *International Journal of Transitional Justice* 4, no. 1 (2010): 110–29.

Boggs, Abigail, Eli Meyerhoff, Nick Mitchell, and Zach Schwartz-Weinstein. "Abolitionist University Studies: An Invitation." *Abolition: A Journal of Insurgent Politics* (August 28, 2019). https://abolitionjournal.org/abolitionist-university-studies-an-invitation/.

Bosco, David. "Why Is the International Criminal Court Picking Only on Africa?" *Washington Post*, March 29, 2013.

Brandt, Michelle. "*Doe v. Karadzic*: Redressing Non-state Acts of Gender-Specific Abuse under the Alien Tort Statute." *Minnesota Law Review* 79 (1994): 1413–46.

Brockes, Emma. "#MeToo Founder Tarana Burke: 'You Have to Use Your Privilege to Serve Other People.'" *Guardian*, January 15, 2018. https://www.theguardian.com/world/2018/jan/15/me-too-founder-tarana-burke-women-sexual-assault.

Brown, Wendy. *States of Injury: Power and Freedom in Late Modernity*. Princeton, NJ: Princeton University Press, 1995.

Brownmiller, Susan. *Against Our Will: Men, Women, and Rape*. New York: Ballantine, 1993.

Broz, Svetlana. *Good People in an Evil Time: Portraits of Complicity and Resistance in the Bosnian War*. New York: Penguin Random House, 2005.

Buchwald, Emilie, Pamela R. Fletcher, and Martha Roth, eds. *Transforming a Rape Culture*. Minneapolis: Milkweed Editions, 2005.

Bumiller, Kristin. *In an Abusive State: How Neoliberalism Appropriated the Feminist Movement against Sexual Violence*. Durham, NC: Duke University Press, 2008.

Burns, John F. "Oct. 24–30: Croatian Slaughter; A Massacre Ghoulish Even According to Bosnian Standards." *New York Times*, October 31, 1993.

Bush, George W. "President Bush Signs Military Commissions Act of 2006." White House, October 17, 2006. https://georgewbush-whitehouse.archives.gov/news/releases/2006/10/20061017-1.html.

Buss, Doris E. "Rethinking 'Rape as a Weapon of War.'" *Feminist Legal Studies* 17, no. 2 (2009): 145–63.

Buss, Doris E. "Sexual Violence, Ethnicity, and Intersectionality in International Criminal Law." In *Intersectionality and Beyond: Law, Power, and the Politics of Location*, edited by Emily Graham, Davina Cooper, Jane Krishnadas, and Didi Herman, 105–23. New York: Routledge-Cavendish, 2008.

Buss, Doris E. "Women at the Borders: Rape and Nationalism in International Law." *Feminist Legal Studies* 6, no. 2 (1998): 171–203.

Butler, Judith. *Bodies That Matter: On the Discursive Limits of Sex*. New York: Routledge, 1993.

Butler, Judith. *Frames of War: When Is Life Grievable?* New York: Verso, 2016.

Byrd, Jodi A. *The Transit of Empire: Indigenous Critiques of Colonialism*. Minneapolis: University of Minnesota Press, 2011.

Byrd, Jodi A., Alyosha Goldstein, Jodi Melamed, and Chandan Reddy. "Predatory Value: Economies of Dispossession and Disturbed Relationalities." *Social Text* 36, no. 2 (2018): 1–18.

Cacho, Lisa Marie. "Civil Rights, Commerce, and US Colonialism," *Social Text* 36, no. 2 (2018): 63–82.

Cantalupo, Nancy Chi. "For the Title IX Civil Rights Movement: Congratulation and Cautions." *Yale Law Journal Forum* 125 (2015–2016): 281–303.

Carpenter, R. Charli. "Surfacing Children: Limits to Genocidal Rape Discourse." *Human Rights Quarterly* 22, no. 2 (2000): 428–77.

Castillo, R. Aída Hernández. *Multiple Injustices: Indigenous Women, Law, and Political Struggle in Latin America*. Tucson: University of Arizona Press, 2016.

Castro, Mary Garcia. "Engendering Powers in Neoliberal Times in Latin America: Reflections from the Left on Feminisms and Feminisms." Translated by Laurence Hallewell. *Latin American Perspectives* 28, no. 6 (2001): 17–37.

Center for Constitutional Rights. "FAQs: Military Commission Act of 2006." October 17, 2007. https://ccrjustice.org/home/get-involved/tools-resources /fact-sheets-and-faqs/faqs-military-commisions-act.

Charlesworth, Hilary, Christine Chinkin, and Shelly Wright, "Feminist Approaches to International Law." *American Journal of International Law* 85, no. 4 (1991): 613–45.

Chemerinsky, Erwin. "Presidential Powers Including Military Tribunals in the October 2005 Term." *Touro Law Review* 22, no. 4 (2006): 897–916.

Cherniavsky, Eva. "On (the Impossibility of) Teaching Gayle Rubin. " *Feminist Formations* 32, no. 1 (2020): 88–95.

Chinkin, Christine M. "Kosovo: A 'Good' or 'Bad' War?" *American Journal of International Law* 93, no. 4 (1999): 841–47.

Chinkin, Christine M. "Rape and Sexual Abuse of Women in International Law." *European Journal of International Law* 5, no. 3 (1994): 326–41.

Chow, Rey. *The Age of the World Target: Self-Referentiality in War, Theory, and Comparative Work*. Durham, NC: Duke University Press, 2006.

Chowdury, Rumna. "*Kadic v. Karadzic*: Rape against Women as a Class." *Law and Social Inquiry* 20, no. 1 (2002): 91–124.

Chu, Andrea Long, and Emmett Harsin Drager. "After Trans Studies." *Transgender Studies Quarterly* 6, no. 1 (2019): 103–16.

Chuang, Janie A. "Exploitation Creep and the Unmaking of Human Trafficking Law." *American Journal of International Law* 108, no. 4 (2014): 609–49.

Chuh, Kandice. "Discomforting Knowledge: Or, Korean 'Comfort Women' and Asian Americanist Critical Practice." *Journal of Asian American Studies* 6, no. 1 (2003): 5–23.

Cohen, Ed. *A Body Worth Defending: Immunity, Biopolitics, and the Apotheosis of the Modern Body*. Durham, NC: Duke University Press, 2009.

Cohen, Roger. "Croat-Muslim Link as Flimsy as a Bridge of Rope in Bosnia." *New York Times*, February 13, 1995.

Collective of Women of Color and the Law at the Yale Law School. "Open Letters to Catharine MacKinnon." *Yale Journal of Law and Feminism* 4, no. 1 (1991): 177–90.

Comella, Lynn. "Revisiting the Feminist Sex Wars," *Feminist Studies* 41, no. 2 (2015): 437–62.

Copelon, Rhonda. "End Torture, End Domestic Violence." *On the Issues Magazine* (Winter 2009). http://www.ontheissuesmagazine.com/2009winter /2009winter_7.php.

Copelon, Rhonda. "Gender Crimes as War Crimes: Integrating Crimes against Women into International Criminal Law." *McGill Law Journal* 46, no. 1 (2000): 217–40.

Copelon, Rhonda. "International Human Rights Dimensions of Intimate Violence: Another Strand in the Dialectic of Feminist Lawmaking." *American University Journal of Gender, Social Policy and Law* 11, no. 2 (2003): 865–77.

Copelon, Rhonda. "Recognizing the Egregious in the Everyday: Domestic Violence as Torture." *Columbia Human Rights Law Review* 25, no. 2 (1994): 291–367.

Copelon, Rhonda. "Surfacing Gender: Reconceptualizing Crimes against Women in Time of War." In *Mass Rape: The War against Women in Bosnia-Herzegovina*, edited by Alexandra Stiglmayer, 197–218. Lincoln: University of Nebraska Press, 1994.

Copelon, Rhonda. "Women and War Crimes." *St. John's Law Review* 69, nos. 1–2 (1995): 61–68.

Copelon, Rhonda, Patrick Cotter, Jennifer Green, and Beth Stephens. "Affecting the Rules for the Prosecution of Rape and Other Gender-Based Violence before the International Criminal Tribunal for the Former Yugoslavia: A Feminist Proposal and Critique." *Hastings Women's Law Journal* 5, no. 2 (1994): 171–221.

Cottom, Tressie McMillan. *Lower Ed: The Troubling Rise of For-Profit Colleges in the New Economy*. New York: New Press, 2017.

Damaska, Mirjan R. "The Shadow Side of Command Responsibility." *American Journal of Comparative Law* 49, no. 3 (2001): 455–96.

Danner, Alison Marston, and Jenny S. Martinez. "Guilty Associations: Joint Criminal Enterprise, Command Responsibility, and the Development of International Criminal Law." *California Law Review* 75, no. 1 (2005): 75–169.

Darton, John. "Does the World Still Recognize a Holocaust?" *New York Times*, April 25, 1993.

Das Gupta, Monisha, and Lynn Fujiwara. "Law and Life: Immigrant and Refugee Acts amid White Nationalism." *Amerasia Journal* 46, no. 1 (2020): 2–16.

Davis, Angela Y. "Rape, Racism and the Capitalist Setting." *Black Scholar: Journal of Black Studies and Research* 12, no. 6 (1981): 39–45.

Davis, Angela Y. "Rape, Racism and the Myth of the Black Rapist." In *Women, Race, and Class*, 172–201. New York: Random House, 1981.

Davis, Jeffrey. *Justice across Borders: The Struggle for Human Rights in US Courts.* New York: Cambridge University Press, 2008.

Deer, Sarah. *The Beginning and End of Rape: Confronting Sexual Violence in Native America.* Minneapolis: University of Minnesota Press, 2015.

de Finney, Sandrina, Lena Palacios, Mandeep Kaur Mucina, Anna Chadwick, and John A. MacDonald. "Refusing Band-Aids: Un-settling 'Care' under the Carceral Settler State." *CYC-Online*, no. 235 (September 2018): 28–38. https://cyc-net.org/cyc-online/sep2018.pdf.

des Forges, Alison. *Leave None to Tell the Story: Genocide in Rwanda.* New York: Human Rights Watch, 1999.

Devic, Ana. "Anti-war Initiatives and the Un-making of Civic Identities in the Former Yugoslav Republics." *Journal of Historical Sociology* 10, no. 2 (1997): 127–56.

Dolan, Chris. *War Is Not Yet Over: Community Perceptions of Sexual Violence and Its Underpinnings in Eastern DRC.* London: International Alert, 2010.

Dolan, Chris, Maria Eriksson Baaz, and Maria Stern. "What Is Sexual about Conflict-Related Sexual Violence? Stories from Men and Women Survivors." *International Affairs* 96, no. 5 (2020): 1151–168.

Dougherty, Tom. "No Way around Consent: A Reply to Rubenfeld on Rape-by-Deception." *Yale Law Journal Online* 123 (2013): 321–34.

Dowds, Eithne. "Conceptualizing the Role of Consent in the Definition of Rape at the International Criminal Court: A Norm Transfer Perspective." *International Journal of Feminist Politics* 20, no. 4 (2018): 624–43.

Doyle, Jennifer. *Campus Sex, Campus Security.* Cambridge, MA: Semiotext(e), 2015.

Driskill, Qwo-Li, Chris Finley, Brian Joseph Gilley, and Scott Lauria Morgensen. Introduction to *Queer Indigenous Studies: Critical Interventions in Theory*, edited by Qwo-Li Driskill, Chris Finley, Brian Joseph Gilley, and Scott Lauria Morgensen, 1–28. Tucson: University of Arizona Press, 2011.

Driskill, Qwo-Li, Chris Finley, Brian Joseph Gilley, and Scott Lauria Morgensen, eds. *Queer Indigenous Studies: Critical Interventions in Theory.* Tucson: University of Arizona Press, 2011.

Drumond, Paula, Elizabeth Mesok, and Marysia Zalewski. "Sexual Violence in the Wrong(ed) Bodies: Moving beyond the Gender Binary in International Relations." *International Affairs* 96, no. 5 (2020): 1145–49.

Duarte, Ángela Ixkic Bastian. "From the Margins of Latin American Feminism: Indigenous and Lesbian Feminisms." *Signs: Journal of Women in Culture and Society* 38, no. 1 (2012): 153–78.

Duggan, Lisa. *The Twilight of Equality? Neoliberalism, Cultural Politics, and the Attack on Democracy.* Boston: Beacon, 2003.

Duggan, Lisa, and Nan Hunter. *Sex Wars: Sexual Dissent and Political Culture.* New York: Routledge, 1995.

Echols, Alice. *Daring to Be Bad: Radical Feminism in America, 1967–75.* Minneapolis: University of Minnesota Press, 1995.

Eichstadt, Peter H. *Consuming the Congo: War and Conflict Minerals in the World's Deadliest Place*. Chicago: Lawrence Hill Books, 2011.

Engle, Karen. "Calling in the Troops: The Uneasy Relationship among Women's Rights, Human Rights, and Humanitarian Intervention." *Harvard Human Rights Journal* 20, no. 1 (2007): 189–226.

Engle, Karen. "Feminism and Its (Dis)contents: Criminalizing Wartime Rape in Bosnia and Herzegovina." *American Journal of International Law* 99, no. 4 (2005): 778–817.

Engle, Karen. *The Grip of Sexual Violence in Conflict: Feminist Interventions in International Law*. Stanford, CA: Stanford University Press, 2020.

Engle, Karen. "Liberal Internationalism, Feminism, and the Suppression of Critique: Contemporary Approaches to Global Order in the United States." *Harvard International Law Journal* 46, no. 2 (2005): 427–40.

Engle, Karen, Zinaida Miller, and Denys Mathias Davis, eds. *Anti-impunity and the Human Rights Agenda*. New York: Cambridge University Press, 2016.

Eriksson, Maria. *Defining Rape: Emerging Obligations for States under International Law?* Leiden: Koninklijke Brill, 2011.

Falcón, Sylvanna M. *Power Interrupted: Anti-racist and Feminist Activism Inside the United Nations*. Seattle: University of Washington Press, 2017.

Falk, Patricia J. "Not Logic, but Experience: Drawing on Lessons from the Real World in Thinking about the Riddle of Rape-by-Fraud." *Yale Law Journal Online* 123 (2013): 353–70.

Fanon, Frantz. *Black Skin, White Masks*. Translated by Charles Lam Markmann. New York: Grove, 1967.

Farris, Sara. *In the Name of Women's Rights: The Rise of Femonationalism*. Durham, NC: Duke University Press, 2017.

Farris, Sara, and Catherine Rottenberg. "Introduction: Righting Feminism." *new formations: a journal of culture/theory/politics* 91, no. 1 (2017): 5–15.

Feimster, Crystal. *Southern Horrors: Women and the Politics of Rape and Lynching*. Cambridge, MA: Harvard University Press, 2009.

Ferber, Alona. "Judith Butler on the Culture Wars, JK Rowling and Living in 'Anti-intellectual Times.'" *New Statesman*, September 22, 2020. https://www.newstatesman.com/international/2020/09/judith-butler-culture-wars-jk-rowling-and-living-anti-intellectual-times.

Ferguson, Roderick A. *Aberrations in Black: Toward a Queer of Color Critique*. Minneapolis: University of Minnesota Press, 2004.

Ferguson, Roderick A. "Queer of Color Critique." In *Oxford Research Encyclopedia of Literature*, 2018. https://oxfordre.com/literature/view/10.1093/acrefore/9780190201098.001.0001/acrefore-9780190201098-e-33.

Ferguson, Roderick A. *The Reorder of Things: The University and Its Pedagogies of Minority Difference*. Minneapolis: University of Minnesota Press, 2012.

Ferreira da Silva, Denise. *Toward a Global Idea of Race*. Minneapolis: University of Minnesota Press, 2007.

Ferzan, Kimberly, and Peter Westen. "How to Think (Like a Lawyer) about Rape." *Criminal Law and Philosophy* 11, no. 4 (2017): 759–800.

Fineman, Martha. "The Vulnerable Subject: Anchoring Equality in the Human Condition." *Yale Journal of Law and Feminism* 20, no. 1 (2008): 1–24.

Finnemore, Martha. *The Purpose of Intervention: Changing Beliefs about the Use of Force*. Ithaca, NY: Cornell University Press, 2003.

Fischel, Joseph. *Screw Consent: A Better Politics of Sexual Justice*. Minneapolis: University of Minnesota Press, 2019.

Fisher, Siobhan. "Occupation of the Womb: Forced Impregnation as Genocide." *Duke Law Journal* 46, no. 1 (1996): 91–133.

Foucault, Michel. *The Archaeology of Knowledge; and, The Discourse on Language*. Translated by Alan Sheridan. New York: Pantheon, 1972.

Foucault, Michel. *The Birth of Biopolitics: Lectures at the Collège de France, 1978–1979*. Edited by Michael Senellart and translated by Graham Burchell. New York: Palgrave Macmillan, 2008.

Foucault, Michel. *Security, Territory, Population: Lectures at the Collège de France, 1977–1978*. Edited by Michael Senellart and translated by Graham Burchell. New York: Palgrave Macmillan, 2007.

Franco, Jean. "Rape: A Weapon of War." *Social Text* 91, no. 2 (2007): 23–37.

Franke, Katherine. "Putting Sex to Work." *Denver University Law Review* 75, no. 4 (1998): 1139–80.

Franke, Katherine. "Theorizing Yes: An Essay on Feminism, Law, and Desire." *Columbia Law Review* 101 (2001): 181–208.

Fredman, Sandra. *Comparative Human Rights Law*. Oxford: Oxford University Press, 2018.

Freeman, Elizabeth. "Time Binds, or Erotohistoriography." *Social Text* 23, nos. 3–4 (2005): 58–68.

Freedman, Estelle B. *Redefining Rape: Sexual Violence in the Era of Suffrage and Segregation*. Cambridge, MA: Harvard University Press, 2013.

Friedman, Elisabeth Jay, ed. *Seeking Rights from the Left: Gender, Sexuality, and the Latin American Pink Tide*. Durham, NC: Duke University Press, 2019.

Fukuyama, Francis. *The End of History and the Last Man*. New York: Avon, 1992.

Gagnon, V. P., Jr. *The Myth of Ethnic War: Serbia and Croatia in the 1990s*. Ithaca, NY: Cornell University Press, 2004.

Gago, Verónica. *Feminist International: How to Change Everything*. New York: Verso, 2020.

Gersen, Jacob, and Jeannie Suk. "The Sex Bureaucracy." *California Law Review* 104, no. 4 (2016): 881–948.

Gettleman, Jeffrey. "Clinton Presents Plan to Fight Sexual Violence in Congo." *New York Times*, August 11, 2009.

Gettleman, Jeffrey. "Clinton Presses Congo on Minerals." *New York Times*, August 10, 2009.

Gettleman, Jeffrey. "Symbol of Unhealed Congo: Male Rape Victims." *New York Times*, August 4, 2009.

Gillette, Jodi, and Charlie Galbraith. "President Signs 2013 VAWA—Empowering Tribes to Protect Native Women." *The White House: President Barack Obama* (blog), March 7, 2013. https://obamawhitehouse.archives.gov/blog/2013/03/07/president-signs-2013-vawa-empowering-tribes-protect-native-women.

Gill-Peterson, Julian. *Histories of the Transgender Child*. Minneapolis: University of Minnesota Press, 2018.

Gilmore, Ruth Wilson. "Abolition Geography and the Problem of Innocence." In *Futures of Black Radicalism*, edited by Gaye Theresa Johnson and Alex Lubin, 225–40. Brooklyn: Verso, 2017.

Glasius, Marlies. *The International Criminal Court: A Global Civil Society Achievement*. New York: Routledge, 2006.

Goldscheid, Julie. "Elusive Equality in Domestic and Sexual Violence Law Reform." *Florida State University Law Review* 34, no. 3 (2007): 731–78.

Goldstein, Alyosha, ed. *Formations of United States Colonialism*. Durham, NC: Duke University Press, 2014.

Goldstone, Richard J. "Prosecuting Rape as a War Crime." *Case Western Reserve Journal of International Law* 34, no. 3 (2002): 277–86.

Gopinath, Gayatri. *Impossible Desires: Queer Diasporas and South Asian Public Cultures*. Durham, NC: Duke University Press, 2005.

Gopinath, Gayatri. *Unruly Visions: The Aesthetic Practices of Queer Diaspora*. Durham, NC: Duke University Press, 2018.

Grandin, Greg. *Empire's Workshop: Latin America, the United States, and the Rise of the New Imperialism*. New York: Metropolitan, 2006.

Grandin, Greg. "The Latin American Exception: How a Washington Global Torture Gulag Was Turned into the Only Gulag-Free Zone on Earth." *Le Monde Diplomatique*, February 19, 2013. https://mondediplo.com/openpage/the-latin-american-exception.

Greppi, Edoardo. "The Evolution of Individual Criminal Responsibility under International Law." *International Review of the Red Cross* 81, no. 835 (1999): 531–54.

Gross, Aeyal. "Rape by Deception and the Policing of Gender and Nationality Borders." *Tulane Journal of Law and Sexuality* 24 (2015): 1–34.

Gruber, Aya. "Consent Confusion." *Cardozo Law Review* 38, no. 2 (2016): 425–48.

Gruber, Aya. *The Feminist War on Crime: The Unexpected Role of Women's Liberation in Mass Incarceration*. Oakland: University of California Press, 2020.

Gruber, Aya. "Rape, Feminism, and the War on Crime." *Washington Law Review* 84, no. 4 (2009): 581–660.

Gupta, Amith. "Orientalist Feminism Rears Its Head in India." *Jadaliyya*, January 2, 2013. https://www.jadaliyya.com/Details/27746.

Gutman, Roy. "A Daily Ritual of Sex Abuse." *Newsday*, April 19, 1993.

Gutman, Roy. "Rape Camps: Evidence Serb Leaders in Bosnia OKd Attacks."
   Newsday, April 19, 1993.

Gutman, Roy. *A Witness to Genocide*. New York: Lisa Drew Books, 1993.

Haag, Pamela. *Consent: Sexual Rights and the Transformation of American Liberalism*. Ithaca, NY: Cornell University Press, 1999.

Hajjar, Lisa. "American Torture: The Price Paid, the Lessons Learned." *Middle East Report* 39, no. 251 (2009): 14–19.

Hajjar, Lisa. "From Nuremberg to Guantánamo: International Law and American Power Politics." *Middle East Report* 33, no. 229 (2003): 8–15.

Halley, Janet. "The Move to Affirmative Consent." *Signs: Journal of Women in Culture and Society* 42, no. 1 (2016): 257–79.

Halley, Janet. "Rape at Rome: Feminist Interventions in the Criminalization of Sex-Related Violence in Positive International Criminal Law." *Michigan Journal of International Law* 30, no. 1 (2009): 1–123.

Halley, Janet. "Rape in Berlin: Reconsidering the Criminalisation of Rape in the International Law of Armed Conflict." *Melbourne Journal of International Law* 9 (2008): 1–47.

Halley, Janet. "Where in the Legal Order Have Feminists Gained Inclusion?" In *Governance Feminism: An Introduction*, edited by Janet Halley, Pranha Kotiswaran, Rachel Rebouché, and Hila Shamir, 3–22. Minneapolis: University of Minnesota Press, 2018.

Halley, Janet. "Which Forms of Feminism Have Gained Inclusion?" In *Governance Feminism: An Introduction*, edited by Janet Halley, Pranha Kotiswaran, Rachel Rebouché, and Hila Shamir, 23–55. Minneapolis: University of Minnesota Press, 2018.

Halley, Janet, Prabha Kotiswaran, Rachel Rebouché, and Hila Shamir, eds. *Governance Feminism: Notes from the Field*. Minneapolis: University of Minnesota Press, 2019.

Halley, Janet, Prabha Kotiswaran, Rachel Rebouché, and Hila Shamir. Preface to *Governance Feminism: Notes from the Field*, edited by Janet Halley, Pranha Kotiswaran, Rachel Rebouché, and Hila Shamir, ix–xxxviii. Minneapolis: University of Minnesota Press, 2019.

Hansen, Lene. "Gender, Nation, Rape: Bosnia and the Construction of Security." *International Feminist Journal of Politics* 3, no. 1 (2000): 55–75.

Hanssens, Catherine, Aisha C. Moodie-Mills, Andrea J. Ritchie, Dean Spade, and Urvashi Vaid. "A Roadmap for Change: Federal Policy Recommendations for Addressing the Criminalization of LGBT People and People Living with HIV." Center for Gender and Sexuality Law, Columbia Law School, 2014. http://www.law.columbia.edu/gender-sexuality/roadmap-change.

Haraway, Donna. *Staying with the Trouble: Making Kin in the Chthulucene*. Durham, NC: Duke University Press, 2016.

Harney, Stefano, and Fred Moten. *The Undercommons: Fugitive Planning and Black Study*. Wivenhoe, UK: Minor Compositions, 2013.

Harris, Angela P. 1990. "Race and Essentialism in Feminist Legal Theory." *Stanford Law Review* 42, no. 3 (1990): 581–616.

Harris, Cheryl. "Whiteness as Property." *Harvard Law Review* 106, no. 8 (1993): 1707–91.

Harris, Leslie M., James T. Campbell, and Alfred L. Brophy, eds. *Slavery and the University: Histories and Legacies*. Athens: University of Georgia Press, 2019.

Hartman, Saidiya. "The Belly of the World: A Note on Black Women's Labors." *Souls* 18, no. 1 (2016): 166–73.

Hartman, Saidiya V. *Scenes of Subjection: Terror, Slavery, and Self-Making in Nineteenth-Century America*. New York: Oxford University Press, 1997.

Hathaway, Oona, Aileen Nowlan, and Julia Spiegel. "Tortured Reasoning: The Intent to Torture Under International and Domestic Law." *Virginia Journal of International Law* 52, no. 4 (2012): 791–837.

Heineman, Elizabeth. "The History of Sexual Violence in Conflict Zones: Conference Report." *Radical History Review* 101, no. 1 (2008): 5–21.

Heineman, Elizabeth, ed. *Sexual Violence in Conflict Zones: From the Ancient World to the Era of Human Rights*. Philadelphia: University of Pennsylvania Press, 2011.

Herr, Ranjoo Sedou. "Reclaiming Third World Feminisms: Or Why Transnational Feminism Needs Third World Feminisms." *Meridians* 12, no. 1 (2014): 1–30.

Hobson, Emily K. *Lavender and Red: Liberation and Solidarity in the Gay and Lesbian Left*. Oakland: University of California Press, 2016.

Holland, Sharon Patricia. *The Erotic Life of Racism*. Durham, NC: Duke University Press, 2012.

Holloway, Karla F. C. "'Cruel Enough to Stop the Blood' Global Feminisms and the US Body Politic, or: 'They Done Taken My Blues and Gone.'" *Meridians* 7, no. 1 (2006): 1–18.

Holmes, Caren. "Carceral Feminisms, Femonationalism, and Quarantine." *Abolition Journal* (July 12, 2020). https://abolitionjournal.org/carceral-feminism-pandemic/.

Hong, Grace Kyungwon. *Death beyond Disavowal: The Impossible Politics of Difference*. Minneapolis: University of Minnesota Press, 2015.

Hong, Grace Kyungwon. "The Ghosts of Transnational American Studies: A Response to the Presidential Address." *American Quarterly* 59, no. 1 (2007): 33–39.

Howe, Sara Eleanor. "The Madres de la Plaza de Mayo: Asserting Motherhood; Rejecting Feminism?" *Journal of International Women's Studies* 7, no. 3 (2006): 43–50.

Hua, Julietta. *Trafficking Women's Human Rights*. Minneapolis: University of Minnesota Press, 2011.

Human Rights Watch. "Untold Terror: Violence against Women in Peru's Armed Conflict." Report, 1992. https://www.hrw.org/report/1992/12/01/untold-terror-violence-against-women-perus-armed-conflict#.

Independent International Commission on Kosovo. *The Kosovo Report: Conflict, International Response, Lessons Learned*. New York: Oxford University Press, 2000.

Irwin, Jennifer. "Civil Actions Offer Some Closure for Bosnia Victims." Institute for War and Peace Reporting, April 26, 2011. https://iwpr.net/global-voices /civil-actions-offer-some-closure-bosnia-victims.

Jain, Dipika, and Debanuj DasGupta. "Law, Gender Identity, and the Uses of Human Rights: The Paradox of Recognition in South Asia." *Journal of Human Rights* 20, no. 1 (2020): 1–21.

Jakobsen, Janet R. "Perverse Justice." *GLQ: A Journal of Lesbian and Gay Studies* 18, no. 1 (2012): 19–45.

Jaleel, Rana M. "The Wages of Human Trafficking." *Brooklyn Law Journal* 81, no. 2 (2016): 563–625.

Jaleel, Rana M. "Weapons of Sex, Weapons of War: Feminisms, Ethnic Conflict and the Rise of Rape and Sexual Violence in Public International Law during the 1990s." *Cultural Studies* 27, no. 1 (2013): 115–35.

Jefremovas, Villia. *Brickyards to Graveyards: From Production to Genocide in Rwanda*. Albany: SUNY Press, 2012.

Jefremovas, Villia. "Contested Identities: Power and the Fictions of Ethnicity, Ethnography and History in Rwanda." *Anthropologica* 39, nos. 1–2 (1997): 91–104.

Jefremovas, Villia. "Treacherous Waters: The Politics of History and the Politics of Genocide in Rwanda and Burundi." *Africa: Journal of the International African Institute* 70, no. 2 (2000): 298–308.

Jordan, June. "Poem about My Rights." Poetry Foundation. Accessed February 21, 2021. https://www.poetryfoundation.org/poems/48762/poem-about-my -rights.

Kajevska, Ana Miškovska. *Feminist Activism at War: Belgrade and Zagreb Feminists in the 1990s*. New York: Routledge, 2017.

Kaldor, Mary. *New and Old Wars: Organized Violence in a Global Era*. Stanford, CA: Stanford University Press, 1999.

Kamola, Isaac A. *Making the World Global: US Universities and the Production of the Global Imaginary*. Durham, NC: Duke University Press, 2019.

Kang, Laura Hyun Yi. *Compositional Subjects: Enfiguring Asian/American Women*. Durham, NC: Duke University Press, 2002.

Kaplan, Caren, and Inderpal Grewal, eds. *Scattered Hegemonies: Postmodernity and Transnational Feminist Practices*. Minneapolis: University of Minnesota Press, 1994.

Kapur, Ratna. *Erotic Justice: Law and the New Politics of Postcolonialism*. New York: Routledge, 2013.

Kapur, Ratna. "Human Rights in the 21st Century: Take a Walk on the Dark Side." *Sydney Law Review* 28, no. 4 (2006): 665–88.

Kesic, Vesna. "A Response to Catharine MacKinnon's Article 'Turning Rape into Pornography: Postmodern Genocide.'" *Hasting's Women's Law Journal* 5, no. 2 (1994): 267–81.

Kinzer, Stephen. "Ethnic Conflict Is Threatening in Yet Another Region of Yugoslavia: Kosovo." *New York Times*, November 9, 1992.

Kinzer, Stephen. "U.N. Official Warns Europe on Ethnic Strife." *New York Times*, May 18, 1993.

Kipnis, Laura. *Unwanted Advances: Sexual Paranoia Comes to Campus*. New York: Harper Collins, 2017.

Kirby, Paul. "How Is Rape a Weapon of War? Feminist International Relations, Modes of Critical Explanation and the Study of Wartime Sexual Violence." *European Journal of International Relations* 19, no. 4 (2013): 797–821.

Koh, Harold Hongju. "*Filártiga v. Peña-Irala*: Judicial Internalization into Domestic Law of the Customary International Norm against Torture." In *International Law Stories*, edited by John E. Noyes, Laura A. Dickinson, and Mark W. Janis, 45–76. New York: Foundation Press, 2007.

Krieger, Heike. 2001. *The Kosovo Conflict and International Law: An Analytical Documentation 1974–1999*. Cambridge: Cambridge University Press, 2001.

Kunstle, David P. "*Kadic v. Karadžić*: Do Private Individuals Have Enforceable Rights and Obligations under the Alien Tort Claims Act?" *Duke Journal of Comparative and International Law* 6, no. 2 (1996): 319–46.

Leatherman, Janie. *Sexual Violence and Armed Conflict*. Malden, MA: Polity, 2011.

Lee, Roy S. "Introduction: The Rome Conference and Its Contributions to International Law." In *The International Criminal Court: The Making of the Rome Statute*, 1–40. The Hague: Kluwer Law International, 2002.

LaFleur, Greta. *The Natural History of Sexuality in Early America*. Baltimore: Johns Hopkins University Press, 2020.

Leval, Pierre N. "Beyond *Kiobel*: The Future of Human Rights Litigation in US Courts." UCLA *Journal of International Law and Foreign Affairs* 19, no. 1 (2015): 1–18.

Lewin, Tamar. "The Balkans Rapes: A Legal Test for the Outraged." *New York Times*, January 15, 1993.

Li, Darryl. "Jihad in a World of Sovereigns: Law, Violence, and Islam in the Bosnia Crisis." *Law and Social Inquiry* 41, no. 2 (2016): 371–401.

Li, Darryl. *The Universal Enemy: Jihad, Empire, and the Challenge of Solidarity*. Stanford, CA: Stanford University Press, 2020.

Lieberwitz, Risa, Rana Jaleel, Tina Keheller, Anita Levy, Joan Scott, and Donna Young. "The History, Uses, and Abuses of Title IX." American Association of University Professors, June 2016. https://www.aaup.org/sites/default/files/TitleIXreport.pdf.

Liu, Petrus. *Queer Marxism in Two Chinas*. Durham, NC: Duke University Press, 2015.

Lowe, Lisa. *The Intimacies of Four Continents*. Durham, NC: Duke University Press, 2015.

MacKinnon, Catharine A. *Are Women Human? And Other International Dialogues*. Cambridge, MA: Harvard University Press, 2006.

MacKinnon, Catharine A. "Crimes of War, Crimes of Peace." *UCLA Women's Law Journal* 4, no. 1 (1993): 59–86.

MacKinnon, Catharine A. "Defining Rape Internationally: A Comment on Akayesu." *Columbia Journal of Transnational Law* 44, no. 3 (2006): 940–58.

MacKinnon, Catharine A. "Feminism, Marxism, Method, and the State: Toward Feminist Jurisprudence." *Signs: Journal of Women in Culture and Society* 8, no. 4 (1983): 635–58.

MacKinnon, Catharine A. *Feminism Unmodified: Discourses on Life and Law*. Cambridge, MA: Harvard University Press, 1987.

MacKinnon, Catharine A. "From Practice to Theory, or What Is a White Woman Anyway?" *Yale Journal of Law and Feminism* 4 (1991): 13–22.

MacKinnon, Catharine A. "International Gender Justice Dialogue: Professor Catharine A. MacKinnon." Nobel Women's Initiative, April 20, 2010. http://nobelwomensinitiative.org/2010/04/session-ii-prosecutions-and -jurisprudence.

MacKinnon, Catharine A. "In Their Hands: Restoring Institutional Liability for Sexual Harassment in Education." *Yale Law Journal* 125, no. 7 (2016): 2038–2105.

MacKinnon, Catharine A. "#MeToo Has Done What the Law Could Not." *New York Times*, February 4, 2018.

MacKinnon, Catharine A. "Rape, Genocide, and Women's Human Rights." *Harvard Women's Law Journal* 17, no. 1 (1994): 5–16.

MacKinnon, Catharine A. "Rape Redefined." *Harvard Law and Policy Review* 10 (2016): 431–78.

MacKinnon, Catharine A. "Reflections on Sex Equality under Law." *Yale Law Journal* 100, no. 5 (1991): 1281–1328.

MacKinnon, Catharine A. "Turning Rape into Pornography: Postmodern Genocide." In *Mass Rape: The War against Women in Bosnia-Herzegovina*, edited by Alexandra Stiglmayer, 73–81. Lincoln: University of Nebraska Press, 1994.

MacKinnon, Catharine A. "Where #MeToo Came from, and where It's Going: The Movement Is Moving the Culture beneath the Law of Sexual Abuse." *Atlantic*, March 24, 2019. https://www.theatlantic.com/ideas/archive/2019 /03/catharine-mackinnon-what-metoo-has-changed/585313/.

MacKinnon, Catharine A. *Women's Lives, Men's Laws*. Cambridge, MA: Harvard University Press, 2007.

Mahoney, Martha R. "Whiteness and Women, in Practice and Theory: A Reply to Catharine MacKinnon." *Yale Journal of Law and Feminism* 5, no. 2 (1992): 217–52.

Mamdani, Mahmood. *When Victims Become Killers: Colonialism, Nativism, and the Genocide in Rwanda*. Princeton, NJ: Princeton University Press, 2002.

Marcus, Sharon. "Fighting Bodies, Fighting Words: A Theory and Politics of Rape Prevention." In *Feminists Theorize the Political*, edited by Judith Butler and Joan Scott, 385–403. New York: Routledge, 1992.

Marvel, Stu. "The Vulnerable Subject of Rape Law: Rethinking Agency and Consent. A Response to Deborah Tuerkheimer, Rape on and off Campus." *Emory Law Journal Online* 65 (2015): 2035–50.

Marx, Karl. *Capital: Volume One*. New York: Courier Dover, 2019.

Mbembe, Achille. "Necropolitics." Translated by Libby Meintjes. *Public Culture* 15, no. 1 (2003): 11–40.

McClintock, Michael. *Instruments of Statecraft: US Guerilla Warfare, Counter-Insurgency, Counter-Terrorism, 1940–1990*. New York: Pantheon, 1992.

McDuff, Robin, Deanne Pernell, and Karen Saunders. "Open Letter to the Anti-rape Movement." 1977. https://issuu.com/projectnia/docs/letter-to-the-antirape-movement.

McGlynn, Clare, and Vanessa E. Munro, eds. *Rethinking Rape Law: International and Comparative Perspectives*. New York: Routledge, 2010.

McGuire, Danielle. *At the Dark End of the Street: Black Women, Rape, and Resistance: A New History of the Civil Rights Movement from Rosa Parks to the Rise of Black Power*. New York: Random House, 2011.

McKittrick, Katherine. *Demonic Grounds: Black Women and the Cartographies of Struggle*. Minneapolis: University of Minnesota Press, 2006.

Meger, Sara. "The Fetishization of Sexual Violence." *International Studies Quarterly* 60, no. 1 (2016): 149–59.

Meger, Sara. "Rape in Contemporary Warfare: The Role of Globalization in Wartime Sexual Violence." *African Conflict and Peacebuilding Review* 1, no. 1 (2011): 100–132.

Meger, Sara. *Rape Loot Pillage: The Political Economy of Sexual Violence in Armed Conflict*. New York: Oxford University Press, 2016.

Melamed, Jodi. *Represent and Destroy: Rationalizing Violence in the New Racial Capital*. Minneapolis: University of Minnesota Press, 2011.

Melamed, Jodi. "The Spirit of Neoliberalism: From Radical Liberalism to Neoliberal Multiculturalism." *Social Text* 24, no. 4 (2006): 1–24.

Melamed, Jodi, and Chandan Reddy. "Using Rights to Enforce Racial Capitalism." *Items: Insights from the Social Sciences*, February 20, 2019. https://items.ssrc.org/race-capitalism/using-liberal-rights-to-enforce-racial-capitalism/ 2019.

Meron, Theodor. "On a Hierarchy of International Human Rights." *American Journal of International Law* 80, no. 1 (1986): 1–23.

Meron, Theodor. "Rape as a Crime under International Law." *American Journal of International Law* 87, no. 3 (1993): 424–28.

Merry, Sally Engle. *Human Rights and Gender Violence: Translating International Law into Local Justice*. Chicago: University of Chicago Press, 2009.

Mills, Charles W. *The Racial Contract*. Ithaca, NY: Cornell University Press, 1997.

Mingus, Mia. "Transformative Justice: A Brief Description." TransformHarm.org. Accessed February 20, 2021. https://transformharm.org/transformative -justice-a-brief-description/.

Mitchell, Timothy. "Society, Economy, and the State Effect." In *State/Culture: State-Formation after the Cultural Turn*, edited by George Steinmetz, 76–97. Ithaca, NY: Cornell University Press, 1999.

Moloney, Anastasia. "Guatemalan War Rape Victims Break Silence in Genocide Trial." *Thomson Reuters Foundation News*, May 10, 2013. https://news.trust .org/item/20130510144558-362tb.

Morgan, Jennifer L. "Accounting for 'The Most Excruciating Torment': Gender, Slavery, and Trans-Atlantic Passages." *History of the Present* 6, no. 2 (2016): 184–207.

Morgan, Jennifer L. *Laboring Women: Reproduction and Gender in New World Slavery*. Philadelphia: University of Pennsylvania Press, 2011.

Morgan, Jennifer L. "*Partus sequitur ventrem*: Law, Race, and Reproduction in Colonial Slavery." *Small Axe* 22, no. 1 (2018): 1–17.

Morgensen, Scott Lauria. *Spaces between Us: Queer Settler Colonialism and Indigenous Decolonization*. Minneapolis: University of Minnesota Press, 2012.

Moten, Fred. "The Subprime and the Beautiful." *African Identities* 11, no. 2 (2013): 237–45.

Muñoz, José Esteban. *Cruising Utopia: The Then and There of Queer Futurity*. Durham, NC: Duke University Press, 2009.

Murphy, Michelle. *The Economization of Life*. Durham, NC: Duke University Press, 2017.

Musser, Amber Jamilla. "Consent, Capacity, and the Non-narrative." In *Queer Feminist Science Studies: A Reader*, edited by Cyd Cipolla, Kristina Gupta, David A. Rubin, and Angela Willey, 221–33. Seattle: University of Washington Press, 2017.

Musser, Amber Jamilla. "Queering Sugar: Kara Walker's Sugar Sphinx and the Intractability of Black Female Sexuality." *Signs: Journal of Women in Culture and Society* 42, no. 1 (2016): 153–74.

Nadj, Daniela. "The Culturalisation of Identity in an Age of 'Ethnic Conflict'— Depoliticised Gender in ICTY Wartime Sexual Violence Jurisprudence." *International Journal of Human Rights* 15, no. 5 (2011): 647–63.

Nash, Jennifer C. *Black Feminism Reimagined: After Intersectionality*. Durham, NC: Duke University Press, 2018.

Nash, Jennifer C. "Pedagogies of Desire." *differences: A Journal of Feminist Cultural Studies* 30, no. 1 (2019): 197–217.

New York Times. "'Ask First' at Antioch." October 16, 1993.

New York Times. "Turning Back the Clock on Rape." September 23, 2006.

Nguyen, Mimi Thi. *The Gift of Freedom: War, Debt, and Other Refugee Passages.* Durham, NC: Duke University Press, 2012.

Nobel Women's Initiative. "From Survivors to Defenders: Women Confronting Violence in Mexico, Honduras, and Guatemala." June 11, 2012. http://nobelwomensinitiative.org/wp-content/uploads/2012/06/Report _AmericasDelgation-2012.pdf?ref=18.

Ochoa, Christiana. "Access to U.S. Federal Courts as a Forum for Human Rights Disputes: Pluralism and the Alien Tort Claims Act." *Indiana Journal of Global Legal Studies* 12, no. 2 (2005): 631–50.

Ohlin, Jens David. "Three Conceptual Problems with the Doctrine of Joint Criminal Enterprise." *Journal of International Criminal Justice* 5, no. 1 (2007): 69–90.

Ong, Aihwa. "Strategic Sisterhood or Sisters in Solidarity? Questions of Communitarianism and Citizenship in Asia." *Indiana Journal of Global Legal Studies* 4, no. 1 (1996): 107–35.

Oosterveld, Valerie. "The Definition of 'Gender' in the Rome Statute of the International Criminal Court: A Step Forward or Back for International Criminal Justice?" *Harvard Human Rights Journal* 18, no. 1 (2005): 55–84.

Oosterveld, Valerie. "Sexual Slavery and the International Criminal Court: Advancing International Law." *Michigan Journal of International Law* 25, no. 3 (2004): 605–51.

Oosterveld, Valerie. "When Women Are the Spoils of War." *UNESCO Courier* 51, nos. 7–8 (1998): 64–66.

"Open Letters to Catharine MacKinnon." *Yale Journal of Law and Feminism* 4 (1991): 177–90.

Orford, Anne. *International Authority and the Responsibility to Protect.* New York: Cambridge University Press, 2011.

Orford, Anne. *Reading Humanitarian Intervention: Human Rights and the Use of Force in International Law.* New York: Cambridge University Press, 2007.

Owens, Emily A. "Keyword 7: Consent." *differences: A Journal of Feminist Cultural Studies* 30, no. 1 (2019): 148–56.

Pace, William R., and Jennifer Schense. "Coalition for the International Criminal Court at the Preparatory Commission." In *The International Criminal Court: Elements of Crimes and Rules of Procedure and Evidence*, edited by Roy S. Lee, 705–34. Ardsley, NY: Transnational, 2001.

Parra, Juliana Rincón. "Guatemala: Speaking Out on the Genocide of Indigenous Women." *Global Voices*, February 22, 2012. http://globalvoicesonline .org/2012/02/22/guatemala-speaking-out-o-the-genocide-of-indigenous -women/.

Pateman, Carole. *The Sexual Contract.* Cambridge: Polity, 1988.

Perluss, Deborah, and Joan F. Hartman. "Temporary Refuge: Emergence of a Customary Norm." *Virginia Journal of International Law* 26, no. 3 (1986): 551–626.

Petrovic, Dranzen. "Ethnic Cleansing: An Attempt at Methodology." *European Journal of International Law* 5, no. 3 (1994): 342–59.

Philipose, Elisabeth. "Feminism, International Law, and the Spectacular Violence of the 'Other': Decolonizing the Laws of War." In *Theorizing Sexual Violence*, edited by Victoria Grace and Renée J. Heberle, 176–204. New York: Routledge, 2009.

Phipps, Alison, Jessica Ringrose, Emma Renold, and Carolyn Jackson, "Rape Culture, Lad Culture and Everyday Sexism: Researching, Conceptualizing and Politicizing New Mediations of Gender and Sexual Violence." *Journal of Gender Studies* 27, no. 1 (2018): 1–8.

Portman, Roland. *Legal Personality in International Law*. New York: Cambridge University Press, 2010.

Posner, Theodore R. "Kadic v. Karadzic. 70 F.3d 232." *American Journal of International Law* 90, no. 4 (1996): 658–63.

Post, Robert C., and Reva B. Siegel. "Equal Protection by Law: Federal Antidiscrimination Legislation after *Morrison* and *Kimel*." *Yale Law Journal* 110, no. 3 (2000): 441–526.

Potter, Claire Bond. "Taking Back Times Square: Feminist Repertoires and the Transformation of Urban Space in Late Second Wave Feminism." *Radical History Review*, no. 113 (2012): 67–80.

Puar, Jasbir K. *Terrorist Assemblages: Homonationalism in Queer Times*. Durham, NC: Duke University Press, 2007.

Puar, Jasbir K., and Amit Rai. "Monster, Terrorist, Fag: The War on Terrorism and the Production of Docile Patriots." *Social Text* 20, no. 3 (2002): 117–48.

Radcliffe, Sarah A. "Women's Place/El Lugar de Mujeres: Latin America and the Politics of Gender Identity." In *Place and the Politics of Identity*, edited by Michael Keith and Steve Pile, 100–114. New York: Routledge, 1993.

Ramachandran, Gowri. "Delineating the Heinous: Rape, Sex, and Self-Possession." *Yale Law Journal Online* 123 (2013): 371–78.

Rana, Junaid. "The Racial Infrastructure of the Terror-Industrial Complex." *Social Text* 34, no. 4 (2016): 111–38.

Rao, Rahul. *Out of Time: The Queer Politics of Postcoloniality*. Oxford: Oxford University Press, 2020.

Ratner, David. "Haifa Transgender Sex Scandal Ends with a Plea and Community Service." *Ha'aretz*, September 8, 2003. https://www.haaretz.com/1.5371800.

Reddy, Chandan. *Freedom with Violence: Race, Sexuality, and the US State*. Durham, NC: Duke University Press, 2011.

Reid-Pharr, Robert. *Archives of Flesh: African America, Spain, and Post-Humanist Critique*. New York: New York University Press, 2016.

Reuters. "'Rape Epidemic' in African Conflict Zones—UNICEF." February 12, 2008. https://www.reuters.com/article/idINIndia-31908520080212.

Riding, Alan. "France Presses US for Stronger Stand on Bosnia." *New York Times*, January 6, 1994.

Ritchie, Beth E. *Arrested Justice: Black Women, Violence, and America's Prison Nation*. New York: New York University Press, 2012.

Rivera, Taracila. *El Andar de las Mujeres Indígenas* [The movements of indigenous women]. Lima: Chiparac, 1999.

Rodríguez, Dylan. "Racial/Colonial Genocide and the 'Neoliberal Academy': In Excess of a Problematic." *American Quarterly* 64, no. 4 (2012): 809–13.

Rodríguez, Carmen. "Fifth Feminist Conference of Latin America and the Caribbean: A Bet on the Future." *Aquelarre*, no. 6. (1990): 33–34.

Rodríguez, Juana María. "Keyword 6: Testimony." *differences: A Journal of Feminist Cultural Studies* 30, no. 1 (2019): 119–25.

Roht-Arriaza, Naomi. "Prosecuting Genocide in Guatemala: The Case before the Spanish Courts and the Limits to Extradition." Center for Global Studies: Project on Human Rights, Global Justice and Democracy, Working Paper no. 2 (2009): 1–20.

Romany, Celina. "Women as Aliens: A Feminist Critique of the Public/Private Distinction in International Human Rights Law." *Harvard Human Rights Journal* 6, no. 1 (1993): 87–125.

Rosay, André B. "Violence against American Indian and Alaska Native Women and Men." *National Institute of Justice Journal* (June 1, 2016). https://nij.ojp.gov/topics/articles/violence-against-american-indian-and-alaska-native-women-and-men.

Rosén, Hannah. *Terror in the Heart of Freedom: Citizenship, Sexual Violence, and the Meaning of Race in the Postemancipation South*. Chapel Hill: University of North Carolina Press, 2009.

Rosenberg, Jordy, and Amy Villarejo. "Queerness, Norms, Utopia." *Gay and Lesbian Studies Quarterly* 18, no. 1 (2012): 1–18.

Roy, Olivier. *The Failure of Political Islam*. Translated by Carol Volk. Cambridge, MA: Harvard University Press, 1994.

Rubenfeld, Jed. "The Riddle of Rape by Deception and the Myth of Sexual Autonomy." *Yale Law Journal* 122, no. 6 (2013): 1372–443.

Russell-Brown, Sherrie L. "Rape as an Act of Genocide." *Berkeley Journal of International Law* 21, no. 2 (2003): 350–74.

Savcı, Evren. *Queer in Translation: Sexual Politics under Neoliberal Islam*. Durham, NC: Duke University Press, 2021.

Schabas, William. "Theoretical and International Framework: Punishment of Non-state Actors in Non-international Armed Conflict." *Fordham International Law Journal* 26, no. 4 (2003): 907–33.

Scheffer, David. "Corporate Liability under the Rome Statute." *Harvard International Law Journal* 57 (2016): 36–39.

Scheffer, David. "Rape as Genocide." *New York Times*, November 3, 2008.

Schmidt, Caroline S. "What Killed the Violence against Women Act's Civil Rights Remedy before the Supreme Court Did?" *Virginia Law Review* 101, no. 2 (2015): 501–57.

Schomberg, Wolfgang, and Ines Peterson. "Genuine Consent to Sexual Violence under International Criminal Law." *American Journal of International Law* 101, no. 1 (2007): 121–40.

Schuller, Kyla. *The Biopolitics of Feeling: Race, Sex, and Science in the Nineteenth Century*. Durham, NC: Duke University Press, 2018.

Schultz, Vicki. "Reconceptualizing Sexual Harassment, Again." *Yale Law Journal Forum* 128 (2018–19): 22–66.

Schwartz-Weinstein, Zach. "Not Your Academy: Occupation and the Futures of Student Struggles." In *Is This What Democracy Looks Like?*, edited by Cristina Beltrán, A. J. Bauer, Rana Jaleel, and Andrew Ross, 2013. https://what-democracy-looks-like.org/not-your-academy-occupation-and-the-futures-of-student-struggles/.

Sellers, Patricia Viseur. "The Context of Sexual Violence: Sexual Violence as Violations of International Humanitarian Law." In *Substantive and Procedural Aspects of International Humanitarian Law: Commentary*, edited by Gabrielle Kirk MacDonald and Olivia Swaak-Goldman, 263–332. Cambridge: Kluwer Law International, 2000.

Sellers, Patricia Viseur. "The Cultural Value of Sexual Violence." In *Proceedings of the ASIL Annual Meeting* 93, 312–24. Cambridge: Cambridge University Press, 1999.

Sellers, Patricia Viseur. "The Prosecution of Sexual Violence in Conflict: The Importance of Human Rights as Means of Interpretation." UN Human Rights, Office of the High Commissioner, Women's Human Rights and Gender Unit, 2008. https://www2.ohchr.org/english/issues/women/docs/Paper_Prosecution_of_Sexual_Violence.pdf.

Shakhsari, Sima. *Politics of Rightful Killing: Civil Society, Gender, and Sexuality in Weblogistan*. Durham, NC: Duke University Press, 2020.

Shamir, Hila. "A Labor Paradigm for Human Trafficking." *UCLA Law Review* 60, no. 1 (2012): 76–137.

Sharlach, Lisa. "Gender and Genocide in Rwanda: Women as Agents and Objects of Genocide." *Journal of Genocide Research* 1, no. 3 (1999): 387–99.

Sieder, Rachel. "Contested Sovereignties: Indigenous Law, Violence and State Effects in Postwar Guatemala." *Critique of Anthropology* 31, no. 3 (2011): 161–84.

Sieder, Rachel. "Sexual Violence and Gendered Subjectivities: Indigenous Women's Search for Justice in Guatemala." In *Gender Justice and Legal Pluralities: Latin American and African Perspectives*, edited by Rachel Sieder and John-Andrew McNeish, 121–44. New York: Routledge, 2013.

Smith, Andrea. *Conquest: Sexual Violence and American Indian Genocide*. Durham, NC: Duke University Press, 2015.

Smith, Andrea. "Not an Indian Tradition: The Sexual Colonization of Native Peoples." *Hypatia* 18, no. 2 (2003): 70–85.

Smith, Andrea. "Queer Theory and Native Studies: The Heteronormativity of Settler Colonialism." *GLQ: A Journal of Lesbian and Gay Studies* 16, nos. 1–2 (2010): 41–68.

Snorton, C. Riley. *Black on Both Sides: A Racial History of Trans Identity*. Minneapolis: University of Minnesota Press, 2017.

Somerville, Siobhan. "Queer Loving." *GLQ: A Journal of Lesbian and Gay Studies* 11, no. 3 (2005): 335–70.

Soto, Sandra. "Transnational Knowledge Projects and Failing Racial Etiquette." National Association for Chicana and Chicano Studies Annual Conference Paper, April 1, 2008. http://citeseerx.ist.psu.edu/viewdoc/download?doi =10.1.1.864.6488&rep=rep1&type=pdf.

Spade, Dean. *Normal Life: Administrative Violence, Critical Trans Politics, and the Limits of Law*. Durham, NC: Duke University Press, 2015.

Spade, Dean. "Their Laws Will Never Make Us Safer." In *Everyday Women's and Gender Studies: Introductory Concepts*, edited by Ann Braithwaite and Catherine M. Orr, 156–61. New York: Routledge, 2017.

Spees, Pam. "Women's Advocacy in the Creation of the International Criminal Court: Changing the Landscapes of Justice and Power." *Signs: Journal of Women in Culture and Society* 28, no. 4 (2003): 1233–54.

Spillers, Hortense J. "Mama's Baby, Papa's Maybe: An American Grammar Book." *diacritics* 17, no. 2 (1987): 65–81.

Stephens, Beth. "Individuals Enforcing International Law: The Comparative and Historical Context." *DePaul Law Review* 52, no. 2 (2002): 433–72.

Stephens, Beth. "Translating *Filártiga*: A Comparative and International Law Analysis of Domestic Remedies for Human Rights Violations." *Yale Journal of International Law* 27, no. 1 (2002): 1–57.

Sternbach, Nancy Saporta, Marysa Navarro-Aranguren, Patricia Chuchryk, and Sonia E. Alvarez. "Feminisms in Latin America: From Bogotá to San Bernardo." *Signs: Journal of Women in Culture and Society* 17, no. 2 (1992): 393–434.

Stoler, Ann Laura. "On Degrees of Imperial Sovereignty." *Public Culture* 18, no. 1 (2006): 125–46.

Stoler, Ann Laura. *Race and the Education of Desire: Foucault's "History of Sexuality" and the Colonial Order of Things*. Durham, NC: Duke University Press, 1995.

Suchland, Jennifer. *Economies of Violence: Transnational Feminism, Postsocialism, and the Politics of Sex Trafficking*. Durham, NC: Duke University Press, 2015.

Suchland, Jennifer. "Is Postsocialism Transnational?" *Signs: Journal of Women in Culture and Society* 36, no. 4 (2011): 837–62.

Sudetic, Chuck. "U.S. Envoy Issues Warning to Serbs." *New York Times*, April 15, 1993.

Suk, Jeannie. "'The Look in His Eyes': The Story of *State v. Rusk* and Rape Reform." In *Criminal Law Stories*, edited by Robert Weisberg and Donna Coker, 10–23. New York: Foundation Press/Reuters, 2013.

Slye, Ronald C. "The Dayton Peace Agreement: Constitutionalism and Ethnic-ity." *Yale Journal of International Law* 21, no. 2 (1996): 459–74.

Tadiar, Neferti X. M. "Life-Times of Disposability within Global Neoliberalism." *Social Text* 31 no. 2 (2013): 19–48.

Tadiar, Neferti X. M. "Sexual Economies of the Asia-Pacific." In *What's in a Rim? Critical Perspectives of the Pacific Region Idea*, edited by Arif Dirlik, 219–50. Boulder, CO: Westview, 1998.

Tadiar, Neferti X. M. *Things Fall Away: Philippine Historical Experience and the Makings of Globalization*. Durham, NC: Duke University Press, 2009.

TallBear, Kim. "Making Love and Relations beyond Settler Sex and Family." In *Making Kin, Not Population*, edited by Adele E. Clarke and Donna Haraway, 145–64. Chicago: Prickly Paradigm, 2018.

Thuma, Emily L. *All Our Trials: Prisons, Policing, and the Feminist Fight to End Violence*. Champaign: University of Illinois Press, 2019.

Thuma, Emily L. "Lessons in Self Defense: Gender Violence, Racial Criminaliza-tion, and Anti-carceral Feminism." *WSQ: Women's Studies Quarterly* 43, nos. 3–4 (2015): 52–71.

Todorova, Maria. *Imagining the Balkans*. New York: Oxford University Press, 1997.

Tompkins, Kyla Wazana. "Intersections of Race, Gender, and Sexuality: Queer of Color Critique." In *The Cambridge Companion to American Gay and Lesbian Literature*, edited by Scott Herring, 173–79. New York: Cambridge University Press, 2015.

Tompkins, Kyla Wazana. *Racial Indigestion: Eating Bodies in the 19th Century*. New York: New York University Press, 2013.

Tripp, Aili Mari. "Challenges in Transnational Feminist Mobilization." In *Global Feminism: Transnational Women's Activism, Organizing, and Human Rights*, edited by Myra Marx Ferree and Ali Mari Tripp, 296–312. New York: New York University Press, 2006.

True, Jacqui. *The Political Economy of Violence against Women*. New York: Oxford University Press, 2012.

Tuerkheimer, Deborah. "Rape on and off Campus." *Emory Law Journal* 65, no. 1 (2015): 14–53.

Tuerkheimer, Deborah. "Sex without Consent." *Yale Law Journal Online* 123, no. 335 (2013): 335–52.

United Nations. "Framework of Analysis for Atrocity Crimes: A Tool of Pre-vention." 2014. https://reliefweb.int/sites/reliefweb.int/files/resources /framework%20of%20analysis%20for%20atrocity%20crimes_en.pdf.

United Nations. "The Prijedor Report." December 28, 1994. http://balkanwitness .glypx.com/un-annex5-prijedor.htm.

United Nations Population Fund. "From Conflict and Crisis to Renewal: Gen-erations of Change." State of World Population 2010 Report. https://www .unfpa.org/publications/state-world-population-2010.

US Department of Justice. "Department of Justice Withdraws 'Enemy Combatant' Definition for Guantanamo Detainees." March 13, 2009. https://www
.justice.gov/opa/pr/department-justice-withdraws-enemy-combatant
-definition-guantanamo-detainees.

Van Sliedregt, Elies. *Individual Criminal Responsibility in International Law.*
Oxford: Oxford University Press, 2012.

Vance, Carole S., ed. *Pleasure and Danger: Exploring Female Sexuality.* London:
Pandora, 1989.

Vimalassery, Manu, Juliana Hu Pegues, and Alyosha Goldstein. "Introduction:
On Colonial Unknowing." *Theory and Event* 19, no. 4 (2016). muse.jhu.edu
/article/633283.

Volpp, Leti. "The Indigenous as Alien." *Immigration and Nationality Law Review*
36, no. 1 (2015): 773–812.

Vulliamy, Ed. 1994. *Seasons in Hell: Understanding Bosnia's War.* New York:
St. Martin's, 1994.

Walters, Suzanna Danuta. "Introduction: The Dangers of a Metaphor—Beyond
the Battlefield in the Sex Wars." *Signs: Journal of Women in Culture and
Society* 42, no. 1 (2016): 1–9.

Weheliye, Alexander G. *Habeas Viscus: Racializing Assemblages, Biopolitics, and
Black Feminist Theories of the Human.* Durham, NC: Duke University Press,
2014.

Weinbaum, Alys Eve. *The Afterlife of Reproductive Slavery: Biocapitalism and
Black Feminism's Philosophy of History.* Durham, NC: Duke University
Press, 2019.

West, Robin. "Sex, Law and Consent." Georgetown Law Faculty Working Papers,
2008. http://scholarship.law.georgetown.edu/fwps_papers/71.

White, Richard. 2004. *Breaking Silence: The Case That Changed the Face of
Human Rights.* Washington, DC: Georgetown University Press, 2004.

Wiegman, Robyn. *Object Lessons.* Durham, NC: Duke University Press, 2012.

Wiegman, Robyn, Wahneema Lubiano, and Michael Hardt. "In the Afterlife of
the Duke Case." *Social Text* 25, no. 4 (2007): 1–16.

Williams, Randall. *The Divided World: Human Rights and Its Violence.* Minneapolis: University of Minnesota Press, 2010.

Winichakul, Thongchai. *Siam Mapped: A History of the Geo-Body of a Nation.*
Honolulu: University of Hawai'i Press, 1994.

Wolfe, Patrick. "Settler Colonialism and the Elimination of the Native." *Journal
of Genocide Research* 8, no. 4 (2006): 387–409.

Wood, Elisabeth. "Rape as a Practice of War: Towards a Typology of Political
Violence." *Politics and Society* 46, no. 4 (2018): 513–37.

Wood, Elisabeth. "Variation in Sexual Violence during War." *Politics and Society*
34, no. 3 (2006): 307–41.

Woodward, Susan L. "Violence-Prone Area or International Transition? Adding the Role of Outsiders in Balkan Violence." In *Violence and Subjectivity,* edited by Veena Das, Arthur Kleinman, Mamphela Ramphele, and Pamela Reynolds, 19–45. Durham, NC: Duke University Press, 1997.

Wynter, Sylvia, and Katherine McKittrick. "Unparalleled Catastrophe for Our Species? Or, To Give Humanness a Different Future: Conversations." In *Sylvia Wynter: On Being Human as Praxis*, edited by Katherine McKittrick, 9–89. Durham, NC: Duke University Press, 2015.

Wynter, Sylvia. "Unsettling the Coloniality of Being/Power/Truth/Freedom: Towards the Human, after Man, Its Overrepresentation—An Argument." *CR: The New Centennial Review* 3, no. 3 (2003): 257–337.

Yoneyama, Lisa. *Cold War Ruins: Transpacific Critique of American Justice and Japanese War Crimes*. Durham, NC: Duke University Press, 2016.

Žarkov, Dubravka. *The Body of War: Media, Ethnicity, and Gender in the Breakup of Yugoslavia*. Durham, NC: Duke University Press, 2007.

Žarkov, Dubravka. "Gender, Orientalism and the History of Ethnic Hatred in the Former Yugoslavia." In *Crossfires: Nationalism, Race and Gender in Europe*, edited by Helma Lutz, Ann Phoenix, and Nira Yuval-Davis, 121–42. London: Pluto, 1995.

Zimmerman, Warren. "Impressions of Karadžić." *Frontline*. Accessed February 15, 2021. http://www.pbs.org/wgbh/pages/frontline/shows/karadzic/radovan /impressions.html.

Index

Deer, Sarah, 11–14, 167, 198n5

Democratic Republic of the Congo, 49, 86, 104, 119

Detainee Treatment Act of 2005, 134

DeVos, Betsy, 160, 225n66

Dirty Wars (Latin America), 3, 88, 96, 191n52

disappearances, 93, 96, 99–101, 178, 191n52, 212n81

Doe v. Haskell Indian Nations University, 168

Doe v. Karadzic, 126–28, 217n42. See also *Kadic v. Karadzic*

Dolan, Chris, 219n78

domestic violence. *See* intimate violence

dominance theory, 17, 161, 202n71, 212n83; heterosexuality of 75, 79, 82, 121, 158; nonplace of women of color in, 67–73, 86, 128, 191n51, 198n19; and rape as genocide, 37, 51–54, 61, 64–66. *See also* governance feminism; MacKinnon, Catharine

Doyle, Jennifer, 171, 227n104

Duarte, Ángela Ixkic Bastian, 96

Du Bois, W. E. B., 43

Dworkin, Andrea, 37, 52, 67–68, 76–79

Ecuador, 89

Egypt, 10

El Salvador, 93, 96

Encuentros Feministas, 97–99, 192, 210n44, 212n69

Engels, Friedrich, 64

Engle, Karen, 2, 191n49, 205n147

English, 143, 189n36, 199n32

Espinosa, Gisela, 96

Essence magazine, 174

ethnic cleansing, 56–62, 72, 75, 79–81, 89, 199n27

ethnic wars, 2–7, 18–20, 135, 138, 187n6; Balkan, 54–57, 74–76, 86–89, 100, 152–54, 179, 208n20; and sex in legal debates, 26, 32–37, 45, 52, 63–65, 92–93, 113–17, 130

ethnonationalism, 18, 77, 85, 87, 152. *See also* nationalism

ethnoreligious sexualized violence, 16, 57, 69, 72–86, 112, 127–35, 138

ethnosexual violence, 5, 16, 21, 56–57, 86–87

etničko čišćenje (ethnic cleansing), 56–62, 72, 75, 79–81, 89, 199n27

European Convention for the Protection of Human Rights and Fundamental Freedoms, 85

Falcón, Sylvanna, 188n8, 196n103, 210n46

Fanon, Frantz, 164

Farris, Sara, 179, 228n5

Federal Bureau of Investigation (FBI), 180, 183–84

Federal Rules of Evidence (US), 221n15

feminist carceral logics, 2–4, 17, 30, 67, 79, 179, 191n49, 199n20, 228n5; and VAWA, 149–51, 165–67, 222n27. *See also* carceral logics

Ferguson, Roderick A., 193n55

Ferzan, Kimberly, 225n58

Filártiga v. Peña-Irala, 123–24, 217n37

Filártiga, Dolly, 123

Filártiga, Joel, 123

Filártiga, Joelito, 123

Fineman, Martha, 195n89, 221n6

Fischel, Joseph, 41, 44, 226n70

Foča, 56. *See also* rape camps

forced pregnancy, 32, 59, 81, 125–27, 201n61, 202n68, 218n47, 223n36

Foucault, Michel, 17, 19–20, 94, 193, 195n95

Fourteenth Amendment (US Constitution), 150, 222n22, 222n25

France, 10, 57

Franke, Katherine, 25, 198n18

Freedman, Estelle, 10

Freeman, Elizabeth, 132

French Algerian War, 211n54

Freud, Sigmund, 64

Fujiwara, Lynn, 188n10

Fukuyama, Francis, 54

Furies, 97, 209n40